# SHAKESPEARE'S
## Tragedies of Love

AN EXAMINATION OF THE POSSIBILITY
OF COMMON READINGS OF
*Romeo and Juliet, Othello, King Lear*
*& Anthony and Cleopatra*

BY

## H. A. MASON

1970
## CHATTO & WINDUS
### LONDON

Published by
Chatto and Windus Ltd
40 William IV Street
London W.C.2

*

Clarke, Irwin & Co. Ltd
Toronto

ISBN 0 7011 1609 9

Printed in Great Britain by
R. and R. Clark Ltd
Edinburgh

# SHAKESPEARE'S TRAGEDIES
## OF LOVE

*By the same Author*

✱

HUMANISM AND POETRY IN THE
EARLY TUDOR PERIOD
(*Routledge*)

# Contents

# Acknowledgments

Thanks are due to the Executors of the John Middleton Murry Estate and to The Society of Authors for permission to quote from *Between Two Worlds* by John Middleton Murry (London, Jonathan Cape Ltd); and to Quentin Bell, Angelica Garnett and The Hogarth Press Ltd for permission to quote from 'Mr. Bennett and Mrs. Brown' in volume 1 of *Collected Essays* by Virginia Woolf.

# Preface: Author to Reader

THAT the most indulgent reader will find much in these pages to puzzle, irritate and exasperate him is, alas, only too certain, just as it is certain that no prefatory words of mine can wholly remove the chief difficulties in the way of smooth reading. The damaging truth is that I began with a very clear scheme of considering the rôle of love in Shakespeare's plays and of distinguishing the circumstances in which we could describe the treatment as tragic. Something more obviously connected with my title might have emerged if I had not at about the same time taken an opportunity to offer a set of public lectures on the selected plays and to conduct discussion classes with people who came together with no examinations to pass and no great interest in the academic Shakespeare who in one way or another had been a hardy annual in my professional life for very many years. To effect a genuine meeting of minds, I attempted to throw myself into the position of my youngest listeners, who were reading the plays for the first time, and I tried to set up conditions that would make the text of the plays as vividly present to beginners as it eventually becomes to the regular student. The essence of these 'extra-mural' performances consisted in meditations during the week in whatever leisure was available on selected portions of a chosen play followed by meetings in which with the help of tape-recorders an acted version (or several versions) of the portion was listened to, and, while the words were still in the air, the participants in the discussion were invited to give vent to whatever strong impressions prevailed from the week's meditation immediately after the impact of a quasi-theatrical experience.

These meetings undermined the projected book, for I had not been expecting to have any fresh views on the four plays in which love figured prominently in relation to death. Yet as I tried to follow in the beginners' tracks and to distinguish my real feelings in the spirit of Arnold's formulation:

> Below the surface-stream, shallow and light,
> Of what we *say* we feel—below the stream,
> As light, of what we *think* we feel—there flows
> With noiseless current strong, obscure and deep,
> The central stream of what we feel indeed:

I found myself parting with a long-familiar friend and receiving in exchange views on each of the four selected plays that I never would have thought possible. These changes changed my sense of priorities, and in the interest of group discussions I subordinated everything to the possibility of creating a basis of general agreement upon which private disagreement would be fruitful and interesting. In searching for this basis I found myself making one or two large assumptions about the plays themselves and the possibility of meeting over them that crop up in appropriate places in the following pages.

The next stage in the formation of this volume came when I tried out what had been thrown up on these extra-mural occasions inside lecture and other rooms in colleges and faculties of the Universities of Cambridge and Oxford, and met with substantial encouragement from my betters and my peers to work from the extra-mural basic scripts towards some form of print. I owe so much to these voluntary meetings and free exchanges that I would wish a gratified reader to know who and what I have to thank if at any point I seem to have become a true common reader and to be speaking of a human Shakespeare. For it is to the credit of these places that though they harbour and encourage the study of an intra-mural Shakespeare, people there also strive to break away from the merely academic and to get into touch with an author who speaks to the world as a whole. It was also a help to me to be allowed to offer my comments on two of the plays in the form of articles in the *Cambridge Quarterly*, since the public response to them taught me to be modest in my expectations of winning an instant audience for my views or of living long enough to see any form of general agreement about Shakespeare.

My text is far more optimistic about the possibility of getting agreement than it has any right to be. I therefore give here the substance of what I learned from the greatest privilege I enjoyed: long talks with friends who bothered with my scripts and told me how the plays had shaped themselves in their minds. It was that if we cease to insist on our personal views, we can form, dimly and intermittently, a sense of what, for our times, must impose itself as the *common sense* about *main* things in the plays. Tolerance of the differences that were finally set up between friends enables me to say in turn to a disgruntled reader, 'Don't let me get in your way, don't let me have my way at all save in being permitted once to place before you a *large general suggestion*—do that, and then if need be put me aside for ever.' In order to get the suggestion properly mounted, I have had, with each play, to make many detailed remarks just to prove that I was in fact speaking from a grasp of each play as an independent whole. But I do not cling to any of the particular remarks since I

know from these friends that there are many different ways of reaching
my general conclusions—and these 'conclusions', after all, are more like
hints suggesting a sway of the mind in one direction different from that
which happens to be the fashion of the moment. For instance, the general
drift of my remarks on *King Lear* can be shared by readers who differ
from me over the opening scenes and would quarrel with my formulation
of the *donnée*. (There is a term that I use for the want of a better, but the
reader will find it properly defined wherever it occurs. For it designates
one of the 'main things' I had in mind, for the sake of which I urge that we
sacrifice, temporarily, of course, all other considerations. For if we can
come to agree on what the author appears to be driving at as he, as it were,
sets out his stall to catch our attention, then the further discussion of the
way the play hangs together will almost look after itself.)

Although I have allowed it to become my main business to ask what
each of the chosen plays is principally about, and found 'love and death'
to be the answer in only one, *Romeo and Juliet*, yet my original design is
not after all neglected. If the reader will move from my third chapter to
my last, from the consideration of immature love to that of love where it
begins to pass from ripe to rotten, or will allow the themes of *Othello* to
mingle and clash with those of *King Lear*, he can bring to the surface
what I originally planned to treat by abstraction from the plays. My
original themes, in fact, may now have just the prominence and no more
than I would wish them to have in the minds of other common readers.

A general objection I anticipate because I have had to listen to it so
often from readers of the published portion of this work, is that I am
better at finding faults than in exposing hidden beauties. My own self-
criticism is that the faults do not worry me *enough*. It is so wonderful to
have Shakespeare at all that I do not grieve as I should that the artistic
sense is not gratified as it might be and that we cannot claim perfection
for any of his works. In these matters I have no special insights. The only
novelty, if it is one, is to find no great difference in artistic conscience
between Shakespeare the comedian and Shakespeare the tragedian.
Hence I merely follow my 'authority' in these matters, but extend the
particular comment to the whole work:

> . . . And often, when he came to parts of his scheme that were necessary but
> not interesting to him, he wrote with a slack hand, like a craftsman of genius
> who knows that his natural gift and acquired skill will turn out something
> more than good enough for his audience: wrote probably fluently but cer-
> tainly negligently, sometimes only half saying what he meant, and some-
> times saying the opposite, and now and then, when passion was required,

lapsing into bombast because he knew he must heighten his style but would
not take the trouble to inflame his imagination. It may truly be said that
what injures such passages is not inspiration, but the want of it. But, as they
are mostly passages where no poet could expect to be inspired, it is even
more true to say that here Shakespeare lacked the conscience of the artist
who is determined to make everything as good as he can. Such poets as
Milton, Pope, Tennyson, habitually show this conscience. They left probably scarcely anything that they felt they could improve. No one could
dream of saying that of Shakespeare.[1]

It seems to me to matter so much to come to possess a Shakespeare play
in common as to its essential features that I have been unable to follow up
the question of faults as far as it ought to be taken. For I think our enjoy-
ment of Shakespeare is lacking in sincerity so long as we do not give full
expression to our detestations. But that is only one of many other large
matters that I have deliberately set aside as not in place in a book of first
thoughts about the four plays. I will therefore wind up with two trifling
(I hope) sources of irritation. 'Why must you quote from a largely un-
edited Folio?' I have been asked. If I could feel confidence in any modern
edition of the plays I would gladly use it. But I have no special feeling for
my practice. If the reader will allow me to tell him how I would like my
book to be read, I would advise returning as far as possible to the conditions from which it started — to the extent at any rate of keeping the ratio
of my text very low to the frequency of application to the words of each
play. I count on the reader starting from Shakespeare and constantly
checking and in particular noting whether I am not silently passing over
features that might force me to drop my 'line' of the moment. So my
quotations are merely reminders to the reader of just which portions of
the text are to be under focus. I should be very sorry to be distracting
attention by (as I sometimes have done) printing lines that obviously
cannot stand as the Folio printers left them. I at least know what an
ignoramus I am in textual matters and how little flair I possess. Yet I
could not resist once or twice making small 'fiddles' of amateur editing,
but I hope no reader will discover them.

Similarly, no claim to special knowledge is implied by my quoting
from the so-called Bishops' Bible of 1568. I should very much like to
know whether Shakespeare had a favourite edition, but the extant au-
thorities who have debated the question have not converted me. I trust
that the slight unfamiliarity of my texts will as often prove a stimulus as a
hindrance.

[1] A. C. Bradley, *Shakespearean Tragedy* (1904), pp. 76–77.

An unexpected result of these close readings has been that I lost any sense of Shakespeare's chronological order of composition. It follows that the reader can take these four studies in any order that is convenient. People who dislike being reminded of the times in which the plays were composed are advised to skip the first two chapters of the study of *Romeo and Juliet.*

Cambridge, June 1969

# Romeo and Juliet

# CHAPTER 1

# Fate or Fortune?

THE most stimulating conditions for a common reading of the play might be brought about by having before us the results of the following three exercises; first, an attempt by a reader knowing nothing of the 'source' to guess which parts of the play were inherited by Shakespeare from his narrative-verse predecessor and which were 'free' creation; then an effort by one who had never read the play to sketch a tragedy keeping as close as possible to the plot of *The Tragicall Historye of Romeus and Iuliet*[1] by Arthur Brooke, and, lastly, a rehandling of Shakespeare's plot by a writer of Thomas Hardy's genius to make it correspond to some of the current critical descriptions of Shakespeare's play, such as: '. . . the atmosphere of Fate, of oncoming doom, which overhangs the play . . .' and '[Romeo and Juliet] are the helpless victims of a malevolent, or at least capricious, universal force. The philosophy underlying this conception of tragedy is a profoundly pessimistic philosophy.' The reader familiar with the body of current writing on the play who could easily suggest alternative exercises might agree that something as powerful as this is needed to give us the possibility of fresh vision, to enable us

> to arrive where we started
> And know the place for the first time.

At all events when I read critics who claim to have made out the 'tragic inevitability' or the 'all-embracing pattern' or the 'basic design' of the play I am reminded of the words of a revered master trying to restrain my hasty efforts to get a meaning at all costs out of some difficult Greek author, 'why won't you let the poor blighter say what he wants?'

We have a right, it seems to me, to ask those who are sure that Shakespeare intended to write a play on a conventional tragic plan what gave them the over-riding assurance in face of the fact that Shakespeare obviously intended for so much of the play to be more than a little merry, and to ask those who are sure that the play is merely a simple love story

[1] THE TRAGICALL HIS- / torye of Romeus and Juliet, writ- / ten first in Italian by Bandell, / and nowe in Englishe by / Ar. Br. . . Imprinted at London in / Flete strete within Temble barre, at / the signe of the hand and starre, by / Richard Tottill the .xix. day of / Nouember. An. do. 1562.

how they explain away the presence of so much and often unpleasant bawdy talk. In the next chapter I shall pose similar questions to those who see great significance in the family feud. And a whole series of questions about the kinds and quality of verse writing in this play ought to be put to those who find it embodying deep philosophical thought. If we take up every disparate feature of the play in this spirit and ask what it is doing as a contribution to a whole, we may carry scepticism so far as to say that Shakespeare had no intention, plan or design other than to turn Arthur Brooke's poem into a play. But if we reach this point it becomes clear that we have gone too far. Although Shakespeare has, I think, retained far more of the poem than most of us would if we had merely to make any kind of play out of it, he has powerfully modelled it in several aspects and the simple comparison of poem and play would alone compel us to approach *Romeo and Juliet* with a question expecting an answer about its main point.

But before we examine the answer: *fate or fortune*: we might very profitably consider the possible meanings of the two words and their natural contexts, or rather, bring to mind the meanings that arise naturally out of the occurrences of the words in our play and its 'source'. The latter immediately tells us something that is worth taking in even imprecisely: that the two words were not ultimately serious. They had a full dramatic life and no doubt meant something quite substantial in popular superstition and so were common property to Shakespeare and his audience, and could therefore figure in serious plays such as *King Lear*, but real thinking in real life was carried on in theological terms under the headings of Divine Providence, Predestination, etc. Secondly, and perhaps because of this, the two words began to overlap and mix their meanings, as may be seen from this snippet from Thomas Becon[1]: '*What is fortune?* It is fate, or destiny chaunsing to any man by the will of God, without mans prouidence.'

In making this observation we have unwittingly made another: that serious thought would condemn many of the actions in the play that pass unreproved before our eyes. Because of this lack of condemnation in the text some critics have supposed that Shakespeare wrote the play and we should witness it with that portion of our nature which represents our unforced moral interest shut off, as if writing a play and watching it were like attending a game of football with a rule about the use of hands: 'In this play it is a rule that your normal (or the Christian) condemnation of suicide is to be suspended'. But although moral rules may be likened to rules of games by philosophers and sociologists, ordinary people, seeing

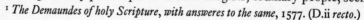

[1] *The Demaundes of holy Scripture, with answeres to the same*, 1577. (D.ii *recto*.)

a play in which a prominent personage is a *religious* and treated as such
by all the other personages, will find it impossible both to play the religious game and suspend its rules. The absence of moral comment at the
end of the play would cause a shock if we had been taking Romeo as
standing for a whole man and the whole of humanity and not for the embodiment of a Love that must perish with the beloved, or if the monument to the dead lovers were to be set up in Cheapside and proposed as a
shrine of pilgrimage. But does the more serious set of rules cancel the
other? I was certainly shocked when I first read *The Tragicall Historye* to
find such a very severe summary of the tale in his prose address to the
reader. The author, it is true, promised to give us when more mature
(after poems that would tell of battles) others that would 'geue rules of
chast and honest lyfe . . .', yet nothing had prepared me for the following
passage:

> And to this ende (good Reader) is this tragicall matter written, to describe
> vnto thee a coople of vnfortunate louers, thralling themselues to vnhonest
> desire, neglecting the authoritie and aduise of parents and frendes, confer-
> ring their principall counsels with dronken gossyppes, and superstitious
> friers (the naturally fitte instrumentes of vnchastitie) attemptyng all ad-
> uentures of peryll, for thattaynyng of their wished lust, vsing auriculer con-
> fession (the kay of whoredome, and treason) for furtheraunce of theyr purpose,
> abusing the honorable name of lawefull mariage, to cloke the shame of stolne
> contractes, finallye, by all meanes of vnhonest lyfe, hastyng to most vn-
> happye deathe. This president (good Reader) shalbe to thee, as the slaues of
> Lacedemon, oppressed with excesse of drinke, deformed and altered from
> likenes of men, both in mynde, and vse of body, were to the free borne chil-
> dren, so shewed to them by their parentes, to thintent to rayse in them an
> hatefull lothyng of so filthy beastlynes. Hereunto if you applye it, ye shall
> deliuer my dooing from offence, and profit your selues . . .[1]

followed by so frank a relish in every part of his verse narrative of the very
features here condemned. My first thoughts were to treat this preface as
the humbug it would no doubt be in Defoe's pages, but as I read more
authors of the years between Brooke and Shakespeare I came to see that
ordinary people were able without hypocrisy to move on two planes, one
overtly Christian, the other more or less coloured by pagan and superstitious thought. Shakespeare, I now assume, counted on our applying the
two moral schemes simultaneously, that of Brooke's prose, and that
implied in his verse, and so on our accepting that what is called *filthy
beastlynes* in the one should appear as

[1] Op. cit., ii *verso* to iii *recto*.

> so perfect, sound,
> and so approued loue . . . (fo: 84 *verso*)

in the other.

The clergy, however, were uncompromising in their condemnation of rival views of the laws governing the universe. Since they all say more or less the same thing there is no point in preferring one voice to another, and I have consulted my own convenience in offering Roger Hutchinson's *The Image of God* (1550), fo: lxii *verso*, for this: 'I wold denye all thinges to be ruled by necessitie, by fate and destinie, for almightie God worketh what he wyll in them . . .' and John Bradford's *An other treatise of election and freewill*[1] (1562), p. v *recto* for:

> . . . the Stoikes opynion is to be condemned as concerninge fatall necessitie . . . we shoulde certaynelye knowe that it is God whyche is the ruler and arbyter of all thynges . . . I thinke there be none nowe whiche bee of this opynyon, to attrybute thinges to fortune, a word vnsemly for Christians.

and his *An exhortation to the patient sufferyng of trouble, etc.*[2] for '. . . there is no crosse which commeth vpon any of vs without the counsel of our heauenly father (for as for the fansie of fortune, it is wicked, as many places of the scripture do teach) . . .' where he refers us to passages such as these: 'What is he then that saith, there should some thing be done without the Lordes commaundement? Out of the mouth of the most highest goeth not euyll and good? (from *The lamentations of Ieremie* The .iij. Chapter, 37–38).' and

> I am the Lord, and there is none other, for without me there is no God: I haue prepared thee or euer thou knewest me. Therfore they shall knowe from the rising of the sunne, vnto the goyng downe of the same, that all is nothing without me: for I am the Lorde, and there is els none. It is I that created light and darknesse, I make peace and trouble: yea euen I the Lorde do all these thinges (from *The Prophecie of Esai*, The .xlv. Chapter, 5–7).

Even more impressive are the incidental reflections of this belief which crop up in narratives, such as these:

> They that with reuerence will consider Gods secret prouidence, and care that he hath for his people, how he gouerneth all things yea euen those that

---

[1] In *Godlie meditations vpon the Lordes prayer, the beleefe, and ten commaundementes . . . gathered by the constant martyr of God John Bradford in the tyme of his imprisonment.*
[2] printed under this title in Coverdale's 1564 collection *Certain most godly, fruitful, and comfortable letters of such true Saintes and holy Martyrs of God, as in the late bloodye persecution here within this Realme, gaue their lyues for the defence of Christes holy gospel: written in the tyme of theyr affliction and cruell imprysonment.* p. 437.

seeme outwardly of no value, after such a sorte, that his heauenly wisdome and fatherly loue doeth most manyfestly appeare in them, toward those that seeke him, may here see a manifest example of it. Not by chaunce (for so nothing falleth out) but by gods great prouidence, the king had wyne afore him. . . . (fo: 12 *recto*)

> (*A Godlie Exposition vpon Certeine Chapters of Nehemiah, etc.* (1585) by James Pilkington)

and 'And like as David . . . was letted by Deathe, . . . Even so ẙ noble Kynge Henry. . . . was by th Vnsearchable Desteny of god preventid by Deathe . . .[1] Obedient to this principle they condemned astrology as a breach of the commandment: *Thow shalt haue no strange Godes before my face*:

> Souche as be yeuen to Astronomie, or other that supersticiouslie obserue the course and reuolution of the heauens thinke they can do good or harme, yeue good fortune or ile as those thinke and iudge that eleuate the figure of heauen [calculate the disposition of the heavenly bodies at any given time] to iudge what shall folow them, when they perceaue by there Natyuites vnder what signe the[y] were born: offend against this commaundement . . .

John Hooper, from whose *A Declaration of the ten holy commaundementes, etc.* (1548), fo. lx, I have taken this, gives us there (fo: lxi) the orthodox view:

> . . . well we be assurid by the scripture [Thus saith the Lord: ye shal not learne after the maner of the heathen, and ye shall not be afraide for the tokens of heauen: for the heathen are afraide of suche. *Ier.x.2.*] . . . that no constellation of heauen, mistemperature of the ayre, water, or earthe can hurt him that feryth god . . . only the disobedience of man towardes god makith man subiect vnto these diseacis and sikenis that man is troblyd withe all. . .

If something of this sort is granted about the standing of the two words we can proceed to make a rough distinction between them, to the extent at least of saying that one word is less frightening than the other. I shall take Fortune to be what we find it is in *The Tragicall Historye* and in a moment quote passages to illustrate the present summary account. Fortune, I shall be arguing, is less formidable than Fate. It has an indifferent side covered by the words 'hap', 'chance' and 'change'; these represent the less eventful moments of the eternal wheel but at the same time the only moments that affect everybody. Fortune is only to be feared when it, or now we should say she, *smiles*. For her law is eternal inconstancy and

---

[1] John Philpot in Ms. Bibl. Reg. 17 C IX, fo: 2 *verso*.

eternal caprice. She elects her victim on a whim, raises him to the top of
the wheel and then plunges him down. The wheel image is unfortunate in
suggesting *regularity* of ups and downs. As we shall be seeing, Fortune is
capricious in this, too, and can award suffering out of proportion to
previous felicity. The worst Fortune can do is to terminate life and with
it her own power. But as long as you live, if you are in adversity you can
hope for a change, since Fortune of her nature cannot bear eternal ill-will.
Fortune cannot be constantly malignant just as she cannot be constantly
kind: she is by definition heartless, fickle. She can cause pain but never
despair, since she cannot depart from her rôle of eternal change. Fortune,
then, is the presiding genius of Comedy, though the play must abandon
her just as the wheel comes up.

If we take the word 'lot' (as, with our eye on *Sors* and *Lachesis*, we may)
as the corresponding word for Fate, we see at once how near it comes to
Fortune and in fact coincides with Fortune thought of as 'it' rather than
'she'. It is least painful when felt as impersonal: '. . . what is fate and
destinye? a stedfaste & immutable order of causes, whereby all thynges
chaunce of necessitie, called in greke, *Eimarmene* . . .'[1] which is virtually
Cicero's: 'Fatum autem id appello quod Graeci εἱμαρμένην, id est, ordi-
nem seriemque causarum, cum causa causae nexa rem ex se gignat. . . .'[2]
Although the Greeks and Romans had their weird sisters, this fate is
essentially impersonal. There is no personal intention or special feeling
about the doling out of lots. In this sense fate is something that, if we
follow Sir Walter Scott, we *dree*: there is no point in making a fuss since
fate unlike fortune cannot change for better or for worse. As long as the
doom is hidden from us it is very little more than a law of nature. It
is a pathetic fallacy to call this fate 'cruel' or 'kind'. What frightens us is
the apparent crossing of our actions when we attempt to do something
which is inconsistent with what has been allotted to us. We are terrified
when we find ourselves mysteriously unable to prevent some disaster or
when an act in itself harmless inexplicably brings on disaster. Most
appalling is to appear to collaborate with our Fate, as Samuel Johnson[3]
imagined:

> Fate wings with ev'ry Wish th' afflictive Dart,
> Each Gift of Nature, and each Grace of Art,
> With fatal Heat impetuous Courage glows,
> With fatal Sweetness Elocution flows,

[1] Hutchinson, *op. cit.*, fo: lxii *verso*.          [2] *De Divinatione*, I. LV. 125.
[3] in *The Vanity of Human Wishes. The Tenth Satire of Juvenal*, imitated by Samuel
Johnson, London, M. DCC. XLIX.

Impeachment stops the Speaker's pow'rful Breath,
And restless Fire precipitates on Death.

Fate frightens us most when it is felt as in us rather than set over against us.

It is some mitigation that Fate in this sense has nothing to do with *deserts*, and so long as such fate is a mere force otherwise unconnected with our lives the ordinary 'doom of man' need not be overwhelming. Nor, unless we are its victims, is Nemesis a notion from which we shrink, since we are presumably not *driven* to commit Hubris and if we find ourselves excessively fortunate it is in our power to behave warily. A more fearful thought is that we could become an object of attention to 'the gods' and to gods as capricious as Fortune but worse than Fortune in that they could exercise a *fixed* ill-will, as in the epics of Homer and Virgil. I don't know whence Gloucester was supposed to derive his bitter lesson:

> I haue heard more since:
> As Flies to wanton Boyes, are we to th' Gods,
> They kill vs for their sport.

This seems to me to go as much beyond the evidence as the Fate discovered by the modern critic in *Romeo and Juliet*: 'The lovers are the predestined victims of a malicious Fate . . .' That is to say, not only is their death-day fixed by their nativity, but Fate is not satisfied with mere doom and intervenes repeatedly:

> Fate . . . works against them . . . by contriving a deadly series of accidents . . . Shakespeare does not want us to think of these 'accidents' as merely fortuitous. We cannot avoid the impression that he asks us to think of them as intentionally arranged by Fate. Fate deliberately works against the lovers . . . Fate is here operating against Romeo and Juliet through the fact that Tybalt and Mercutio have false ideals, false values . . . by means of accident and coincidence, and by means of character-flaws in others . . .

Here, it seems to me, we have an unjustified transposition. Although we are not given the nativities of Romeo and Juliet, it may well be that the signs of heaven were technically 'malign' when they were born. But to create from this an unsleeping fiend contriving a series of petty accidents and to call it a 'cosmic force' into the bargain is to put into the play something more than anybody else could find.

And here there would be a very serious conflict for the spectator who noticed that the personages of the play shared with him a belief in Divine Providence, a just dispensation where afflictions are sent to warn and grace is given to assist repentance. The doctrine, it is true, could be correspondingly frightening for those not chosen or for reprobates, especially when we recall that, as Longfellow said in *Retribution*, translating Friedrich von Logau's *Sinngedicht*, 'Göttliche Rache',

Though the mills of God grind slowly, yet they grind exceeding small;

or as Pilkington puts it[1]: 'Thus of smale occasions God worketh great things, that we may know that he ruleth all things, be they neuer so smale in mans sight'. But if God is thought of as merely Fate and as having doomed us from the beginning, then we cannot have tragedy but only what the French call *pièces noires*. Similarly, if we know that we are saved there can be no tragedy, for tragedy inhabits a twilight region between hope and despair: tragedies are plays of dreadful possibilities but not of certainties.

But *did* Shakespeare suppose he was writing a tragedy, and if he did, what did he mean by the word? Was he consciously creating something new or was he merely taking over the word along with the rest of his 'source'? Neither Brooke nor the author of his 'source' meant anything specific by the description of their stories as tragedies, nor should *we* think of applying the word to either their prose or their verse. We may therefore alter our original question and ask: did Shakespeare see any significance in the events of the story other than that to be found in the two preceding works? And with this change we come near to answering the question whether Fortune is the organising term in Shakespeare's play. For although in Brooke's source the story is thought of as a piece of history exemplifying the truth that Love issues significantly in Death, this story is knit together by the notion of Fortune, as we may plainly see from William Painter's version of the French, entitled 'The goodly Hystory of the true, and constant Loue betweene RHOMEO and IVLIETTA, the one of whom died of Poyson, and the other of sorrow, and heuinesse: wherein be comprysed many aduentures of Loue, and other deuises touchinge the same'.[2]

Their marriage thus consumate, *Rhomeo* perceyuing the morning make to hasty approch, tooke his leaue, making promise that he would not fayle wythin a day or two to resort agayne to the place by lyke meanes, and sem-

[1] *Op. cit.*, fo: 12 *verso*.
[2] The Second / Tome of the Palace of / Pleasure contayning store of goodlye / Histories, Tragical matters, & other / Morall argumentes, very requi- / site for delight and / profyte. / Chose*n* and selected out / of diuers good and commendable Au- / thors, and now once agayn correc / ted and encreased. / By Wiliam Painter, Clerke of the / Ordinance and Armarie / Imprinted at London / In Fleatstrete by Thomas / Marshe. The author's 'Epistle' is dated: From my pore house besides the / Towre of London, the iiij / of Nouember. / 1567.

blable time, vntil Fortune had prouided sure occasion vnfearfully to many-fest their marriage to the whole Worlde. And thus a month or twayne, they continued their ioyful mindes to their incredible satisfaction, vntil Lady fortune enuious of their prosperity, turned hir Wheele to tumble them into sutch a bottomlesse pit, as they payed hir vsury for their pleasures past, by a certayne most cruell and pitifull death, as you shal vnderstand hereafter by the discourse that followeth . . . (fo: 187 *recto*).

and

"Myne owne dearest freend *Iulietta*, I am not now determined to recite the particulars of the straung happes of frayle and inconstaunte Fortune, who in a moment hoisteth a man vp to the hyghest degree of hir wheele, and by and by, in lesse space than in the twynckeling of an eye, she throweth hym downe agayne so lowe, as more misery is prepared for him in one day, than fauour in one hundred yeares: Whych I now proue, & haue experience in my selfe, which haue bene nourished delicately amonges my frends, and maynteyned in sutch prosperous state . . . . . . (hoping for the full perfection of my feli-city) by meanes of our mariage to haue reconciled our Parents, and frends, and to conduct the residue of my lyfe, according to the scope and lot de-termined by Almighty God . . ." (fo: 190 *recto*).

This last reference is a reminder that the Fortune of Brooke's source is subordinate to Providence. The story indeed ends on a pious note: Romeo dies on his knees with this prayer:

O my Lord God, which to redeeme me didest discend from the bosom of thy Father, and tookest humane fleshe in the Wombe of the Vyrgine . . . (fo: 199 *recto*) *Ie te supply prendre compassion de cette pauure ame affligée: car ie congnoy bien, que ce corps n'est plus que terre. . . .*[1]

and Juliet dies in the hope 'that our soules passing from this light, may eternally liue together in the place of euerlasting ioy'(fo: 200 *recto*). (I can now insert an apology to the reader who may have been wondering why I was lingering among the 'sources' when there was such a delightful play waiting to be discussed. Now that Brooke's poem is so easy to come by,[2] I should like to inform the reader that it is a genuine poem, a true 'creative' translation. It would now be well known to every student of Tudor literature if it had appeared a few years earlier in Tottel's

---

[1] *Histoires Tragiques extraictes des oeuvres italiennes de Bandel, & mises en nostre langue Françoise, par Pierre Boaistuau surnommé Launay, natif de Bretagne . . . A Paris . . . 1559. Histoire Troisiesme, de deux amans, dont l'vn mourut de venin, l'autre de tristesse,* fo: 78 *recto*.

[2] in *Narrative and Dramatic Sources of Shakespeare*, edited by G. Bullough, Vol. I, 1957, pp. 284–363.

*Miscellany*. It fired Shakespeare's imagination by the very features that distinguish it from its French source and remained in his memory long after he had used it for two of his plays[1]). Brooke could not altogether eliminate the Christian bias of his source but he quite deliberately tried to increase the emphasis on Fortune as an agent and the scope of her rôle. Thus where the French—though for convenience I revert to Painter's translation—gave us:

> Madame aunswered *Rhomeo*, my Lyfe is in the Hand of God, who only can dispose the same: howbeyt yf any Man had soughte menes to beryeue mee of my Lyfe, I should (in the presence of you) haue made him knowen what mine ability had ben to defend the same . . . (fo: 184 *recto*).

Brooke rewrites as follows:

Fayre lady myne dame Iuliet
my lyfe (quod hee)
Euen from my byrth committed was
to fatall sisters three.
They may in spyte of foes,
draw foorth my liuely threed:
And they also, who so sayth nay,
a sonder may it shreed.
But who to reaue my lyfe,

---

[1] For this reason alone some readers may not be displeased to have here a contemporary's tribute:

An Epitaph on the death of Maister
Arthur Brooke, drownde in passing to New Hauen.

At pointe to ende and finishe this my Booke,
    Came good report to mee, and wild me write
A dolefull Uerse, in praise of *Aurthur Brooke*,
    That age to come lament his fortune might.
Agreede (quoth J) for sure his Uertues were
    As many as his yeares in number few:
The Muses him in learned laps did beare,
    And *Pallas* Dug this daintie Bab did chew.
*Apollo* lent him Lute for solace sake
    To sound his Uerse by touch of stately string,
And of the neuer fading Baye did make
    A Lawrell Crowne, about his browes to cling,
Jn proufe that he for Myter did excell,
    As may be iudge by *Iuliet* and hir Mate:
For there he shewde his cunning passing well
    When he the Tale to Englishe did translate. . .

George Turbervile in *Epitaphes, Epigrams, Songs and Sonets* . . . 1567 (pp. 257–258 of the Collier reprint, fols. 143v–144v of the edition of 1570).

his rage and force would bende,
Perhaps should trye vnto his payne
how I it could defende.      (fo: 14 *verso*)

Although Brooke's poem will give us a perfect touchstone for trying
Shakespeare's, since it will shew us what the story looks like when sub-
jected to Fortune as its organising idea, it is by no means a thorough-
going reworking in the light of a general *philosophic* concept. The crucial
events are never explained as part of Fortune's plan. Thus there is no
suggestion of a supernatural agency in the failure of the monk's message
to reach Romeo or in the sudden opportunity of the handy means to get
the poison or the last-minute liberty accorded to Juliet to stab herself.
Nevertheless although Romeus and the author invoke the Fates in the
spirit of Chaucer's Troilus:

O fatal sustren, which, er any cloth
Me shapen was, my destine me sponne,

it is not a story of Fate but of Fortune, which both initiates the whole
action and constantly intervenes to promote it both in favouring the
lovers and in ruining them. It is roughly summarized here:

There were two auncient stocks,
whiche Fortune hygh did place
Aboue the rest, indewd with welth,
and nobler of their race.
Loued of the common sorte,
loued of the Prince alike:
And lyke vnhappy were they both,
when Fortune list to stryke.      (fo: 1 *verso*)

Similarly Romeus is described as *high in Fortunes grace*, and Fortune
assists him with Juliet at the banquet; though the bringing him there
might have been thought of as fatal:

False fortune cast for him poore wretch,
a mischiefe newe to brewe . . .      (fo: 5 *recto*)

and Romeus reacts sharply when he discovers that Juliet is a Capulet:

feerce Fortune doth he blame:
That in his ruth and wretched plight
doth seeke her laughing game . . .  (fo: 10 *recto*)

Fortune, however, continues to smile, and though Romeus calls her
*cruell Fortune* and *my dedly foe*, he has to acknowledge her favour:

Since Fortune of her grace
    hath place and time assinde
Where we with pleasure may content
    our vncontented minde. . . .    (fo: 25 *recto*)

which also in Brooke's poem lasts two months. The author comments:

The blindfyld goddesse that
    with frowning face doth fraye,
And from theyr seate the mighty kinges
    throwes downe with headlong sway:
Begynneth now to turne,
    to these her smyling face,
Nedes must they tast of great delight,
    so much in Fortunes grace.    (fo: 26 *recto*)

Brooke's poem might well have been called *The Two Faces of Fortune* since he marks off the smiling from the frowning face by a direct address to the reader, which gives us his fundamental idea:

(fo: 26 *verso*)    But who is he that can
    his present state assure?
And say vnto himself, thy ioyes
    shall yet a day endure.
So wauering Fortunes whele
    her chaunges be so straunge.
And euery wight ythralled is
    by fate vnto her chaunge,
(fo: 27 *recto*)    Who raignes so ouer all,
    that eche man hath his part:
(Although not aye perchaunce alike)
    of pleasure and of smart.
For after many ioyes,
    some feele but little paine:
And from that little greefe they toorne
    to happy ioy againe.
But other somme there are,
    that liuing long in woe,
At length they be in quiet ease,
    but long abide not so.
Whose greefe is much increast
    by myrth that went before:

> Because the sodayne chaunge of thinges
>           doth make it seeme the more.
>     Of this vnlucky sorte
>           our Romeus is one. . . .

We do not readily see the true point of balance here for the story is after all now really just beginning: we are to hear of a *heauy happe*, a *wofull chaunce*, and the *straungenes of the chaunce*. But one dominating feature of the next two thirds of the poem (which exasperates the modern reader) is a series of laments that Fortune should have these two faces. All the actors are posed with the question: what is to be done when Fortune frowns? The lovers have one consolation: that of innocence. The author exonerates Romeus from any share of responsibility for Tybalt's death. Fortune is the criminal:

> The lookeles lot by Fortunes gylt,
>           that is so late befall,
>     (Without his falt,) vnto
>           the seely Romeus. . . .            (fo: 30 *recto*)

an argument also used by the Nurse:

>           for though that Fortunes cryme
> Without your falt, to both your greefes
>           depart you for a time. . . .        (fo: 34 *verso*)

Yet the lovers are not thought of as *victims*. Every lament is opposed by an argument for doing something in the face of Fortune and not for taking things too hard.

There are two such debates, one between the Friar and Romeus, and the other, more serious, between Romeus and Juliet just before he leaves for Mantua. The first scene may very well be entirely Brooke's own, since there is no corresponding scene in the French, and here above all we see, what critics have often pointed out, how much *Chaucer* is responsible for the general shaping of Brooke's version. This Chaucer is, of course, the author of *Troilus and Criseyde*, where a long discourse on predestination is inserted at a critical point. The immediate parallel here, however, is in Book IV:

> Right as the wylde bole bygynneth sprynge,
> Now her, now ther, idarted to the herte,
> And of his deth roreth in compleynynge,
> Right so gan he aboute the chaumbre sterte,
> Smytyng his brest ay with his fistes smerte;

His hed to the wal, his body to the grounde
Ful ofte he swapte, hymselven to confounde.

His eyen two, for piete of herte,
Out stremeden as swifte welles tweye;
The heighe sobbes of his sorwes smerte
His speche hym refte; unnethes myghte he seye,
"O deth, allas! why nyltow do me deye? . . ."

as we may see from the following:

(fo: 36 *verso*)   These heauy tydinges heard,
     his golden lockes he tare:
  And like a frantike man hath torne
    the garments that he ware.
    And as the smitten deere,
     in brakes is waltring found:
  So waltreth he, and with his brest
    doth beate the troden grounde.
    He rises eft, and strikes
     his head against the wals,
  He falleth downe againe, and lowde
    for hasty death he cals. . . .
(fo: 37 *recto*) And two great streames of bitter teares,
     ran from his swowlen eyes. . . .

But the structure of the scene and the argument come from Book I,
where Troilus complains *Fortune is my fo* and Pandarus makes the equally
traditional rejoinder:

      "Than blamestow Fortune
  For thow art wroth; ye, now at erst I see.
  Woost thow nat wel that Fortune is comune
  To everi manere wight in som degree?
  And yet thow hast this comfort, lo, parde,
  That, as hire joies moten overgon,
  So mote hire sorwes passen everechon.

  For if hire whiel stynte any thyng to torne,
  Than cessed she Fortune anon to be.
  Now, sith hire whiel by no way may sojourne,
  What woostow if hire mutabilite
  Ryght as thyselven list, wol don by the,
  Or that she be naught fer fro thyn helpynge?
  Paraunter thow hast cause for to synge."

This is substantially what Lawrence has to say to Romeus:

> The world is alway full
> of chaunces and of chaunge,
> Wherfore the chaunge of chaunce must not
> seeme to a wise man straunge.  (fo: 39 *verso*)
> For tickel Fortune doth,
> in chaunging, but her kind:
> But all her chaunges can not chaunge,
> a steady constant mynd.
> Though wauering Fortune toorne
> from thee her smyling face,
> And sorow seeke to set himselfe
> in banished pleasures place,
> Yet may thy marred state,
> be mended in a whyle,
> And she eftsones that frowneth now,
> with pleasant cheere shall smyle,
> For as her happy state,
> no long whyle standeth sure,
> Euen so the heauy plight she brings,
> not alwayes doth endure.  (fo: 40 *recto*)

So fickle is Fortune, he goes on to argue, that the present bad luck may be designed to give Romeus greater relish of even greater felicity to come.

The most serious discussion in the poem occurs when Romeus returns to comfort Juliet before his withdrawal to Mantua. Here he clearly has three forces in mind as governors of his fate, but the two most important (the Christian God and the pagan *Parcae*) are not allowed consideration. Instead the doctrines about Fortune are given full treatment. It is here that occurs the speech I took from Painter on page 11. Juliet then takes up the tale:

> So that iust cause I haue,
> to thinke (as seemeth me)
> That froward Fortune did of late,
> with cruell death agree
> To lengthen lothed life,
> to pleasure in my payne,
> And tryumph in my harme, as in
> the greatest hoped gayne.

And thou the instrument
of Fortunes cruell will,
Without whose ayde she can no way,
her tyrans lust fulfill:                    (fo: 45 *recto*)

but Romeus shews that he has taken in Lawrence's lesson and closes the
debate with:

For Fortune chaungeth more,
then fickel fantasie,
In nothing Fortune constant is,
saue in vnconstancie.
Her hasty ronning wheele,
is of a restles coorse,
That turnes the clymers hedlong downe,
from better to the woorse.
And those that are beneth,
she heaueth vp agayne,
So we shall rise to pleasures mount,
out of the pit of payne.                    (fo: 47 *recto*)

In Brooke's poem, as in his source, Romeus dies as a Christian with no
mention of Fortune. Juliet, however, when she sees his dead body,
exclaims:

How could thy dainty youth
agree with willing hart,
In this so fowle infected place
(to dwell) where now thou art?
Where spitefull Fortune hath
appoynted thee to bee,
The dainty foode of greedy woormes,
vnworthy sure of thee.                    (fo: 77 *recto*)

But this is her rhetoric: she dies as in the French with the hope of joint
immortality in heaven. The Friar, too, speaks of the corpses as

. . . . this heauy sight, the wreke,
of frantike Fortunes rage,                    (fo: 79 *verso*)

but the story ends on the note with which it began: *The straungenes of the
chaunce.*

The advantage of pursuing this poem into such detail is that it forces
us to say of Shakespeare both that he always and that he never had such
doctrines about Fortune as were plainly used by Brooke in an effort to

give a significant shape and inner coherence to his story. We find Shakespeare in his earliest plays as in *King Lear* drawing on the commonplaces about Fortune but they never have a serious shaping force; they are never used to give tragic colouring to events. A random example will serve for all. At the end of the First Act and the opening of the Second of *Twelfe Night* we find the following lines:

> Fate, shew thy force, our selues we do not owe,
> What is decreed, must be: and be this so . . .
> . . . . . . . my starres shine darkely ouer me; the
> malignancie of my fate, might perhaps distemper
> yours . . .

Here we have the very language of a serious doctrine, but nobody in the play is affected by it. Fortune is not so dead a notion in our play as Fate in *Twelfe Night*, but it is obviously not bearing a part similar to that governing Brooke's poem. Hence, if we are seeking for the central thing in *Romeo and Juliet*, we must turn elsewhere.

*     *     *

Another advantage of the comparison with Brooke's poem is that it gives us one clear instance of a general critical decision that Shakespeare must have taken. He must have said, 'Here I part company; my play will *not* be essentially about Fortune'. Did he go on to say 'it *will* be principally about Fate'? If he did, this, too, will have been a conscious critical decision, since his sources keep Fate in a markedly subordinate position and nowhere pose the question that must always arise when Fate and Necessity are prominent in a story: have the characters lost their free will? Now if it is true that Shakespeare would have had to make serious modifications to his story to create a play governed and permeated by a doctrine of Fate, it is a striking argument that he cannot have had any such intentions since he makes no modification of the story in those very aspects that were handed down to him as pure accidents or at most unlucky chance. The conformity of Shakespeare's ending and Brooke's ought to arrest and puzzle those who speak of *inevitability* or of the young people's love as *doomed*. Shakespeare might still have kept this series of improbable accidents and let his personages interpret them as the work of an interfering 'cosmic force'. But Romeo dies without a word to assist us. If it is true that Shakespeare introduced the death of Paris into the story, is it not significant that Romeo's comment should be merely

One writ with me in sowre misfortunes booke . . . ?

And when he himself comes to die, do we not get the impression that he shrugs off the talk of Fate as not serious in the face of Death?

> O here
> Will I set vp my euerlasting rest:
> And shake the yoke of inauspicious starres
> From this world wearied flesh. . .

Lastly, Shakespeare might have made us feel the events as fatal by allowing others than the victims to call them so. But the Friar's first reaction is: *lamentable chance*, just as if Shakespeare had been content to take over without change what he found in Brooke's poem. Shakespeare even retains a device that might pass in a narrative but is tedious in a play, that of having the main events, which the audience have taken in, resumed for the benefit of personages in the play who make no serious impact on us as a result of their enlightenment. The friar is content to describe the fatal impediment of his message as a mere *accident*. That Shakespeare's mind had left the play by this time is made clear by the perfunctory words spoken to wind matters up, particularly these:

> A glooming peace this morning with it brings,
> The Sun for sorrow will not shew his head:
> Go hence to haue more talke of these sad things,
> Some shall be pardoned, and some punished. . .

Indeed if only the end of our 'sources' had survived we might easily have supposed that Shakespeare had had no other intention than to write as they did. Consider, for instance, this, from Painter:

> And for the compassion of so straunge an infortune, the *Montesches*, and *Capellets* poured forth sutch abundaunce of teares, as with the same they did euacuate their auncient grudge and choler, whereby they were then reconciled. And they which coulde not bee brought to attonement by any wisedome or humayne councell, were in the ende vanquished and made frends by pity. . .  (fo: 202 *verso*).

At this point it may occur to the reader that we have been paying a very poor compliment to Shakespeare in supposing his intelligence to be of the same order as Brooke's and assuming that he would be merely substituting one *doctrine* about the goverment of the universe for another. When a great artist finds himself grappling with the ultimate causes of things he does not characteristically produce a doctrine of any kind. I cannot see even a remote sign that Shakespeare was here grappling with ultimate causes, but he was evidently fascinated by a possibility that a man might somehow become aware that he was under the control of forces outside himself. The play has certain arresting moments of this kind which it is natural to turn to. There is a striking instance at a crucial moment in the play, at the first fatal step, we might say, in the action. Certainly, as we look back, we see that the beginning of what ended in the Capulets' tomb was the visit to the banquet where Romeo first met Juliet. Did Romeo then have a premonition, a sense of fate now taking a hand in his life?

It is true that something new enters into his mind as Romeo lingers with his friends outside the Capulet house. At first he seems to be totally pre-occupied with the hopelessness of his love for Rosaline. He cannot put himself into the sportive, holiday spirit: he has no appetite for the adventures and the possible flirtations of the dance. Shakespeare then goes out of his way to say something that is true of many of the significant acts of his story, that in themselves they are innocent, well-meant. Why do they turn out to be uniformly disastrous? Romeo says here:

> And we meane well in going to this Mask,
> But tis no wit to go.

But when asked for his reason for saying that, he does not speak of pre-monition—at least, not directly: his answer is

> I dreampt a dreame to night.

It seems to me characteristic of the largeness of Shakespeare's mind that just at the point where he is suggesting that dreams tell us of our destiny he gives Mercutio a long speech which brings into our minds other thoughts about the significance of dreams, other fears and fancies. By the time Mercutio has got through his speech he has done all the needful illustration for what he now states:

> . . . I talke of dreames,
> Which are the children of an idle braine,
> Begot of nothing but vaine phantasie:
> Which is as thin of substance as the ayre,
> And more inconstant then the wind. . . .

Yet this is not allowed to settle the matter: it does not rid Romeo of his mood:

> . . . my mind misgiues,
> Some consequence yet hanging in the starres,
> Shall bitterly begin his fearful date,
> With this nights reuels, and expire the terme
> Of a despised life, closde in my brest,
> By some vile forfeit of vntimely death:

STL B

but nothing in the mood prevents Romeo from submitting to the ruling
of . . . Providence!

> But he that hath the stirrage of my course,
> Direct my sute. . . .

This has the effect of dissipating thought and we lose the sense of fate
until Juliet says goodnight to Romeo:

> . . . although I ioy in thee,
> I haue no ioy of this contract to night,
> It is too rash, too vnaduisd, too sudden,
> Too like the lightning which doth cease to bee,
> Ere one can say, it lightens. . . .

Here, however, one is not forced to suppose Juliet has any inkling of her
fate. I do not in fact think that when we first read the play we entertain
any dark thoughts of fate until the death of Mercutio. Romeo in fact
creates the Fate he dreads. We are certainly alarmed when we hear him
say

> I thought all for the best

and are therefore sympathetic to his foreboding:

> This dayes blacke fate on mo daies doth depend,
> This but begins the wo others must end. . .

but we do not see it as a truth until he says

> This shall determine that

and kills Tybalt. But then we see that Romeo does not regard this as fate
but fortune:

> O I am fortunes foole.

Juliet's second misgiving seems like the first, an inevitable accompani-
ment of being in love, and not a reference to fate:

> O God I haue an ill diuining soule,
> Me thinkes I see thee, now thou art so lowe,
> As one dead in the bottome of a tombe . . .

and if we were still inclined to take these moods as evidence of fate's
finger touching the spirit, surely Romeo's happy dream just before he
learns the news of Juliet's supposed death would be enough to make us
dismiss the thought? But all these scattered references to fate do not

amount to very much; they do not set a stamp on the play. We can therefore say that the first prologue gives us a misleading account of the main
interest of Shakespeare in presenting this story, and therefore it would be
a relief if the textual critics could step in and give us conclusive evidence
that Shakespeare had no part in it; for although no good critic can have
been misled, those readers who for other reasons wanted Shakespeare to
have written a play about Fate have been all too willing to make the prologue do for what the play conspicuously fails to support.

# CHAPTER 2

# Shakespeare the Opportunist

WHEN I opened this discussion by proposing as one of the best ways into the play the task of turning Brooke's poem into a tragedy, I was taking for granted that (supposing we did not know how Shakespeare had managed it) we should all agree in *simplifying* the story and subordinating it to one leading 'idea' or at least in treating it in a manner so very different from the one chosen by Shakespeare as to raise doubts in our minds whether he had ever intended anything of the sort himself. And when we observe, by comparing the poem and the play, how many features *Romeo and Juliet* has that we should not expect to see figuring in one and the same play, it is natural to raise the hypothesis that the only connecting thread is the story, and what I have called its features are the signs of a number of unrelated interests that Shakespeare happened to have when he took up the poem to see what he could make of it. Such a hypothesis would place all those many critics on the defensive who affirm that the play has one main theme: the termination of a feud by 'the sacrifice of the innocents'.

The feud is certainly a necessary part of the story as Brooke took it over from his French source. The story is formally framed at the beginning and at the close by a feud involving two houses which was brought to an end by the deaths of the two youngest members, one from each of the feuding families. It was because he hoped to reconcile these families by the marriage of these two members that the Friar consented to an otherwise reprehensible act:

> Part wonne by ernest sute,
> the frier doth graunt at last:
> And part, because he thinkes the stormes
> so lately ouerpast,
> Of both the housholdes wrath
> this mariage might apease,
> So that they should not rage agayne
> but quite for euer cease. (fo: 17 *verso*)

It would be a reasonable way of turning the story into a tragedy to subordinate the love to such a social purpose. Many people have felt the persistence of civil strife inside a natural community to be the very type of tragedy. It comes under the heads imagined by Gloucester in *King Lear*:

> Loue cooles, friendship falls off, Brothers diuide. In Cities, mutinies; in Countries, discord. . .

The strife between the Guelphs and the Ghibellines, for instance, or that between the Orsini and the Colonna families, has something mysterious about it: we feel that all the rational causes alleged could never suffice to explain why neighbours should be for so many generations at each other's throats and murder on one side should in such numbers be followed by murder on the other.

It is a natural slip—as we may see from the early writings of W. H. Auden—to invest the members of feuding families with a tragic halo. Their lives are likely to be short: danger is ever present: opportunities for heroics are always occurring. The very madness of the whole enterprise may strike us as evidence that we have here a 'sacred' activity. We can play with sophisticated variants of this thought: we can see communal hate as the necessary obverse of communal love: we can imagine love shading off into hate, love and hate changing places. And we particularly relish the rich contrasts provided by savage feuds in societies possessing strict codes of honour or chivalry. A further rich source of human interest lies in the attempt to imagine how feuds could be stopped, to think of forces more powerful than those which compel members of one family to kill members of another. Countless plays have been written and stories told in which sexual love has joined a couple who in all else are literally at daggers drawn. We are forced to think how great the force is that could hold such a couple together in a raging feud. And the idea that this great love must be *sacrificed* to appease the family hatred is one that I can well believe has deep roots in our imagination. But even if we think of the greatest values as inherent in the feuding families' code of honour, we cannot altogether exclude our disapproval of a feud. It is at best nature going against nature and at the worst it is childish.

Some of a mature man's thoughts about feuds are unforgettably embodied in Mark Twain's *Huckleberry Finn*.[1] There he does full justice to the fine old aristocrat—as it were, the head of his Capulets—, shews his goodness in all else save the prosecution of the feud, displays his courtesy and majesty even, and his family are seen to be a fine breed of men and women. Mark Twain has his Juliet, too, but his main thought is for the

---

[1] *The Adventures of Huckleberry Finn* (*Tom Sawyer's Comrade*) by Mark Twain (Samuel L. Clemens), London, 1884.

violation of reason, nature and of civilization. Huck, the wise innocent, is astonished when a boy of his own age shoots at the Romeo of the story from behind a tree:

> 'Did you want to kill him, Buck?'
> 'Well, I bet I did.'
> 'What did he do to you?'
> 'Him? He never done nothing to me.'
> 'Well, then, what did you want to kill him for?'
> 'Why, nothing—only it's on account of the feud.'
> 'What's a feud?'
> 'Why, where was you raised? Don't you know what a feud is?'
> 'Never heard of it before—tell me about it.'
> 'Well,' says Buck, 'a feud is this way. A man has a quarrel with another man, and kills him; then that other man's brother kills *him*; then the other brothers, on both sides, goes for one another; then the *cousins* chip in—and by-and-by everybody's killed off, and there ain't no more feud. But it's kind of slow, and takes a long time.'[1]

This feud has been going on for so long that its origin has been forgotten. There has been a 'right smart chance of funerals' on both sides. The latest outburst was the shooting of a fourteen-year-old boy of the Capulets by the old head of the Montagues. Yet in spite of this cowardly behaviour, the families are generally brave:

> 'I reckon that old man was a coward, Buck.'
> 'I reckon he *warn't* a coward. Not by a blame' sight. There ain't a coward amongst them Shepherdsons—not a one. And there ain't no cowards amongst the Grangerfords, either. Why, that old man kep' up his end in a fight one day, for a half an hour, against three Grangerfords, and come out winner. They was all a-horseback; he lit off of his horse and got behind a little wood-pile, and kep' his horse before him to stop the bullets; but the Grangerfords staid on their horses and capered around the old man, and peppered away at him, and he peppered away at them. Him and his horse both went home pretty leaky and crippled, but the Grangerfords had to be *fetched* home—and one of 'em was dead, and another died the next day. No, sir, if a body's out hunting for cowards, he don't want to fool away any time amongst them Shepher[d]sons, becuz they don't breed any of that *kind*.'
>
> (pp. 166-167).

This is very like the account in Painter:

[1] *Op. cit.*, pp. 164–165.

But they were so egre and furious one agaynst the other, as they gaue no audience to *Rhomeo* his councel and bent theymselues too kyll, dysmember and teare eche other in pieces. And the fyght was so cruell and outragious betweene them as they which looked on, were amased to see theym endure those blowes, for the grounde was all couered with armes, legges[,] thighes, and bloude, wherein no signe of cowardnes appeared . . .     (fo: 187 *verso*).

Like Shakespeare, Mark Twain draws the contrast between this primitive behaviour and the observance of civilised forms:

Next Sunday we all went to church, about three mile, everybody a-horse-back. The men took their guns along, so did Buck, and kept them between their knees or stood them handy against the wall. The Shepherdsons done the same. It was pretty ornery preaching—all about brotherly love, and such-like tiresomeness; but everybody said it was a good sermon, and they all talked it over going home, and had such a powerful lot to say about faith, and good works, and free grace, and preforeordestination, and I don't know what all, that it did seem to me to be one of the roughest Sundays I had run across yet (p. 167).

In Mark Twain's story, the flight of his Juliet with his Romeo brings about a general catastrophe. Huck has to witness the murder of his friend and another boy:

The boys jumped for the river—both of them hurt—and as they swum down the current the men run along the bank shooting at them and singing out, 'Kill them, kill them!' It made me so sick I most fell out of the tree. I ain't a going to tell *all* that happened—it would make me sick again if I was to do that. I wished I hadn't ever come ashore that night, to see such things. I ain't ever going to get shut of them—lots of times I dream about them. . . .

When I got down out of the tree, I crept along down the river bank a piece, and found the two bodies laying in the edge of the water, and tugged at them till I got them ashore; then I covered up their faces and got away as quick as I could . . . (pp. 174–175).

In proposing the other exercise, that of trying to guess which features in Shakespeare's play were owing to his 'source', I had in mind among other things an impression that would arise when the play was over of a contrast between the formal importance attributed to the feud at the close and the ludicrous opening of the play, and the many comic touches associated with the feuding families, and I could well imagine a reader attributing this incongruous comic strain to the 'source'. When we discover that it is in fact almost all Shakespeare's invention, we may well wonder what interest it was serving. One little detail suggests how very far that interest

was taking Shakespeare from a possible tragic theme, *i.e.*, his forgetting
to mention that there was any family obstacle to Romeo's pursuit of
Rosaline. On further reflection we may decide that some parts of Shakespeare's invention may be an indirect tribute to Brooke. For Brooke, too,
warmed to the 'bourgeois' aspects of his story, and the portion beginning
with the proposal of marriage made with the best of intentions and ending
with the brutal outburst when the father is thwarted is one of the best
pieces in the poem. We know how well Shakespeare took to it from his
own rewriting. Shakespeare's free creation of the banquet atmosphere
may be a natural overflow from this. It is one of the moments of social
depth which counteract a slight tendency towards a fairy-tale atmosphere
in other parts of the play. Our richest impressions of the head of the
Capulets are not of a tragic protagonist but of a bourgeois gentleman in
two contrasted rôles—the genial host and the bullying parent. Here we
do not have to fill in his character from our sympathetic imagination, he
abounds in suggestive words, particularly where his two parts are com-
bined in the chiding of Tybalt. We are worlds apart from Mark Twain's
feud *here*:

> —Vncle, this is a *Mountague*, our foe,
>    A villaine that is hither come in spight,
>    To scorne at our solemnitie this night.
> —Young *Romeo* is it?
> —Tis he, that villaine *Romeo*.
> —Content thee, gentle Coze, let him alone,
>    A beares him like a portly Gentleman:
>    And to say truth, *Verona* brags of him,
>    To be a vertuous and a welgouernd youth,
>    I would not for the wealth of all this Towne,
>    Here in my house doe him disparagement:
>    Therefore be patient, take no note of him,
>    It is my will; the which if thou respect,
>    Shew a faire presence, and put off these frownes,
>    An illbeseeming semblance for a feast.
> —It fits when such a villaine is a guest,
>    Ile not endure him.
> —He shall be endured:
>    What goodman boy, I say he shall, go too,
>    Am I the master here or you? go too,
>    Youle not endure him, god shall mend my soule,
>    Youle make a mutinie among my guests:

You wil set cock a hoope, youle be the man.
—Why Vncle, tis a shame.
—Go too, go too,
   You are a sawcie boy, ist so indeed?
   This trick may chance to scath you; I know what,
   You must contrarie me, marrie tis time,
   Well said, my hearts. You are a princox, go,
   Be quiet, or more light, more light, for shame,
   Ile make you quiet; what! Chearely, my hearts.

Comparison of poem and play makes it seem very likely that Shakespeare decided that in a general way the play needed as much comedy as he could get in. The comedy, however, does not seem to be there to make any critical point about the feud. Apparently we are not to think of the feud as silly because the heads of both houses are shewn in rather a foolish light. Shakespeare, in fact, appears to have no thought of his own in the matter. He brings the feud in and leaves it out on the apparent principle that what was good enough for Brooke would do for him. Now we have seen that Brooke was following a version of the story in which the feud and the reconciliation were trifling appendices to a love story, a sort of 'and so they all lived happily for ever after' closing tag. There is a memorable similarity in the closing couplets of both compositions which can safely represent the lack of independence of Shakespeare in this part of the play.

> For neuer was a storie of more wo,
>   Then this of *Iuliet* and her *Romeo* . . .

is too like Brooke's close:

> There is no monument
>   more worthy of the sight,
> Then is the tombe of Iuliet,
>   and Romeus her knight. (fo: 84 *verso*)

for us to think it an accident. 'The feud', therefore, does not deserve to figure as a respectable answer to the question: what is the principal concern of *Romeo and Juliet*, that which gives significance to the play as a whole?

It is generally agreed among those who see Shakespeare as writing up his play from the occasional suggestions of Brooke's poem that the most surprising departure from this practice is the almost total recreation and virtually new creation of the character of Mercutio. He has always aroused such a strong interest that it has been a puzzle to see just why he was not given even greater scope. And it is particularly puzzling that he himself though not on either side and so not obliged to join in the feud is shewn as deliberately picking a quarrel and egging Tybalt on. Since he is obviously not the central thing, that for which the rest of the play was written, I shall be brief. Since that for which he is liked seems to be present to almost everybody who reads or sees the play, there will be no harm in rubbing in how much of a desperado he was, almost a potential suicide, and a figure that might attract the modern sociologist who has to deal with the prolonged juvenile delinquent, the former 'teddy boy' of the 1950's who has been unable to settle down in marriage and a job. More puzzling still is the moment that for me 'steals' the play, and for many playgoers is the only *serious* part of the whole. Mercutio dies indeed and we are made to feel it. Here is one of the places that join all readers and playgoers:

> No, tis not so deepe as a well, nor so wide as a Church doore, but tis inough, twill serue: aske for me to morrow, and you shall finde me a graue man. I am peppered I warrant, for this world, a plague a both your houses, sounds, a dog, a rat, a mouse, a cat, to scratch a man to death: a braggart, a rogue, a villaine, that fights by the book of arithmatick, why the deule came you betweene vs? I was hurt vnder your arme.
> —I thought all for the best.
> —Helpe me into some house, *Benuolio*,
>   Or I shall faint, a plague a both your houses.
>   They haue made wormes meate of me,
>   I haue it, and soundly . . .

The moment remains so powerful that the deaths at the end of the play seem by contrast merely parts of a story. I cannot, however, bring myself to believe, as some have done, that the dying man's curse doomed the lovers. If it had so much power it ought to have prevented the 'happy' ending.

In the present uncertainty about Shakespeare's intention it may not be out of place to hazard the conjecture that the interest in Mercutio and Tybalt was also sociological; that he was turning what to Brooke was an exotic and incredible custom into something that contemporary playgoers would recognize as reflecting the quarrels in their London streets. If this conjecture will pass, I would go on to suggest that what distressed Shakespeare most was not that society contained an unruly element but that these murderous passions were shared by the most cultivated men of the day. I was prompted to this reflection by the evident complacency with which Ben Jonson looked back on his younger days both as a soldier and a duellist:

> Jn his servuce in the Low Countrise, he had jn the face of both the Campes Killed ane Enimie taken opima spolia from him, and since his comming to England being appealed to the fields he had Killed his adversarie, which had hurt him jn the arme & whose sword was 10 jnches Longer than his, for the which he was Emprissoned and almost at the Gallowes.[1]

A more outrageous case is presented by Edward Herbert, George Herbert's brother. In his old age he was clearly living over and rekindling the passions of his youth. The following account from his own life story should be thought of as bloodthirsty recreation, perhaps, rather than exact recollection, but if so, it is all the more valuable in taking us into the mind of a cultivated poet, historian and philosopher, who had been living the life of a scholar and a recluse.

The incident itself occurred in 1610, when Sir John Ayres, a gentleman who moved in court circles, thought Herbert had, as he said, whored his wife. His first project was to kill the adulterer in his bed. Herbert protested his innocence and challenged his opponent to a duel, which he declined:

> After this, finding he cou'd take no advantage against me, then in a treacherous way he resolv'd to assassinate me in this manner; hearing I was to come to Whitehall on Horseback with two Lackies only, he attended my coming back in a place called Scotland-Yard, at the hither end of Whitehall, as you come to it from the Strand, hiding himself here with four men armed on purpose to kill me. I took Horse at Whitehall Gate and passing by that place, he being armed with a Sword and Dagger, without giving me so much as the least warning, ran at me furiously, but instead of me wounded my Horse in the brisket, as far as his Sword cou'd enter for the bone; my Horse hereupon starting aside, he ran him again in the shoulder, which, thô it made the Horse more timerous, yet gave me time to draw my Sword; his men thereupon encompassed me and wounded my Horse in three places more; this made my Horse kick and fling in that manner as his men durst not come near me, which advantage I took to strike at Sir John Ayres with all my force, but he warded the blow both with his Sword and Dagger: instead of doing him harm, I broke my Sword within a foot of the hilt; hereupon some Passenger that knew me, and observing my Horse bleeding in so many places, and so many men assaulting me, and my Sword broken, cried to me several times, ride away, ride away; but I scorning a base flight upon what terms

[1] *Ben Jonson's Conversations with William Drummond of Hawthornden*, transcribed by Sir Robert Sibbald, fols. 25-31, National Library of Scotland, Ms. 33.3.19.

soever, instead thereof alighted as well as I cou'd from my Horse; I had no sooner put one foot upon the ground, but Sir John Ayres pursuing me, made at my Horse again, which the Horse perceiving pressed on me on the side I alighted, in that manner that he threw me down, so that I remained flat upon the ground, only one foot hanging in the stirrop, with that piece of a Sword in my right hand; Sir John Ayres hereupon ran about the Horse and was thrusting his Sword into me, when I finding myself in this danger did with both my arms reaching at his legs pull them towards me, 'till he fell down backwards on his head; one of my Footmen hereupon, who was a little Shropshire Boy, freed my foot out of the stirrop, the other which was a great Fellow having run away as soon as he saw the first assault; this gave me time to get upon my legs, and to put myself in the best posture I cou'd with that poor remnant of a weapon: Sir John Ayres by this time likewise was got up, standing betwixt me and some part of Whitehall, with two men on each side of him, and his brother behind him, with at least 20 or 30 Persons of his Friends or Attendants of the Earl of Suffolk; observing thus a body of men standing in opposition against me, 'thô to speak truly I saw no Swords drawn but by Sir John Ayres and his men, I ran violently against Sir John Ayres, but he knowing my Sword had no point, held his Sword and Dagger over his head, as believing I cou'd strike rather than thrust, which I no sooner perceiv'd but I put a home thrust to the middle of his breast, that I threw him down with so much force, that his head fell first to the ground, and his heels upwards; his men hereupon assaulted me, when one Mr. Mansel, a Glamorganshire gentleman, finding so many set against me alone, closed with one of them, a Scotch gentleman also closing with another, took him off also; all I cou'd well do to those two which remained, was to ward their thrusts, which I did with that resolution that I got ground upon them. Sir John Ayres was now got up a third time, when I making towards him with intention to close, thinking that there was otherwise no safety for me, put by a thrust of his with my left hand, and so coming within him, receiv'd a stab with his Dagger on my right side, which ran down my ribs as far as my hip, which I feeling did with my right elbow force his hand together with the hilt of the Dagger so near the upper part of my right side, that I made him leave hold. The Dagger now sticking in me, Sir Henry Cary afterwards Lord of Faulkland and Lord Deputy of Ireland, finding the Dagger thus in my body snatcht it out; this while I being closed with Sir John Ayres, hurt him on the head, and threw him down a third time, when kneeling on the ground and bestriding him, I struck at him as hard as I cou'd with my piece of a Sword, and wounded him in four several places, and did almost cut off his left hand; his two men this while struck at me, but it pleased God even miraculously to defend me, for when I lifted up my Sword to strike at Sir John Ayres I bore of[f] their blows half a dozen times; his Friends now finding him in this danger took him by the head and shoulders, and drew him from betwixt my legs, and carrying him along with them through Whitehall, at the Stairs whereof he took Boat. Sir Herbert Croft (as he told me afterwards) met him upon the Water vomiting all the way, which I believe was caused by the violence of the first thrust I gave him; his Servants, Brother, and Friends being now retir'd also, I remained master of the place and his weapons, having first wrested his Dagger from him, and afterwards struck his Sword out of his hand.

This being done, I retired to a Friend's House in the Strand, where I sent for a Surgeon who searching my wound on the right side, and finding it not to be mortal, cured me in the space of some ten days, during which time I receiv'd many noble Visits and Messages from some of the best in the kingdom. Being now fully recover'd of my Hurts, I desired Sir Robert Harley to go to Sir John Ayres, and tell him, that 'thô I thought he had not so much Honor left in him, that I cou'd be any way ambitious to get it, yet that I desired to see him in the field with his Sword in his hand; the Answer that he sent me was, that I had whored his Wife, and that he wou'd kill me with a Musket out of a Window.[1]

Although we can find many places where the Shakespearean verse is very thin on the ground because what we are getting is *The Tragicall Historye* only slightly transposed, the account we must give of the whole is that the poem inspired Shakespeare to some of his most vigorous invention. What is surprising is that some of the best parts of the play come from close imitation of Brooke. One notable example is the incident where the nurse acts the go-between for Juliet:

(fo: 19 *recto*)      I warrant you she shall not fayle
                            to come on Saterday.
                    And then she sweares to him,
                            the mother loues her well:
                    And how she gaue her sucke in youth
                            she leaueth not to tell.
                    A prety babe (quod she)
                            it was when it was yong:
                    Lord how it could full pretely
                            haue prated with it tong.
                    A thousand times and more

[1] *The Life of Edward Lord Herbert of Cherbury, written by himself.* London, 1770, pp. 88–91.

I laid her on my lappe,
And clapt her on the buttocke soft
            and kist her where I did clappe.
And gladder then was I
            of such a kisse forsooth:
Then I had been to haue a kisse
            of some olde lechers mouth.
And thus of Iuliets youth
            began this prating noorse,
And of her present state to make
            a tedious long discoorse.
For though he pleasure tooke
            in hearing of his loue:
The message aunswer seemed him
            to be of more behoue.
But when these Beldams sit
            at ease vpon theyr tayle:
The day and eke the candle light
            before theyr talke shall fayle.
And part they say is true,
            and part they do deuise:
Yet boldly do they chat of both
            when no man checkes theyr lyes.
(fo: 19 *verso*)          Then he .vi. crownes of gold
            out of his pocket drew:
And gaue them her, a slight reward
            (quod he) and so adiew.
In seuen yeres twise tolde
            she had not bowd so lowe,
Her crooked knees, as now they bowe,
            she sweares she will bestowe
Her crafty wit, her time,
            and all her busy payne,
To helpe him to his hoped blisse,
            and cowring downe agayne:
She takes her leaue, and home
            she hyes with spedy pace:
The chaumber doore she shuts, and then
            she saith with smyling face:
Good newes for thee my gyrle,
            good tidinges I thee bring:

> Leaue of thy wonted song of care
>             and now of pleasure sing.
>     For thou mayst hold thy selfe
>             the happiest vnder sonne:
> That in so little while, so well
>             so worthy a knight hast wonne.
>     The best yshapde is he,
>             and hath the fayrest face,
> Of all this towne, and there is none
>             hath halfe so good a grace.
>     So gentle of his speche,
>             and of his counsell wise:
> And still with many prayses more
>             she heaued him to the skies.
>     Tell me els what (quod she)
>             this euermore I thought:
> But of our mariage say at once,
>             what aunswer haue you brought?
> Nay, soft, quod she, I feare
>             your hurt by sodain ioye:
> I list not play quoth Iuliet,
>             although thou list to toye.

(fo: 20 *recto*)

I know of no better way to convince oneself of Shakespeare's talent as distinct from his genius than to note what opportunities he could see and exploit in passages like this. It seems to me a mistake to call it a gift for creating *character*, if by that we mean individual character. Shakespeare, it seems to me, has not thought out his Nurse as an independent creation, her various aspects are not properly related to each other if she was intended to be a real person. She is rather a vehicle for various 'moments' and some of the best are moments of prose speech. Like some of the creations of Dickens, while she is speaking, and only while she is speaking she has abundant life, as here:

> And a speake any thing against me, Ile take him downe, and a were lustier then he is, and twentie such Iacks: and if I cannot, ile finde those that shall: scuruie knaue, I am none of his flurt gills; I am none of his skaines mates . . .

This grafting on to the commonplace of talk of the quicker, livelier, compressed phrase *flurt gills* and the coining under the pressure of passion of a word that could hardly be given a precise meaning—*skaines mates*—give the impression of life. The result is to bring the whole class of *these*

*Beldams* before us in a far more taking way than by mere statement, as in Brooke. Or again here:

> Well sir, my Mistresse is the sweetest Lady, Lord, Lord, when twas a litle prating thing. O there is a Noble man in town, one *Paris*, that would faine lay knife aboord; but she, good soule, had as leeue see a tode, a very tode, as see him . . .

These sentences for me concentrate the type but they do not distinguish the individual from the type.

Nevertheless, although passages like these may set us dreaming of what a fine prose tale Shakespeare might have made of the poem, when we look at the blank verse exploitation of this moment we see that he had not missed his vocation. On the contrary, the challenge of verse[1] roused him to a fuller act of creation:

> Euen or odde, of all daies in the yeare,
> Come *Lammas* Eue at night shal she be fourteen.
> *Susan* and she, God rest all Christian soules,
> Were of an age. Well, *Susan* is with God;
> She was too good for me: But as I said,
> On *Lammas* Eue at night shall she be fourteene;
> That shall shee, marrie; I remember it well.
> Tis since the Earth-quake now eleuen yeares,
> And she was weand, I neuer shall forget it,
> Of all the daies of the yeare vpon that day:
> For I had then laide worme-wood to my dug,
> Sitting in the sun vnder the Doue-house wall.
> My Lord and you were then at *Mantua*:
> Nay, I doo beare a braine. But, as I said,
> When it did taste the worme-wood on the nipple
> Of my dug, and felt it bitter, pretie foole,
> To see it teachie and fall out with the Dugge.
> Shake, quoth the Doue-house: twas no need, I trow,
> To bid me trudge.
> And since that time it is a leuen yeares:
> For then she could stand hylone, nay byth roode
> She could haue run and wadled all about:
> For euen the day before she broke her brow,
> And then my husband, God be with his soule,
> A was a merrie man, tooke vp the child:

---

[1] The passage is printed as prose in the editions of 1597, 1599, and 1623.

'Yea,' quoth he, 'doest thou fall vpon thy face?
Thou wilt fall backward when thou hast more wit,
Wilt thou not, *Iule*? and by my holydam,
The pretie wretch left crying, and said 'I':
To see now how a ieast shall come about!
I warrant, and I should liue a thousand yeares,
I neuer should forget it: 'Wilt thou not, *Iule*?' quoth he;
And, pretie foole, it stinted, and said 'I'.
— Inough of this; I pray thee hold thy peace.
— Yes, Madam, yet I cannot chuse but laugh,
To thinke it should leaue crying, and say 'I':
And yet, I warrant, it had vpon it brow
A bump as big as a young Cockrels stone,
A perillous knock, and it cryed bitterly.
'Yea', quoth my husband, 'fallst vpon thy face?
Thou wilt fall backward when thou commest to age:
Wilt thou not, *Iule*?' It stinted, and said 'I'.
— And stint thou too, I pray thee Nurse, say I.
— Peace, I haue done: God marke thee too his grace,
Thou was the prettiest babe that ere I nurst:
And I might liue to see thee married once,
I haue my wish.

Here too, I think, our attention should not be so much on the character of the speaker as on the amount of *perspective* the speech introduces into the play, not merely of the eleven years behind Juliet but the world of domestic life with its mediaeval mixture of reverence and irreverence. How much is done, for instance, by the little detail of the pigeon-house compared with the overt statement elsewhere about the great rich Capulet!

Another excellent example of Shakespeare's opportunism occurs at the point where Juliet is reflecting before drinking the contents of the Friar's phial. At first Shakespeare seems to be merely translating the idiom of the previous generation into his own, but gradually he reaches out from narrative style towards true drama.

(fo: 66 *verso*)          And what know I (quoth she)
                              if serpentes odious,
                     And other beastes and wormes that are
                              of nature venemous,
                          That wonted are to lurke,
                              in darke caues vnder grounde,

And commonly as I haue heard
                in dead mens tombes are found,
        Shall harme me yea or nay,
                where I shall lye as ded,
Or how shall I that alway haue
                in so freshe ayre been bred
        Endure the lothsome stinke
                of such an heaped store
Of carkases, not yet consumde
                and bones that long before
        Intombed were, where I
                my sleping place shall haue,
Where all my auncesters doe rest,
                my kindreds common graue?
        Shall not the fryer and
                my Romeus when they come,
Fynd me (if I awake before)
                ystyfled in the tombe?
(fo: 67 *recto*)        And whilst she in these thoughts
                doth dwell somwhat to long,
The force of her ymagining
                anon dyd waxe so strong,
        That she surmisde she saw
                out of the hollow vaulte,
(A grisly thing to looke vpon,)
                the carkas of Tybalt,
        Right in the selfe same sort
                that she few dayes before
Had seene him in his blood embrewd,
                to death eke wounded sore.
        And then, when she agayne
                within her selfe had wayde
That quicke she should be buried there,
                and by his side be layde
        All comfortles, for she
                shall liuing feere haue none
But many a rotten carkas, and
                full many a naked bone:
        Her daynty tender partes
                gan sheuer all for dred,
Her golden heares did stand vpright

vpon her chillish hed.
Then pressed with the feare
that she there liued in,
A sweat as colde as mountayne yse,
pearst through her tender skin,
That with the moysture hath
wet euery part of hers,
And more besides, she vainely thinkes,
whilst vainly thus she feares,
A thousand bodies dead
haue compast her about,
And least they will dismember her,
she greatly standes in doute,
(fo: 67 *verso*)    But when she felt her strength
began to weare away,
By little and little, and in her hart
her feare increased ay:
Dreading that weakenes might
or foolish cowardise
Hinder the execution of
the purposde enterprise,
As she had frantike been,
in hast the glasse she cought,
And vp she dranke the mixture quite,
withouten farther thought.

Nothing could convince one more thoroughly that blank verse was a great discovery than the contrast in movement here:

What if it be a poyson which the Frier
Subtilly hath ministered to haue me dead,
Least in this marriage he should be dishonourd,
Because he married me before to *Romeo*?
I feare it is: and yet me thinks it should not,
For he hath still bene tried a holy man.
How if when I am laid into the Tombe,
I wake before the time that *Romeo*
Come to redeeme me? theres a fearfull poynt:
Shall I not then be stiffled in the Vault,
To whose foule mouth no healthsome ayre breaths in,
And there die strangled ere my *Romeo* comes?
Or if I liue, is it not very like,

The horrible conceit of death and night,
Togither with the terror of the place,
As in a Vaulte, an auncient receptacle,
Where for this many hundred yeares the bones
Of all my buried auncestors are packt,
Where bloudie *Tybalt*, yet but greene in earth,
Lies festring in his shroude, where as they say,
At some houres in the night, spirits resort:
Alack, alack! is it not like that I
So early waking, what with loathsome smels,
And shrikes like mandrakes torne out of the earth,
That liuing mortalls hearing them run mad:
O if I wake, shall I not be distraught,
Inuironed with all these hidious feares?
And madly play with my forefathers ioynts?
And pluck the mangled *Tybalt* from his shrowde?
And in this rage with some great kinsmans bone,
As with a club dash out my desprate braines?
O looke, me thinks I see my Cozins Ghost,
Seeking out *Romeo*, that did spit his body
Vpon a Rapiers poynt; stay *Tybalt*, stay!
*Romeo*, [heres drinke], I drinke to thee.

The point of these comparisons is that they put beyond doubt what would have been merely a feeling, a suspicion, if we had lost the poem, that in *Romeo and Juliet* Shakespeare was for much of the time living through and filling out in stage terms what was essentially a narrative, a story, content to reap the full benefit from each incident, but—and this is what matters—not very much concerned with any total significance. Since it is so difficult to find the mind in the play it is desperate to try to find the mind behind the play. Nevertheless if we argue from effect to cause we might reasonably suppose that Shakespeare had something in him to say about love (and perhaps about death) which got itself released and shaped into words through the task of working up the story of *Romeus and Iuliet*. But the same evidence forces us to say that he now felt himself as never before at one with the broad Petrarchist tradition. Could it be that the zest that carries this play forward comes from a double impulse, from literature and from life? That such a thing did happen to Shakespeare and produce an exultant lilt we know from Berowne's famous speech in *Loues Labour's lost*:

But Loue first learned in a Ladies eyes,
Liues not alone emured in the braine:
But with the motion of all elamentes,
Courses as swift as thought in euery power,
And giues to euery power a double power,
Aboue their functions and their offices.
It addes a precious seeing to the eye:
A Louers eyes will gaze an Eagle blinde.
A Louers eare will heare the lowest sound. . . .
Loues feeling is more soft and sensible,
Then are the tender hornes of Cockled Snayles.
Loues tongue proues dainty *Bachus* grosse in taste,
For Valour, is not Loue a *Hercules*
Still climbing trees in the *Hesperides?*
Subtill as *Sphinx*, as sweete and musicall,
As bright *Apollos* Lute, strung with his haire.
And when Loue speakes, the voyce of all the Goddes,
Make heauen drowsie with the harmonie.
Neuer durst Poet touch a pen to write,
Vntill his Inke were tempred with Loues sighes:
O then his lines would rauish sauage eares,
And plant in Tyrants milde humilitie.
From womens eyes this doctrine I deriue.
They sparcle still the right promethean fier,
They are the Bookes, the Artes, the Achademes,
That shew, containe, and nourish all the worlde.
Else none at all in ought proues excellent.

# CHAPTER 3

# Love and Death in *Romeo and Juliet*

WHEN we are looking for the largest possible effects, about which we can expect unanimity of opinion, it is a good general rule that the answer to the question: what is the main thing in the play? should be given in terms that include some actual scene or scenes that once seen are never forgotten and which retain their hold when the play becomes thoroughly familiar. Ideally, they should be those which make the strongest impression after the first visit to the theatre. But as we all know, many an excited visit proves to have been a mere theatrical excitement, due to conditions that are not an inherent part of the play. If we nominate the 'balcony' scene as one of those scenes which on this rule ought to give us a clue or tip about the principal thing in the play and what makes it a whole, we can count on almost universal support, though there is a significant minority view which, as we shall see, condemns it. It will be convenient at the same time to take into consideration another verdict, that the play somehow makes up for its failures by providing glorious poetry. Once again it will serve to let one critic speak for a great many:

> But if Shakespeare failed in these ways, wherein consists the success of the play? For, admitting that 'as a pattern of the idea of tragedy it is a failure', the fact remains that in some way or ways it is a resplendent success, being indeed one of the best-loved and most frequently quoted of the author's works.
>
> The answer is that while the play is in certain important respects a dramatic failure, it is a great poetic success. The thing that most powerfully impressed Shakespeare's imagination as he worked on *Romeo and Juliet* was the emotional richness of the lovers' feeling for each other, and he expresses this in lines of incomparable poetic beauty.

To set up a critical atmosphere we have only to turn to Mr Traversi,[1] who makes very different comments on 'Romeo's familiar apostrophe to Juliet at the balcony':

> But soft, what light through yonder window breaks?
> It is the East, and *Iuliet* is the Sun.
> Arise faire Sun, and kill the enuious Moone,

[1] in *Shakespeare: The Young Dramatist* (1955), an essay in *A Guide to English Literature*, Vol. 2, ed. Boris Ford.

> Who is alreadie sicke and pale with greefe,
> That thou her maide art far more faire then she:
> Be not her maide since she is enuious,
> Her vestall liuery is but sicke and greene,
> And none but fooles do weare it, cast it off:
> It is my lady. ô it is my loue,
> O that she knew she wer.
> She speakes, yet she saies nothing, what of that?
> Her eye discourses, I will answere it.
> I am too bold, tis not to me she speakes:
> Two of the fairest starres in all the heauen,
> Hauing some busines, do entreate her eyes
> To twinckle in their spheres till they returne.
> What if her eyes were there, they in her head?
> The brightnesse of her cheek wold shame those stars,
> As day-light doth a lampe; her eye in heauen
> Would through the ayrie region streame so bright,
> That birds would sing, and thinke it were not night.
> See how she leanes her cheeke vpon her hand.
> O that I were a gloue vpon that hand,
> That I might touch that cheeke!

The logic of this passage is, in spite of its romantic reputation, almost entirely a matter of artifice. The links that bind together the various concepts — 'light', 'sun', 'moon', 'maid' in the first part; 'stars', 'eyes', 'heaven', 'night' in the second — are to a high degree mechanical, and to them corresponds an artificial conception of rhythm based on an abstract construction of carefully rounded periods. Formal considerations, in other words, prevail over the full development of emotion, and the elaborate verbal pattern corresponds to considerations that are primarily literary or rhetorical, and only in a very secondary sense personal or truly dramatic.

Because I am about to offer what may seem some all-too-personal comments on this scene, it may be as well to interpose a hint that Eliot threw out in his memorial lecture of November 21, 1950, *Poetry and Drama*.[1] I call it a hint because I have not been able to make out clearly what he had in mind. It begins with an analysis of the opening scene of *Hamlet*, in the course of which Eliot said, after quoting these lines:

> So haue I heard and doe in part belieue it,
> But looke the morne in russet mantle clad

[1] First published in England in 1951.

> Walkes ore the dewe of yon high Eastward hill,
> Breake we our watch vp . . .

Thisisgreatpoetry, and it is dramatic; but besides being poetic and dramatic, it is something more. There emerges, when we analyse it, a kind of musical design also which reinforces and is one with the dramatic movement. It has checked and accelerated the pulse of our emotion without our knowing it. Note that in these last words of Marcellus there is a deliberate brief emergence of the poetic into consciousness. When we hear the lines

> [But looke . . . . . . .          hill,]

we are lifted for a moment beyond character, but with no sense of unfitness of the words coming, and at this moment, from the lips of Horatio. The transitions in the scene obey laws of the music of dramatic poetry. . . . I think that the examination of this one scene is enough to show us that verse is not merely a formalization, or an added decoration, but that it intensifies the drama. It should indicate also the importance of the unconscious effect of the verse upon us.

At the close of these lectures he made a powerful reference to the balcony scene, which is a challenge for every reader to take up:

> It seems to me that beyond the namable, classifiable emotions and motives of our conscious life when directed towards action—the part of life which prose drama is wholly adequate to express—there is a fringe of indefinite extent, of feeling which we can only detect, so to speak, out of the corner of the eye and can never completely focus; of feeling of which we are only aware in a kind of temporary detachment from action. . . . This peculiar range of sensibility can be expressed by dramatic poetry, at its moments of greatest intensity. At such moments, we touch the border of those feelings which only music can express. We can never emulate music, because to arrive at the condition of music would be the annihilation of poetry, and especially of dramatic poetry. Nevertheless, I have before my eyes a kind of mirage of the perfection of verse drama, which would be a design of human action and of words, such as to present at once the two aspects of dramatic and of musical order. It seems to me that Shakespeare achieved this at least in certain scenes—even rather early, for there is the balcony scene of *Romeo and Juliet*—and that this was what he was striving towards in his late plays.

When Eliot decided to include this lecture in the collection of addresses he published in 1957 under the title *On Poetry and Poets*, he informed the world that the material here quoted was based on a pre-war lecture from which he printed this further extract:

In Romeo's beginning, there is still some artificiality:

[Two of the fairest . . . till they returne.]

For it seems unlikely that a man standing below in the garden, even on a very bright moonlight night, would see the eyes of the lady above flashing so brilliantly as to justify such a comparison. Yet one is aware, from the beginning of this scene, that there is a musical pattern coming, as surprising in its kind as that in the early work of Beethoven. The arrangement of voices— Juliet has three single lines, followed by Romeo's three, four and five, followed by her longer speech—is very remarkable. In this pattern, one feels that it is Juliet's voice that has the leading part: to her voice is assigned the dominant phrase of the whole duet:

[My bountie is as boundlesse as the sea,
My loue as deepe, the more I giue to thee
The more I haue, for both are infinite:]

And to Juliet is given the key-word 'lightning', which occurs again in the play, and is significant of the sudden and disastrous power of her passion, when she says

[It is too rash, too vnaduisd, too sudden,
Too like the lightning which doth cease to bee,
Ere one can say, it lightens.]

In this scene, Shakespeare achieves a perfection of verse which, being perfection, neither he nor anyone else could excel—for this particular purpose. The stiffness, the artificiality, the poetic decoration, of his early verse has finally given place to a simplification to the language of natural speech, and this language of conversation again raised to great poetry, and to great poetry which is essentially dramatic: for the scene has a structure of which each line is an essential part.

The awkward personal statement, which unless the reader endorses it has no standing whatever, is that from adolescence to old age I have so regularly found that this scene has the power to send me off and put me into a trance-like state. No conditions have been able to inhibit this response: a succession of crude Romeos and over-aged Juliets, performances in broad daylight, the sarcasm of Voltaire, the mispronouncings of schoolboys, my own remoteness from sympathy with and indeed my repulsion at hearing the word 'lyrical' applied to the moment; none of these has been able to get in the way of an impression that I hope is based exclusively on the text and might be shared by those who have not been 'got at' by irrelevant criticism. Although, having been bowled over so often, I now 'go off' very fast, sometimes during the very first lines quoted above, the solid recurring impression is not of words or passages but of a whole scene. The first feature of this experience is a strong conviction that it really is *night*, but when I ask myself what leads me to begin with this remark I find I am thinking more of being put into a state of unusual preparedness for what is to be said, and of something analogous to the physical fact that voices sound different at night. I hope that this part of my impression corresponds to the effect Eliot noticed when hearing Marcellus and Horatio: 'It has checked and accelerated the pulse of our emotion without our knowing it'. I feel I am being put into a condition of unusual refinement in which I might become fit to apprehend pure passion, something rare and unearthly and yet of the earth, into a state, in short, on the spiritual plane that would correspond with our taking in on the physical the smell of the ground at night while we gaze up at the stars.

My second impression is the predominance in this scene of the *sacred*, though the word will have to work its passage. I had better start with the milder word 'magic' for the lulling power it exercises over the moral censor in each of us. For Juliet (as she is partly aware) is doing something that ranges from the naughty through the improper to the downright immoral. This is no opera where by convention love can do no wrong. The moral censor is not tricked, the spectator is clear-eyed about the issues of right and wrong, but he becomes aware that their normal operation is suspended, and suspended by the something sacred in Juliet's soliloquy. At first the natural word for it is 'utterly private', since we feel no ear ought to hear what she is saying. Can we assume that at one point she is actually praying? At first, Romeo is not aware of intruding:

> She speakes, yet she saies nothing, what of that?
> Her eye discourses, I will answere it. . .

but then he checks himself and says

> I am too bold, tis not to me she speakes . . .

and he goes on to speak of heaven.

Before developing my sense of the further sacred aspects of the scene, let me say how this impression affects my verdict on the pronouncements of the two critics. Firstly, why don't I take offence at Romeo's string of conceits? I think it is because of the *function* of the speech at the opening of the scene. Romeo, for the moment, is merely background music. He is making the only permissible response in a situation where nobody ought to be present. He is creating an atmosphere that interprets for us what we see Juliet silently doing. In a sense he is not speaking for himself but for

us. He is casting an aura round Juliet's purity and preparing us to accept
the word 'sacred' for what is going on. We may feel a tinge of blasphemy
in the attempt to see Juliet as an angel as we are taken through the stroke
of Petrarchist fancy

> her eye in heauen,
> Would through the ayrie region streame so bright,
> That birds would sing, and thinke it were not night . . .

to the image of

> Oh speake againe bright Angel, for thou art
> As glorious to this night being ore my head,
> As is a winged messenger of heauen
> Vnto the white vpturned wondring eyes
> Of mortalls that fall backe to gaze on him,
> When he bestrides the lazie puffing Cloudes,
> And sayles vpon the bosome of the ayre.

Romeo's character is so little present in subordination to this function
that if this had been the language of character we might have had to put
some severe questions on Mr Traversi's lines: 'were you trying to be
witty? where had your *natural* feelings disappeared to?' If I am right we
should regard such questions as tactless and irrelevant. I join the broad
stream of critics in noting that Romeo's opening is a true prologue and
serves also as a *foil* to what is to come. Everybody has said to himself
what a washout the scene would be if Juliet had persisted long in the same
vein as Romeo. This opening wonder with its suggestions of the supernatural is trumped by the greater wonder of Juliet's naturalness. My reply
to Eliot would be on the lines that he was apprehending the opening of the
scene with the wrong organs. I don't think, when I note how our apprehension of night is heightened, that we feel that we are participating in a
real scene in which it matters how good the visibility is and how much of
Juliet's face Romeo can glimpse. The very fact of talking in conceits puts
normal vision into abeyance and encourages us to join in creating an *aura*,
a supernatural light that never was on land or sea.

But the real meaning of sacred escapes from the fanciful once Juliet is
actively involved. My third main impression is that the point of the scene
lies in the sacredness of promise. For me it is all in this exchange:

—Take all my selfe.
—             I take thee at thy word. . .

What makes the scene strong is the finality and completeness of the trust:
it is a scene of plighting rather than love. To say this does not mean that

we should turn up our noses at all the pretty touches, such as Juliet's practical anxieties. But the emphasis is all on faithfulness and on preserving the sanctity of what was originally a private vow. This impression is sealed by the admirable recovery of poise by Juliet. It is not an Italian love scene: it is the winning of serenity not of tumult. From the moment of the decisive exchange the scene is working steadily towards its close in

> Sleep dwel vpon thine eyes, peace in thy breast.

This putting back of natural excitement—for Juliet is certain of what is to come—gives a richness and potency to the scene.

> This bud of loue by Sommers ripening breath,
> May proue a bewtious floure when next we meete.
> Goodnight, goodnight! as sweete repose and rest
> Come to thy heart, as that within my brest!

There is much knowledge of life hidden in these thoughts, particularly that there must be a pause to allow the new knowledge of mutuality to do its work.

My last main impression—that of *maximum delight*—comes when Juliet returns to the balcony for the last time. The whole scene should be judged by its climax. What this climax does among other things is to quicken to dramatic life a potential moment of deadness, for without this climax we should be left with Romeo's mere sentiment:

> O blessed, blessed night! I am afeard
> Being in night, all this is but a dreame,
> Too flattering sweete to be substantiall.

I am prepared to go a long way with those who note how passive Romeo becomes, how prone to fall back on the expected remark. Juliet is the active partner: she is appetite, Romeo is all sentiment. Something we badly need comes when Juliet reappears and gives us a taste of the spiritual plane of her love. We get this above all from the two bird-images which create for us her feeling of possessiveness. First, she longs to be the falconer and to have the power to whistle the proud bird down: then she longs for the bird to be the pet prisoner. I feel there is much scope in this contrast between the man's bird, the hunter's bird, and the woman's bird, and that we could dwell for ever in this imaginative range. But these two images are powerful as drama because they enclose this moment:

> —I haue forgot why I did call thee backe.
> —Let me stand here till thou remember it.
> —I shall forget to haue thee still stand there,

Remembring how I loue thy companie.
—And Ile still stay, to haue thee still forget,
Forgetting any other home but this.

Here we do not think of the words they use, but of what must be going on
in their minds for them to speak like this. So I conclude that the literary
devices of this scene, which taken separately might seem poor and brittle
stuff, have turned out strong and rich enough to make us live through a
supreme moment in the play.

Once we go on to ask whether this was a tragic situation and what is its
relation to the rest of the play as a whole and to our sense of life as a
whole, we are faced with formidable critical questions, some of which the
indignant reader may feel ought to have been attempted before going
through the play at all. For nothing, he may say, has come up to justify
the inclusion of this play along with those discussed in the rest of the
book, and I might properly be suspected of a very shallow reading of the
serious plays that follow if I thought that love and death became significant issues in *Romeo and Juliet*. I have delayed the introduction of these
indispensable questions so long, first, to allow our minds to play freely
over this play without too much overshadowing from the others. For it is
worth telling ourselves that unsurpassable things can occur in plays that
cannot satisfactorily meet the large, simple questions I am concerned
with. And this in turn tells us, or at least I shall assume so, that perhaps
very few plays in fact are serious and profound works of art with an
organisation that can be found throughout in whole as in part. I am
assuming that there are some such plays and that because there are we
are able to apply standards to all plays. I am assuming, too, that for a play
there is a relation between having such an organisation and being able to
involve us as deeply as any literature can. But above all, I am assuming
that a successful play is one that in its main features we all recognise and
enjoy in similar ways. This is not to deny that plays have other features
that are not so generally appreciated.

Assumptions of this sort, I believe, are made by everybody who supposes we can engage directly in discussions about the world's greatest
plays. Though there is an interest in exploring all the implications of
these assumptions, there is no necessity to do so, and the general form of
my argument does not require that I go further into what is commonly
understood when we ask each other: were you deeply moved and what
moved you deeply? What is, however, required here is some indication of

the grounds for making out the difference between *Romeo and Juliet* and, say, *Othello*, to be very great. When details are compared with details we have no difficulty in admitting the degree of difference. If, for example, while reading the blank verse that I thought such an advance over Brooke's metre,

> What if it be a poyson . . . ,

we happen to recall a soliloquy from *Macbeth*, such as

> Is this a Dagger . . . ,

none of us, I imagine, hesitates. Yet I have seen declarations that the lines

> My bountie is as boundlesse as the sea,
> My loue as deepe, the more I giue to thee,
> The more I haue, for both are infinite. . .

do more than report what Juliet feels; they are said to present us immediately with what the words are saying.

The commonsense reply here is, I hope, the right one: that by taking over so much of Brooke's plot and by handling the sentiments in the type of blank verse characteristic of this play, Shakespeare cut us off from the deep involvement that would be ours if we felt these lines of Juliet's from the inside. The reader will by now have decided whether I have responded adequately to the 'emotional richness' of this scene of plighting. Let him substitute his own higher response, he will still have to ask when he looks at the play as a whole: what became of this plighting? The worth of professions of love lies in what lovers do when put to the test. In our play apart from the choice of marriage without parental but with religious blessing, the lovers are allowed only the choice of death. We are therefore compelled to break off discussion of the little significance of love in this play to ask about the lesser significance of death. But before yielding to this I should like to question the common assumption (taken over by Eliot) that the love in this play is characterised by those lines he quotes:

> It is too rash, too vnaduisd, too sudden,
> Too like the lightning which doth cease to bee,
> Ere one can say, it lightens.

Shakespeare has certainly accelerated the action and shortened the time between first meeting and death, but the love presented nowhere bears the mark easy-come-easy-go. The lovers are doing wonderfully well for their age and limited opportunities. Love like that, we feel, was not destined to disappear in a flash. We think rather of those legends of everlasting briars growing out of the lovers' graves or of the eternity promised by an unbroken chain of audiences who believe in the lasting power of the love so briefly presented.

If we turn to what has been written on the deaths of Romeo and Juliet, we find almost universal agreement that the play would have been more deeply moving if there had been an *essential* connection between love and death, particularly if the deaths had seemed to open out what was implied in the love. The play would still be moving if the deaths brought out and heightened the value of life expressed in the love. It is tempting here to evoke some of the beliefs that have had an unbroken underground life during all recorded history. But to set up a debate which will bring out what considerations sway us when deciding whether we have a trivial or a profound relation when love and death are brought together, let me take an instance that will not affect us too powerfully for genuine play of the mind to begin.

In 1859 Tennyson published four verse tales under the title *Idylls of the King*. One of them tells how Elaine fell in love with Lancelot, who was tied to Guinevere. This is how Tennyson represents the critical moment when the knowledge came to Elaine:

> . . . alone
> She murmur'd 'vain, in vain: it cannot be.
> He will not love me: how then? must I die.'
> Then as a little helpless innocent bird,
> That has but one plain passage of few notes,
> Will sing the simple passage o'er and o'er
> For all an April morning, till the ear
> Wearies to hear it, so the simple maid
> Went half the night repeating, 'must I die?'
> And now to right she turn'd, and now to left,
> And found no ease in turning or in rest;
> And 'him or death' she mutter'd, 'death or him',
> Again and like a burthen, 'him or death'.

The interesting complexity arises when Elaine begins to confuse love and death. As she sat in her tower her father and her brothers came to comfort her:

> But when they left her to herself again,
> Death, like a friend's voice from a distant field
> Approaching thro' the darkness, call'd; the owls
> Wailing had power upon her, and she mixt

Her fancies with the sallow-rifted glooms
Of evening, and the moanings of the wind.

And in those days she made a little song,
And call'd her song 'The Song of Love and Death,'
And sang it, sweetly could she make and sing.

'Sweet is true love tho' given in vain, in vain;
And sweet is death who puts an end to pain:
I know not which is sweeter, no, not I.

'Love, art thou sweet? then bitter death must be:
Love, thou art bitter; sweet is death to me.
O Love, if death be sweeter, let me die.

'Sweet love, that seems not made to fade away,
Sweet death, that seems to make us loveless clay,
I know not which is sweeter, no, not I.

'I fain would follow love, if that could be;
I needs must follow death, who calls for me;
Call and I follow, I follow! let me die.'

Here Tennyson is bringing back into modern consciousness the ancient
heresy which was made so much of in an attractive if not wholly responsible way by Denis de Rougemont in 1939.[1] Although Tennyson's treatment of the story is such as to make me stand some distance from it, the
situation occurring in real life would be very moving. To be denied
mutuality and to be unable to live without it are things we feel compassion
for. Yet if we take Elaine to be a suicide, something in us refuses to call
her situation tragic. Death has somehow been done away with and got
over. The suicide has contracted out of life, turned her face away from us.
The values that concern the living become useless foreign coins to the
suicide in love with death.

So I should argue we are kept at a distance as we notice the change that
comes over Romeo when he learns, as he thinks, that Juliet is dead.
There is a perverse energy, a conviction and solid reality in his

Well *Iuliet*, I will lie with thee to night.

that I do not get from Juliet's lovely imaginings:

. . . come ciuill night,
Thou sober suted matron all in blacke,
And learne me how to loose a winning match,

[1] Translated as *Passion and Society* (1940).

> Plaide for a paire of stainlesse maydenhoods:
> Hood my vnmand bloud bayting in my cheekes,
> With thy blacke mantle, till strange loue grow
> > bold,
> Thinke true loue acted simple modestie:
> Come night, come *Romeo*, come thou day in night,
> For thou wilt lie vpon the winges of night
> Whiter than new snow on a Rauens backe. . .

Romeo strikes us, that is to say, as more manly in his decision to die than in his love-making. Everyone notices how practical and efficient he suddenly becomes in devising the speediest means to encompass his suicide. It is hard to believe that this is the man who a few days before was grovelling on the floor of the Friar's cell. But then to our disappointment we find he is all attitude. He never once looks death in the face as it really is. Death has become for him almost a figure of speech. He does not see Juliet or Tybalt as really dead. All he sees are bodies minus life; but for Romeo the substance is the body; the absence of life hardly matters. And when Romeo thinks of himself as dead, he sees himself as 'out', a mere nothing. Death is for him a relief, a permanent sleeping tablet:

> > O here
> Will I set vp my euerlasting rest,
> And shake the yoke of inauspicious starres
> From this world wearied flesh.

Juliet's death is similar, save that she is all act without reflection:

> Yea noise? then ile be briefe. O happy dagger
> This is thy sheath, there rust and let me dye.

The reader who will now grant that these deaths shut us out may perhaps be willing to entertain the proposition (returning now to consider the love) that Romeo and Juliet had in effect (but not, of course, in intention) been contracting out of society from the first. Those who disapprove of the feud are not sorry to see both young people disregarding those social ties. But if Juliet could help herself, or if she had been merely flirting with Romeo, how could she have excused her behaviour if, say, Tybalt had turned on her? Shakespeare has done a great deal to soften the odium of the deceptions involved in the secret marriage. We are not here concerned much with praise or blame—there is plenty of room for all views ranging from the extremely romantic to the extremely puritanical or even legalistic view of family obligations—as with noting the rôle love plays in the drama.

STL C

So far we have notched up the point that this love isn't given much
chance either by the plot or the style. It doesn't in fact percolate through
the Verona world and join up with all the other human relations there. It
is commonly remarked from the other side that none of the personages
and especially not the Nurse and Mercutio has any conception of what
the love is that fires the young couple. We can reverse the remark and say
that the lovers fail to see what they have in common with such *social*
figures. But this is not the strongest way of making the remark or the most
useful when we are trying to find the meaning of asking whether a play is
a whole. There was a dangerous implication in saying that we are less
moved by an incipient love relation than by one that has been extended to
its final limits: we may come to think that incipient love could never become a significant theme giving unity to a mature play. I find myself
hankering for a sufficient number of gifted amateurs to take up the exercises I mentioned in the first sentences of my first chapter. For if a hundred others would sketch out a tragic scenario on the basis of Brooke's
poem I should like to cheat and see what else could be done with it after
studying *Romeo and Juliet*, not because of any particular twist I might
introduce but for the sake of the general principle I might hope to embody. For it is plain to me that once we have Shakespeare's play before us
we cannot take the raw material of Brooke's poem seriously until the
vision that created the lovers has played over the whole world of Verona.
We can be excited—if the reader will pardon what has become *the* cant
word of these last few years—by the vision but we cannot be profoundly
moved until our sense of life as a whole has been brought into play.

It is perhaps safer to keep to images of light and heat when guessing as
critics what might be the general nature of artistic creation, yet I should
not like to be confined by them or prevented from at least hinting that the
unifying power must be simultaneously described as a form of *intelligence*.
For if part of that 'vision' of young love was the recognition that it must
by its nature contract out from all other relations, another part of *wisdom*
would be to see this unique value in a contrasting context of all the great
values that depend on man entering into multiple relations with other
men. (A similar argument could apply to the lovers by asking what follows
for them as individuals as a result of their love, and answering that the
lovers become subdued to being mere vessels of their passion and so, for
the time, to being out of touch with all their other human potentialities.
We therefore need in the play a plastic intelligence to comprehend *and
criticize* the lovers.) Since it is most unlikely that we shall ever get the
powerful critical jolt we might receive from seeing somebody start
again where Shakespeare did and create a play that would show up

*Romeo and Juliet*, we may re-direct elsewhere the interest aroused by this play and all the topics that have to be left unresolved on the margins just because Shakespeare could not forge a unity out of his materials. If we carry away from the discussion a provisional hypothesis that it might be the special contribution of serious drama to relate love and death in significant wholes, where the whole cannot be significant unless we feel that life as a whole has been re-sourced[1] thereby, we may hope to test the hypothesis by considering three plays in which Shakespeare appears to have been trying to accomplish what he failed to do in *Romeo and Juliet*.

[1] For the term, see *D. H. Lawrence's Early Tales* by J. C. F. Littlewood in *The Cambridge Quarterly*, Vol. 1, No. 2, Spring 1966.

# Othello

# CHAPTER 1

# Overdoing it

'FROM all the Tragedies acted on our English Stage, *Othello* is said to bear the Bell away.'[1] This play, as far as I know, is one of the very few plays by Shakespeare that have never altogether lost their popularity. *Othello* has had critically a continuous run and practically (France being the notorious exception) a world run. It is therefore peculiarly baffling and exasperating to find that *quot homines tot sententiae* holds good here, with each new critic coming along with a fresh interpretation and no single view enlarging its grip on our generation. A special cause must be found for so odd an effect, since nobody finds the play difficult, and I tentatively advance a suggestion which may gradually appear more plausible as the argument develops, that *we cannot face Othello*. Parts, perhaps even great parts, we can enter into with a wonderful feeling of meeting the genius of Shakespeare; yet for every mind there is something in the play that cannot be faced. This unbearable something is never the same for each of us. Indeed, if we examined all the critics and took out of *Othello* everything they cannot stomach, almost every feather would be plucked and not much of *Othello* would be left. That this is true of many people who have written on the play requires no argument: there are entertaining records of critics who could not face Othello's *négritude*, of others who in their anxiety to retain a sense of the hero's *nobility* have erased from the play the fact that he was willing to eavesdrop; we have had productions in which to preserve Desdemona's reputation for *purity* the gossip at the harbour was omitted.

In this preliminary survey of various ways of misreading the play or evading its point I shall lump together matters of very different degrees of importance; and in treating them all lightly I may accidentally appear to be suggesting that I have been successful where great critics have fallen short. The patient reader will eventually discover from my constant recourse to them that this absurd reversal of rôles has not occurred. My aim will be throughout to feel round for the truths we can all join in affirming, since I believe that a right reading of the broadest features of a

[1] Quoted from *A Short View of Tragedy; It's Original, Excellency, and Corruption. With some Reflections on Shakespear, and other Practitioners for the Stage.* By Mr. *Rymer*, Servant to their Majesties, (1693) p. 86.

great play is something that is in our power to attain. The public I am
interested in unifying in terms of an account of the general nature of the
play holds such diverse views that arguments which might prove telling
to one member will not touch another. I have assumed that my major
effort towards an agreed account must lie in persuading many people
that they have been indulging in a wantonly exaggerated interest in
character, that they have assumed that every single personage offered a
consistent character, that the play is a jig-saw puzzle, every piece of
which is made up of 'character-material'; that, in short, the play is *exclusively* 'character in action'. I shall hope to make good the observation that
the first condition for a satisfactory common reading of *Othello* is to hold
in check this wanton and exaggerated interest, of which the following is
a typical specimen:

> Cassio is a ladies' man, that is to say, a man who feels most at home in
> feminine company where his looks and good manners make him popular,
> but is ill at ease in the company of his own sex because he is unsure of his
> masculinity. In civilian life he would be perfectly happy, but circumstances
> have made him a soldier and he has been forced by his profession into a
> society which is predominantly male. Had he been born a generation earlier,
> he would never have found himself in the army at all, but changes in the
> technique of warfare demand of soldiers not only the physical courage and
> aggressiveness which the warrior has always needed, but also intellectual
> gifts.[1]

A second assumption is that similar restraint must be urged on all those
who regard Iago as the central interest of the play. Since the liveliest
readers may be found here, I hope that they will not take offence at my
grudging attitude towards this personage since my numerous sallies at
his expense extend very little further than this claim and a general *caveat*
against importing a significance not obviously there in the text. Here I
judged it to be less important to try to move into what when it comes will
prove to be the sound general line of our day than to irritate and sting
people who are clearly more eccentric one way that I am the other. I have,
however, assumed that here the great Bradley of *Shakespearean Tragedy*
(1904) was excessive and has been a nation's spokesman, and that there
are telling arguments against his in Professor Leavis's famous article in
*Scrutiny* [December 1937].[2]

The reader who finds me a wretched little lap dog yapping at the heels

---

[1] W. H. Auden, in *Encounter* [August 1961].
[2] *Diabolic Intellect and the Noble Hero: A Note on Othello*, reprinted with a small
change of title in *The Common Pursuit* [1952].

of noble animals will perhaps revert to the charge that I have failed to take my own measure when he discovers me, to retain half the image, biting the hand that fed me, and including Professor Leavis's account among those that are not 'dead on'. Any force such a criticism of a great critic may have comes from the plausibility of the general account I am struggling to leave the reader with. From the difficulty I had in surrendering even single sentences I know that considerable violence is needed to shake readers, young as well as old, of what after all these years still seems to me a foundation essay if we are trying to make out what is the general nature of the play and what is its central action. On the other hand, I feel confident that my own suggestions about the general nature of the play are put with all the hesitations I still feel. Nevertheless I am counting on a good deal of assent, from spontaneous to grudging, when I urge all those who are at the moment in agreement with what is common to Bradley's lectures and Leavis's essay to allow for a possibility that they have exaggerated the extent to which the play is, as Professor Leavis wrote, such that 'relevant discussion of . . . [*Othello's*] tragic significance will . . . be mainly a matter of character-analysis' and 'the tragedy may fairly be said to be Othello's character in action'. That is to say, if I may now become a small tug-boat with some great liner to steer or head off, I think I have allies in the minds of all readers who start from the Bradley-Leavis assumption and that very small signals will meet with massive response.

The signals are in themselves so slight, and are so plainly derived from things in the work of both critics—and my debts to other critics will become apparent as I go along—that the opposite charge may be made; that when I have finished my account it appears so like those of Bradley and Leavis that it was hardly worth my while here raising and trying to meet the objection that I was presumptuously challenging their authority. This is the position I would wish to share with the reader: we are as wrens on the shoulders of eagles. But once we have measured and contrasted with our own the upward effort of these mighty birds we may safely concentrate on that final hop into the upper air; for, after all, as long as both critics are flourishing as they are, I have no other justification for asking a reader to bear with so many pages on one play.

*        *        *

The reader who has by now observed how readily I go in for 'character-study' myself may wonder why I make such an issue of it here and what in particular I would have in mind in speaking of a wanton and extravagant interest. It does indeed seem to me the most natural thing in the world to do when going to the theatre. The 'words' of plays are, after all, always in the mouths of personages speaking their parts. The situation of the recipient in an imaginary theatre determines the reader's response. It will always predispose us toward character-mongering at least as much as in ordinary life when we partake in or overhear what appears to be meaningful talk going on between two or more people. The process is so natural that it is hard at first to see how it could be overdone. Yet since this is the principal modification I recommend in the general way of taking *Othello*, I must go out of my way to show that there are conditions where this activity of trying to make out 'characters' from dialogue can become a wanton and improper indulgence.

A remarkably vivid instance of this was provided by Virginia Woolf in a pamphlet[1] written to illustrate what she thought was the novelist's interest in character:

> But novelists differ from the rest of the world because they do not cease to be interested in character when they have learnt enough about it for practical purposes. They go a step further; they feel that there is something permanently interesting in character in itself. When all the practical business of life has been discharged, there is something about people which continues to seem to them of overwhelming importance, in spite of the fact that it has no bearing upon their happiness, comfort, or income. The study of character becomes to them an absorbing pursuit; to impart character an obsession. And this I find it very difficult to explain: what novelists mean when they talk about character, what the impulse is that urges them so powerfully every now and then to embody their view in writing.
>
> So, if you will allow me, instead of analysing and abstracting, I will tell you a simple story which, however pointless, has the merit of being true, of a journey from Richmond to Waterloo, in the hope that I may show you what I mean by character in itself; that you may realise the different aspects it can wear; and the hideous perils that beset you directly you try to describe it in words.
>
> One night some weeks ago, then, I was late for the train and jumped into the first carriage I came to. As I sat down I had the strange and uncomfortable feeling that I was interrupting a conversation between two people who were already sitting there. Not that they were young or happy. Far from it. They were both elderly, the woman over sixty, the man well over forty. They were sitting opposite each other, and the man, who had been leaning over and talking emphatically to judge by his attitude and the flush on his face, sat back and became silent. I had disturbed him, and he was

---

[1] *Mr. Bennett and Mrs. Brown* [1924].

annoyed. The elderly lady, however, whom I will call Mrs. Brown, seemed rather relieved. She was one of those clean, threadbare old ladies whose extreme tidiness—everything buttoned, fastened, tied together, mended and brushed up—suggests more extreme poverty than rags and dirt. There was something pinched about her—a look of suffering, of apprehension, and, in addition, she was extremely small. Her feet, in their clean little boots, scarcely touched the floor. I felt that she had nobody to support her; that she had to make up her mind for herself; that, having been deserted, or left a widow, years ago, she had led an anxious, harried life, bringing up an only son, perhaps, who, as likely as not, was by this time beginning to go to the bad. All this shot through my mind as I sat down, being uncomfortable, like most people, at travelling with fellow passengers unless I have somehow or other accounted for them. Then I looked at the man. He was no relation of Mrs. Brown's I felt sure; he was of a bigger, burlier, less refined type. He was a man of business I imagined, very likely a respectable corn-chandler from the North, dressed in good blue serge with a pocket-knife and a silk handkerchief, and a stout leather bag. Obviously, however, he had an unpleasant business to settle with Mrs. Brown; a secret, perhaps sinister business, which they did not intend to discuss in my presence.

'Yes, the Crofts have had very bad luck with their servants', Mr. Smith (as I will call him) said in a considering way, going back to some earlier topic, with a view to keeping up appearances.

'Ah, poor people', said Mrs. Brown a trifle condescendingly. 'My grandmother had a maid who came when she was fifteen and stayed till she was eighty' (this was said with a kind of hurt and aggressive pride to impress us both perhaps).

'One doesn't often come across that sort of thing nowadays', said Mr. Smith in conciliatory tones.

Then they were silent.

'It's odd they don't start a golf club there—I should have thought one of the young fellows would', said Mr. Smith, for the silence obviously made him uneasy. Mrs Brown hardly took the trouble to answer.

'What changes they're making in this part of the world', said Mr. Smith looking out of the window, and looking furtively at me as he did do (*sic*).

It was plain, from Mrs. Brown's silence, from the uneasy affability with which Mr. Smith spoke, that he had some power over her which he was exerting disagreeably. It might have been her son's downfall, or some painful episode in her past life, or her daughter's. Perhaps she was going to London to sign some document to make over some property. Obviously against her will she was in Mr. Smith's hands. I was beginning to feel a great deal of pity for her, when she said, suddenly and inconsequently,

'Can you tell me if an oak-tree dies when the leaves have been eaten for two years in succession by caterpillars?'

She spoke quite brightly, and rather precisely, in a cultivated, inquisitive voice.

Mr. Smith was startled, but relieved to have a safe topic of conversation given him. He told her a great deal very quickly about plagues of insects. He told her that he had a brother who kept a fruit farm in Kent. He told her what fruit farmers do every year in Kent, and so on, and so on. While he talked a very odd thing happened. Mrs Brown took out her little white handkerchief and began to dab her eyes. She was crying. But she went on listening quite composedly to what he was saying, and he went on talking, a little louder, a little angrily, as if he had seen her cry often before; as if it were a painful habit. At last it got on his nerves. He stopped abruptly, looked out of the window, then leant towards her as he had been doing when I got in, and said in a bullying, menacing way, as if he would not stand any more nonsense,

'So about that matter we were discussing. It'll be all right? George will be there on Tuesday?'

'We shan't be late', said Mrs. Brown, gathering herself together with superb dignity.

Mr. Smith said nothing. He got up, buttoned his coat, reached his bag down, and jumped out of the train before it had stopped at Clapham Junction. He had got what he wanted, but he was ashamed of himself; he was glad to get out of the old lady's sight.

Mrs. Brown and I were left alone together. She sat in her corner opposite, very clean, very small, rather queer, and suffering intensely. The impression she made was overwhelming. It came pouring out like a draught, like a smell of burning. What was it composed of—that overwhelming and peculiar impression? Myriads of irrelevant and incongruous ideas crowd into one's head on such occasions; one sees the person, one sees Mrs. Brown, in the centre of all sorts of different scenes. I thought of her in a seaside house, among queer ornaments: sea-urchins, models of ships in glass cases. Her husband's medals were on the mantlepiece. She popped in and out of the room, perching on the edges of chairs, picking meals out of saucers, indulging in long, silent stares. The caterpillars and the oak-trees seemed to imply all that. And then, into this fantastic and secluded life, in broke Mr. Smith. I saw him blowing in, so to speak, on a windy day. He banged, he slammed. His dripping umbrella made a pool in the hall. They sat closeted together.

And then Mrs. Brown faced the dreadful revelation. She took her heroic decision. Early, before dawn, she packed her bag and carried it herself to the station. She would not let Smith touch it. She was wounded in her pride, unmoored from her anchorage; she came of gentlefolks who kept servants—

but details could wait. The important thing was to realise her character, to steep oneself in her atmosphere. I had no time to explain why I felt it somewhat tragic, heroic, yet with a dash of the flighty, and fantastic, before the train stopped, and I watched her disappear, carrying her bag, into the vast blazing station. She looked very small, very tenacious; at once very frail and very heroic. And I have never seen her again, and I shall never know what became of her.

The story ends without any point to it. But I have not told you this anecdote to illustrate either my own ingenuity or the pleasure of travelling from Richmond to Waterloo. What I want you to see in it is this. Here is a character imposing itself upon another person. Here is Mrs. Brown making someone begin almost automatically to write a novel about her. I believe that all novels begin with an old lady in the corner opposite. I believe that all novels, that is to say, deal with character, and that it is to express character—not to preach doctrines, sing songs, or celebrate the glories of the British Empire, that the form of the novel, so clumsy, verbose, and undramatic, so rich, elastic, and alive, has been evolved. (pp. 5–10)

It is not a necessary stage in my argument but it would certainly help if the reader saw something that had wrongly run away with her in Virginia Woolf's unconscious revelation of her social snobbery and was willing to argue from the readiness she shewed to indulge in 'flights' of fancy that her hold on moral and social realities was less than a firm grasp. Nevertheless I think that the 'brilliance' of this passage represents an ideal to which the young are still being encouraged to aspire. The reason may well be that since prose fiction has become the preponderant reading of the age, the habit of 'romancing' life as distinct from the more rational brilliance of a Sherlock Holmes is on the way to being second nature. 'Reads like a novel' is gradually becoming the criterion for all our reading matter. That there is a different response required from us when we are at the play is not generally recognised. 'Yes, that is all very well,' the reader may retort, 'but surely there are some characters so fully given by Shakespeare that a proper response does not consist of wanton speculation. There are no gaps to be filled out by the Virginia Woolf in us. What about the main character—Iago?'

That this is how many readers are still taking the play is one of those *data* which make the hope of a common reading seem ridiculous. For there is no general reason for discounting such readers: they are just as considerable as those who were convinced by Professor Leavis's essay. Nor will it do to saddle them with all the preconceptions of the Romantics as exhibited in Bradley's lectures. Although this view of Iago comes to us

from the Romantics it has received distinctively modern support. Mr.
Auden's essay begins, 'Any consideration of *The Tragedy of Othello* must
be primarily occupied not with its official hero but with its villain'. Tact,
therefore, commands me to make a very modest opening. Is there such a
thing as overdoing it? Are we bound to press *every* one of Iago's many and
varied appearances, every one of his speeches long and short, into a
single consistent character? Have we no right to describe such attempts
as 'wanton and excessive'?

The question is answered if it can be shewn that Shakespeare himself
was interested in obtaining consistency. (In any full debate we should
have to listen here to Professor Stoll, who might complain with even
greater force than any critic yet mentioned that *his* arguments on this
topic[1] have not carried greater weight.) And here by general agreement
one concession in my favour must be made. For when Shakespeare himself has an interest in character he betrays it by having his personage speak
in a way shared by nobody else in the play. (He doesn't do this so often as
is supposed.) Conversely, when a personage given such distinction loses
it we must argue that Shakespeare's interest in character has yielded to
some greater interest. An instance that strikes every reader occurs here:

> Trifles light as ayre,
> Are to the iealious, confirmations strong,
> As proofes of holy Writ. . . .
> Dangerous conceites, are in their Natures poysons,
> Which at the first are scarce found to distaste:
> But with a little acte vpon the blood,
> Burne like the Mines of Sulphure . . .

> Not Poppy, nor Mandragora,
> Nor all the drowsie Syrrups of the world
> Shall euer medicine thee to that sweete sleepe
> Which thou owd'st yesterday.

If in the spirit of Ben Jonson's (here echoing Vives) phrase—'*Language*
most shewes a man: speake that I may see thee. It springs out of the most
retired, and inmost parts of us, and is the Image of the Parent of it, the
mind . . .'[2] we ask what kind of mind we come into contact with as we
hear these lines spoken by Iago, should we not have to call it large and

---

[1] E. E. Stoll. *Othello*: an historical and comparative study (1915).

[2] TIMBER: / OR, / DISCOVERIES; / MADE VPON MEN / AND MATTER:
AS THEY / have flow'd out of his daily Read- / ings; or had their refluxe to his /
peculiar Notion of the Times / by / Ben: Iohnson. / . . . London / Printed M.D.C.
XLI. p. 120 *Oratio imago animi.*

noble? Must we not salute the power that can rise above events and sum them up in such a general law as

> Trifles light as ayre . . . ,

and, if so, do we not feel it is a power like that we feel in these lines:

> And be these Iugling Fiends no more beleeu'd,
> That palter with vs in a double sence,
> That keepe the word of promise to our eare,
> And breake it to our hope . . . ?

Is not the accent of

> Not Poppy, nor Mandragora . . .

similar to that of

> Better be with the dead,
> Whom we, to gayne our peace, haue sent to peace,
> Then on the torture of the Minde to lye
> In restlesse extasie.
> *Duncane* is in his Graue:
> After Lifes fitfull Feuer, he sleepes well,
> Treason ha's done his worst: nor Steele, nor Poyson,
> Mallice domestique, forraine Leuie, nothing,
> Can touch him further . . . ?

The function of these speeches seems to me plain: they are asking us for the moment to send the interior Virginia Woolf to sleep and to allow another side of the mind to take over, that which is asking what is the significance of this particular set of events that is unrolling itself before us and whether that significance does not extend beyond the particular set of events to the whole of life.

This side of the mind is certainly brought into play by the many references to Heaven and Hell. Although some of the darker allusions appear to bear rather on Othello than Iago, it cannot be denied that we are occasionally forced to think of the Great Tempter when we see Iago at work. But is it not overdoing things to find Iago himself the incarnation of Evil? Here is one critic:

> Evil has nowhere else been portrayed with such mastery as in the character of Iago . . . to compare Iago with the Satan of *Paradise Lost* seems almost absurd, so immensely does Shakespeare's man exceed Milton's Fiend in evil . . . It is only in Goethe's Mephistopheles that a fit companion for Iago can be found . . .

to which another critic replied, 'Iago's overwhelming verisimilitude and fascinating inscrutability . . . put him in a class above Goethe's Mephistopheles'. Granted that these views are excessive, can we say by how much? Their plausibility rests on that of two other views: first, that 'the fall of Othello is the work of another human being; nothing he says and does originates with himself' and, second, that Shakespeare meant us to regard as the *clou* of the play that moment in the final scene where Othello charges Iago,

> Will you, I pray, demand that demy-Diuell,
> Why he hath thus ensnar'd my Soule and Body.

and Iago replies,

> Demand me nothing: what you know, you know.

If confidence is shaken in these two points much of the exaggeration will fall away of itself.


Another form of overdoing it the scheme of this book will not permit me to do justice to, although some mention of it is required here to round off the question: what in general should be our expectation of the play? Here are a couple of quotations:

> . . . the play, everyone agrees, is a brilliantly successful piece of workmanship. . . . 'Clumsy', however, is not the right word for anything in *Othello*. It is a marvellously sure and adroit piece of workmanship.[1]

Is that the voice of the great critic or the inert last gasp of Romantic Bardolatry? That 'everyone' and that 'anything' should put us on our guard. It is a great pity that Rymer and Voltaire introduced into their strictures arguments that any schoolboy could see were irrelevant, for what began in Romantic generosity has ended in national complacency. The assumption that we must swallow every Shakespeare play whole has done much to alienate young minds. There might be some excuse if Shakespeare were a fraud and there were reason to fear that if we were allowed to pick a little hole here and there we should soon find that the whole fabric was rotten, but there is not the slightest danger. If we were to exercise our natural taste we might come to see that one reason why Shakespeare could not have published his own Folio was that the labour of removing his faults would have been too great for him and too painful. If the addition of that last word be thought merely fanciful I would ask:

[1] F. R. Leavis, *op cit.*

why should we deny to Shakespeare consciousness of the difference between his good parts and his bad? Why cannot we suppose that he himself wished that his genius had not been so facile, and that he would have longed in his prime for the leisure needed to bring one play at least to perfection?

> *I remember*, the Players have often mentioned it as an honour to *Shakespeare*, that in his writing, (whatsoever he penn'd) hee never blotted out line. My answer hath beene, would he had blotted a thousand. Which they thought a malevolent speech. I had not told posterity this, but for their ignorance, who choose that circumstance to commend their friend by, wherein he most faulted.[1]

*Othello* seems to me to bear obvious signs of hasty composition and clumsy craftsmanship. I cannot believe that Shakespeare ever re-read his first draft. Moreover, one instance seems to me *proof* that he began the play without knowing how it was going to develop. An important turning point for Othello in his temptation concerns a fact which Desdemona advances and Othello confirms:

> What? *Michael Cassio*,
> That came a woing with you? and so many a time
> (When I haue spoke of you dispraisingly)
> Hath tane your part . . .

In the first act we find that Cassio has no knowledge of these events. He does not know what Othello was doing in the Sagitary:

> —Aunciant, what makes he heere?
> —Faith, he to night hath boarded a Land Carract.
>   If it proue lawfull prize, he's made for euer.
> —I do not vnderstand.
> —He's married.
> —To who?

If Shakespeare had re-read the play after completing it he could not have overlooked this passage.

As for the depths of bad writing I imagine the opening exchanges between the Clown and the Musicians in the third act (themselves a poorer version of a similarly poor episode in the fourth act of *Romeo and Juliet*) are among the feeblest things Shakespeare wrote. Though I can believe that Shakespeare scribbled them in a hurry and very much *inuita Minerua*, yet I can't think him capable, on re-reading, of leaving them in.

[1] Ben Jonson, *op. cit.*, pp. 97–98.

At one point I believe we should refuse to credit Shakespeare with our text. In the third scene of the first Act he gives Brabantio and the Duke a distinctive style, by which we know them, as here:

—Come hither Moore;
  I here do giue thee that with all my heart[1]
  I would keepe from thee. For your sake (Iewell)
  I am glad at soule, I haue no other Child,
  For thy escape would teach me Tirranie
  To hang clogges on them. I haue done my Lord.
—Let me speake like your selfe: And lay a Sentence,
  Which as a grise, or step may helpe these Louers.

The Duke then steps out of his part and speaks lines impossible for the man we have got to know:

When remedies are past, the griefes are ended
By seeing the worst, which late on hopes depended.
To mourne a Mischeefe that is past and gon,
Is the next way to draw new mischiefe on.
Etc. etc.

And Brabantio imitates him:

So let the Turke of Cyprus vs beguile,
We loose it not so long as we can smile:
He beares the Sentence well, that nothing beares,
But the free comfort which from thence he heares.
Etc. etc.

This sketch of the extravagances in our inheritance is far from being complete, but, wanting as it is in features that for different readers would seem very much more pressing than those I have drawn attention to, it is still a formidable total of counter-pulls for the would-be judicious neophyte. All the more reason then for attempting only the first critical step and asking: what sort of thing is *Othello*, has it a main point, what must we at all costs become clearer about in our first readings and what can we safely neglect? These examples of overdoing it give us some negative hints. The hasty composition and clumsiness of craftsmanship warn us not to make too much of faults of detail. At the same time they prevent us from supposing Shakespeare had constructed a novel before he wrote a

[1] The Folio here has a line:
    Which but thou hast already, with all my heart

play, that he had pondered the early career of Cassio or had thought much about Othello's mother. All this has a bearing on the kind of character interest that can be present.

The prime question here, of course, is whether there is one over-riding, controlling interest which can keep us from overdoing the subordinate interests. A second question is whether the play's horizons are so narrow as is supposed by calling *Othello* a *domestic* tragedy. Bradley says:

> If . . . we feel [*Othello*] to occupy a place in our minds a little lower than the other three [tragedies] (and I believe this feeling, though not general, is not rare), the reason lies . . . in . . . the comparative confinement of the imaginative atmosphere. *Othello* has not equally with the other three the power of dilating the imagination by vague suggestions of huge universal powers working in the world of individual fate and passion. It is, in a sense, less 'symbolic'. We seem to be aware in it of a certain limitation, a partial suppression of that element in Shakespeare's mind which unites him with the mystical poets and with the great musicians and philosophers. In one or two of his plays, notably in *Troilus and Cressida*, we are almost painfully conscious of this suppression; we feel an intense intellectual activity, but at the same time a certain coldness and hardness, as though some power in his soul, at once the highest and the sweetest, were for a time in abeyance. In other plays, notably in the *Tempest*, we are constantly aware of the presence of this power; and in such cases we seem to be peculiarly near to Shakespeare himself. Now this is so in *Hamlet* and *King Lear*, and, in a slighter degree, in *Macbeth*; but it is much less so in *Othello*. I do not mean that in *Othello* the suppression is marked, or that, as in *Troilus and Cressida*, it strikes us as due to some unpleasant mood; it seems rather to follow simply from the design of a play on a contemporary and wholly mundane subject. Still it makes a difference of the kind I have attempted to indicate, and it leaves an impression that in *Othello* we are not in contact with the whole of Shakespeare. And it is perhaps significant in this respect that the hero himself strikes us as having, probably, less of the poet's personality in him than many characters far inferior both as dramatic creations and as men.[1]

Are we obliged to follow?

Is it a counter-reply to remind the reader that like *Macbeth* this is a play in which the actual death of the hero is a subordinate matter? The dreadful fact is that Othello is damned, eternally damned, and that both he and we know it before he kills himself. This is not the only fact about the unleashing of evil; the human consequences are fully drawn, which enables us to say that in many respects *Othello* resembles Sophocles'

[1] *Shakespearean Tragedy* (1904), pp. 185–186.

*Antigone*. Negatively, we can say that the one play turns as little on the loss of a handkerchief as the other does on the burial of a brother. Both raise baffling questions about love, both ask what it means to be intelligent about life, both leave us with the tantalising notion of the 'guiltless guilt' of the heroines. Whether *Othello* is the inferior play is too difficult a question for me. On the other hand, this may be the rallying ground for the rival views about *Othello*. Perhaps we are not so much called on to move the play up or down the scale of valuation as to give clear reasons why it is found disturbing rather than profoundly moving. This might involve exposing ourselves to pain rather than pleasure and require a willingness to face in all directions suggestions that we would instinctively avoid.

The critical problem, as I see it, is chiefly to determine how much more we have to face than a play of intrigue, both internal and external. So much of the play can be kept at arm's length and *this by the author's own design*. On the surface we have a predicament that becomes serious only by an improbable series of mischance and only for an exceptional individual. On the surface we are invited merely to consider the mechanics of an extreme case of jealousy. Are we ever drawn closer in, is there anything to make *us* feel *perplexed in the extreame*? Had the author any other design than a well-executed plot, and if so, is it fully drawn?

Lastly, in this very search for significant principles of organisation other than those of plot and characters, is there not also such a thing as overdoing it?

# CHAPTER 2

# The Structure of the First Two Acts

ANYONE seeing *Othello* for the first time who was called away after the first act would have to admit that he might have been witnessing the opening of a comedy. Lovers of 'archetypes' must know of dozens of plays which begin with irate fathers and escaping children and end with reconciliations between parents and children, fathers and sons-in-law. There is hardly a personage in this act who does not at some point raise a smile in us as he unconsciously gives away his ridiculous side. Indeed one figure at least often loses in performance from being treated exclusively as a fool. This part, however, may be the one that has most to tell us about how to take the act as a whole. Shakespeare, I should say, gives us no excuse for overlooking the graver side of Brabantio. For what comes closest to us in all the hurry, excitement and confusion (which prevents our settling down to studying the main characters) is the strong impression of having been plunged into a frightening world. The Venice of this act is not given in any fullness: the area of our acutest uneasiness is confined to sexual morals: it is not such a vicious place as the Vienna of *Measure for Measure* but it is both larger and more disturbing than the Verona of *Romeo and Juliet*. My first impression is of its insecurity and lack of support for any enduring human relations.

The vague frightening feeling first focusses itself round Brabantio and his night alarm and perhaps because of this has some of the fearsomeness of the intrusion of moral knowledge upon our childish imaginings, or rather the uneasy dawning of half-knowledge when for the first time important events are seen to be open to equivocal interpretations. The childish visions of Traherne will remind us of the extreme opposite of Shakespeare's Venice:

All appeared New, and Strange at the first, inexpressibly rare, and Delight-full, and Beautifull. I was a little Stranger which at my Enterance into the World was Saluted and Surrounded with innumerable Joys . . . All Things were Spotles and Pure and Glorious: yea, and infinitly mine, and Joyfull and Precious. I Knew not that there were any Sins, or Complaints, or Laws. I Dreamed not of Poverties Contentions or Vices. All Tears and Quarrels, were hidden from mine Eys. Evry Thing was at Rest, Free, and Immortal. I Knew Nothing of Sickness or Death, or Exaction, in the Absence of these I was Entertained like an Angel with the Works of GOD in their Splendor and Glory . . . O what Venerable and Reverend Creatures did the Aged seem! Immortal Cherubims! And yong Men Glittering and Sparkling Angels and Maids strange Seraphick Pieces of Life and Beauty! Boys and Girles Tumbling in the Street, and Playing, were moving Jewels . . .[1]

'So that', says Traherne, 'with much adoe I was corrupted; and made to learn the Dirty Devices of this World.' We date the birth of our moral consciousness almost from the day when we recognize that the real can never be completely purged of its equivocal interpretations. The choice of Venice was admirable in that its notoriety as a centre of *la dolce vita* permits us to delay the moment when we have to recognize how much that Venice resembles the comparatively decent city or village we may happen to live in.

*Othello* grips us when it forces us simultaneously to take two opposed views both of the main action and its principal actors. It does not grip us when as so often it proposes melodramatic antitheses such as Othello's *sootie bosome* and

> that whiter skin of hers, then Snow,
> And smooth as Monumentall Alablaster:

or when Iago's 'cynicism' is played off against Othello's 'sentimentalism'. The oppositions that grip us are those that give us a pain we cannot easily face. The facile painless oppositions have the effect of making us blush for Shakespeare and the reach-me-down world of

> Theatre business, management of men

in which *Othello* no doubt had to be composed. A great deal of the play does not *speak home* and leaves us very much mere spectators and outsiders. (Here, however, allowance must be made for Shakespeare's deeper knowledge of what an audience could bear. He may have kept aloof from some realities to prevent our running out of the theatre before the end of the play.)

Shakespeare certainly offers us many simple matters, simple at least on the surface, to occupy our attention while the deeply interesting complexities are slowly forming. One such simple matter is Iago: he presents himself with all the artlessness of Richard the Third:

> I follow him, to serue my turne vpon him.
> We cannot all be Masters, nor all Masters

[1] *Thomas Traherne, Centuries, Poems, and Thanksgivings*, edited by H. M. Margoliouth (1958), Vol. I, pp. 110–111.

> Cannot be truely follow'd. You shall marke
> Many a dutious and knee-crooking knaue;
> That (doting on his owne obsequious bondage)
> Weares out his time, much like his Masters Asse,
> For naught but Prouender, & when he's old Casheer'd.
> Whip me such honest knaues. Others there are
> Who trym'd in Formes, and visages of Dutie,
> Keepe yet their hearts attending on themselues,
> And throwing but showes of Seruice on their Lords
> Doe well thriue by them.
> And when they haue lin'd their Coates
> Doe themselues Homage.
> These Fellowes haue some soule,
> And such a one do I professe my selfe.

But he is not only the villain, he is also the rogue and the clown, and as such he has the privilege of speaking the bitter truths that others prefer to hide. He is more interesting to us when he stands for many other Venetians, perhaps for something in every Venetian. But there is no rule to tell which Iago is speaking, and from the beginning to the end of the play we must judge for ourselves what authority to give to anything he says.

In this act he tells us some painful or unpleasant things which we come to see as truths. For instance, his unflattering remarks about Othello:

> But he (as louing his owne pride, and purposes)
> Euades them, with a bumbast Circumstance,
> Horribly stufft with Epithetes of warre . . .

receive immediate partial confirmation in Othello's first speech:

> My Seruices, which I haue done the Signorie
> Shall out-tongue his Complaints. 'Tis yet to know,
> Which when I know that boasting is an Honour,
> I shall prouulgate. I fetch my life and being
> From Men of Royall Seige. And my demerites
> May speake (vnbonnetted) to as proud a Fortune
> As this that I haue reach'd. For know *Iago*,
> But that I loue the gentle *Desdemona*,
> I would not my vnhoused free condition
> Put into Circumscription, and Confine,
> For the Seas worth.

It is only when we find critics calling Othello 'one of the great lovers in the literature of the world' and 'the greatest lover in Shakespeare' that we might be disposed to press the first charge, *louing his owne pride*, but the second, *bumbast Circumstance*, surely sticks. I hope *prouulgate* is the right reading, since it finely expresses Othello's sense of his own superiority and the absence of any consciousness that he might be raising a smile.

A thought which when once put into the mind is hard to dislodge but may not occur in any of the first readings of the play is that we are the more willing to grant that Othello's simplicity is defective because Shakespeare was unwittingly reinforcing it just when he thought he was supporting that other sense of sublime simplicity which settles the issue of scale and grandeur once and for all and makes us see Othello as the biggest man in his world. We see faults where Shakespeare may have thought he was writing especially well. Professor G. W. Knight's essay 'The Othello Music'[1] has made us alert to a fault, noted by Samuel Johnson: 'It is the fate of *Shakespeare* to counteract his own pathos'.[2] One of the passages that would come up in a discussion whether the ruining excesses of contrast were intended by Shakespeare to define a fault in the very moment when the hero is shewing his finest qualities or whether his running on was a vice of style that Shakespeare in this play was impotent to correct, is the following:

> The Tirant Custome, most Graue Senators,
> Hath made the flinty and Steele Couch of Warre
> My thrice-driuen bed of Downe.

Can we help supplying, to match this hyperbole, a sense that the speaker was taking a pride in so thinking and speaking of himself? What should we think of Antony if he had himself regaled Cleopatra with the account of his extremities when retreating from Modena?

A point of debate arises when we try to understand why Othello has chosen Iago for his third-in-command. The play does not allow much free speculation here. Just as I think we have no warrant for saying that no human eye *could* detect that Iago was the Bad Servant, so I must not claim that it was a mark of human unintelligence not to be able to detect that this officer was a low fellow generally and impossible to endure as a companion however useful as a military *aide*, however amusing as an amateur Fool. This act does not force us to accept *Othello* as a *gull* in a strongly pejorative sense. So I should say that everyone is pulled up at the most concentrated and meaningful moment in this act when we hear:

[1] In *The Wheel of Fire* (1930).
[2] *The Plays of William Shakespeare* (1765), Volume the Eighth, page 456.

—Adieu braue Moore, vse *Desdemona* well.

—Looke to her (Moore) if thou hast eies to see:
  She ha's deceiu'd her Father, and may thee.

—My life vpon her faith. Honest *Iago* . . .

but that until the play is over and we discover all that was here concentrated we cannot say for certain where to place the emphasis in Iago's verdict:

> The Moore is of a free, and open Nature,
> That thinkes men honest, that but seeme to be so,
> And will as tenderly be lead by' th' Nose
> As Asses are.

On the other hand, in order to enter into the area of painful speculation, we must tell ourselves in detail just how much an outsider Iago is to the point of wondering how even Roderigo could tolerate him. We begin by learning that he is almost as much a cheat and parasite upon simpletons as Autolycus in *The Winter's Tale*, but the interesting knowledge is of his shocking behaviour, contrasted with the attempted good manners on Roderigo's part, to Brabantio. At this point it is hard to believe that Shakespeare had made up his plot, for it is barely conceivable, given ordinary prudent calculation of probabilities, that Iago would risk using such profane language about a man he knew had been for many months an honoured guest in Brabantio's house. If Iago was risking detection the action is quite incredible, for if one bout of drunkenness was enough to lose Cassio his job, surely Iago's language was bad enough to bar him from any post of honour for the rest of his life.

But nobody, as far as I know, has ever thought like this or attempted to make this action fit any of the more prudent manoeuvres Iago later undertakes. (Nor have I seen any comment on the complete breakdown of Iago's style hereabouts:

> Doe, with like timerous accent, and dire yell,
> As when (by Night and Negligence) the Fire
> Is spied in populous Citties. . . .)

It is, after all, night, and the terrible shouts merge into the frightening background, that is, pass directly into our minds as vivid coarse images long before we know distinctly who are being referred to. (For Brabantio at this moment Iago *is* only a voice.) They form part of the Venice we must take as given: it is a moral world where the most reverend old men may be called out of bed to hear things like this shouted in the street:

Euen now, now, very now, an old blacke Ram
Is tupping your white Ewe . . .
. . . . the deuill will make a Grand-sire of you . . .
you'le haue your Daughter couer'd with a Barbary
                                    horse . . .
. . . your Daughter and the Moore are making the
Beast with two backs.

These shouts might, however, pass away as they came, but when we
hear Roderigo on his best behaviour referring to

. . . . . the grosse claspes of a Lasciuious Moore

and above all when we hear what Brabantio thinks about it we know we
have just heard expressed a truth as Venice sees it. First we learn that a
remark—*the Thickslips*—that we might easily have dismissed as mere
spite, was meiosis. The first and easiest paradox we have to face is that
Othello was in Venetian eyes as ugly as sin but as noble inside as degraded
outside. The point is put beyond all discussion: Othello is not merely
black—there is no trace of racial feeling—but *frighteningly* ugly. That
this is the word to fasten on we see both from what the prejudiced father
brings out before his peers:

To fall in Loue, with what she fear'd to looke on

and what Othello later assents to:

She did deceiue her Father, marrying you,
And when she seem'd to shake, and feare your lookes,
She lou'd them most.

But the rest of the Act is concerned to dismiss the foul charges against
Othello. The vicious images pass through the mind and fall into the
background as we take point after point in favour of Othello's nobility
and purity. Nobody who left the theatre after the first act could guess that
this passive evil in the thoughts of Venice would find lodgement in
Othello's soul and that by the third Act he would be using images every
bit as foul as Iago's.

Since this, as we shall be seeing, turns out to be the general design of
the play, a small question arises about the level of superstition in the
Venetian world. Few people will confess that they have ever entertained
(and none that they have ever acted on) thoughts such as Brabantio
clutched at to explain the black man's hold over his daughter. Though we
have no difficulty in facing the thought that people will and contrive evil,
we don't suppose that there is any means of manipulating evil forces.
Imaginatively, therefore, we must resurrect the belief in black magic and

see it as a plausible charge that such an alliance between black and white requires the explanation that Othello was

> a practiser
> Of Arts inhibited, and out of warrant.

Venice we must see as a city where *Spels and Medicines* could be *bought of Mountebanks*. Such sale was illegal but it went on. Othello's rebuttal is so majestic

> This onely is the witch-craft I haue vs'd

that I cannot believe that when Shakespeare wrote these lines he had already prepared in his mind an event that in his time scheme had occurred a few minutes before:

> That Handkerchiefe
> Did an Ægyptian to my Mother giue:
> She was a Charmer, and could almost read
> The thoughts of people. She told her, while she kept it,
> 'T would make her Amiable, and subdue my Father
> Intirely to her loue: But if she lost it,
> Or made a Guift of it, my Fathers eye
> Should hold her loathed, and his Spirits should hunt
> After new Fancies. She dying, gaue it me,
> And bid me (when my Fate would haue me Wiu'd)
> To giue it her. I did so; and take heede on't,
> Make it a Darling, like your precious eye:
> To loose't, or giue't away, were such perdition,
> As nothing else could match.
> —Is't possible?
> —'Tis true: There's Magicke in the web of it:
> A *Sybill* that had numbred in the world
> The Sun to course, two hundred compasses,
> In her Prophetticke furie sow'd the Worke:
> The Wormes were hallowed, that did breede the Silke,
> And it was dyde in Mummey, which the Skilfull
> Conseru'd of Maidens hearts.

(There are, however, far more serious silences in this act which might all be due to haste and failure to revise. The greatest is the silence of the guilty pair about their failure to try the honourable means of getting married. It is damaging to both—though much more damning against Desdemona—that they never speak as if it had cost them anything to elope. It is a minor matter that we get no light on the nature of the cere-

mony. What Christian priest or if not a priest what authority could make
the marriage irrevocable?)

On the other hand, I do not regard it as the result of haste or in any way
requiring revision that Othello tells such an implausible tale. We in any
case do not expect a proud man to tell all. I take it that once we are assured
that no vile motives are to be imputed we rest on the fact that falling in
love is an irreducible mystery. *Pace* all the critics I cannot see that Othello
comes out of this scene as a distinguished *lover*, but I equally fail to see
that to shew him as such was Shakespeare's major interest. He shews us
other things so much more powerfully that the interest so far aroused in
his guilt is transferred to Desdemona. The design of the act must include
the foundation of Othello's professional *character*.

'We see nothing done by [Othello], nor related concerning him, that
comports with the condition of a General, or, indeed, of a Man . . .'[1] It is
a paradox of the play that Othello is not allowed much scope to shew that
he was a man of action. His one military stroke, it might be said with only
little exaggeration, was the smart execution of the elopement. Nevertheless I would hope for general agreement against Rymer. We form an
almost instantaneous impression that Othello is distinguished both as a
man and a general. It is true that if we are challenged the texts are few.
Yet they are very potent: 'Keepe vp your bright Swords, for the dew will
rust them. Good Signior, you shall more command with yeares, then
with your Weapons'. Yet it must be granted that Othello's character, his
being, is all in his *speech*: 'it is through the characteristic noble verse . . .
that, very largely, we get our sense of the noble Othello. . . .'[2] Nothing
could replace the poetry: infinite prose paraphrase would be needed to
extract the last suggestion of what is conveyed in one grand go when
Othello is given a chance to explain himself.

On the other hand, we are bound to admit that Othello's character is
Othello's *music*. If to have from Shakespeare a poetical character is to be
endowed with a comprehensive soul and immortal charm, we may yet
complain of a lack of definition. There is point in recalling another remark
by Rymer: 'In a Play one should speak like a man of business'. Critics
often fall back on 'romantic valour' to describe Othello's special interest
in his profession; but we can't help noticing that the poetry does not give
us the 'man of action' but a romantic in an older, pejorative sense of the
word. What had Othello to do wandering off about

> Antars vast, and Desarts idle,
> Rough Quarries, Rocks, Hills, whose head touch heauen,

---

[1] Rymer, *op. cit.*, p. 92.          [2] F.R. Leavis, *op. cit.*

The *Antropophague*, and men whose heads
Grew beneath their shoulders . . .?

Though these lines be meat to those who see Othello as a glorified
Caliban, it was not for these tales that Desdemona lost her heart to him.
A concomitant of conveying character through the style of speech is that
faults of style will suggest corresponding faults of character. An actor
would have to decide whether to hide or express something in these lines:

And tell she come, as truely as to heauen,
I do confesse the vices of my blood,
So iustly to your Graue eares . . .

He might decide that such a reference came rather easily to Othello, that
he rather liked the spectacle, and that he saw the penitent in the scene as
rather large than small.

Such a remark, however, could not have been made by a man who felt
the slightest difficulty in defending himself against the abuse and insinuation of Iago. Shakespeare has taken such pains to present Othello as the
keen professional soldier that we might be pardoned if we suspected that
he was not normally eager to consummate the marriage after the long
period of wooing. The elastic rhythms that characterised the hero describing his courtship become stiff and contorted, the suggestion of wit
disappears, when the claims of love and professional duty conflict. We
get lines such as:

I do agnize
A Naturall and prompt Alacratie,
I finde in hardnesse. . .

Shakespeare, I take it, is here giving us something we have to accept as a
fact. We are not to be given the extreme reversal such as we get in Angelo
in *Measure for Measure* but we must begin by divorcing Othello from the
animal suggestions of lust and from any connection with excessively
vehement sexual desire. It is a failure of technique on Shakespeare's part
that the choric figure who should settle such matters for us sounds so
pat and unconvincing that some have supposed that but for the military
necessities he would have sided with Brabantio:

If Vertue no delighted Beautie lacke,
Your Son-in-law is farre more Faire then Blacke.

If Othello suffers in our eyes for giving such a poor account of how he
fell in love, the damage is as nothing compared with that done to Desdemona. It would be unfair to say that he shifts all the blame on to her, but

the effect of his clearing himself is to establish grounds for amazement at if not disparagement of her love for him:

> She lou'd me for the dangers I had past,
> And I lou'd her, that she did pitty them.

Shakespeare, however, knew his powers. Although I think the play could have been improved by himself if he had re-read it while in the heat, I do not think of his haste as reckless. He runs innumerable risks but gives the impression of knowing them all and knowing too how to snatch exhilarating success from each courted disaster. Desdemona, too, is given the style of speech, the manner of action that place her safely out of reach of the most powerful body of suspicion. Yet it will be my argument that if the play could have been made supremely great it would be by giving closer attention to Desdemona. She calls for more interest than Shakespeare in his first draft was prepared to give her. He did not know all she could do to make us take the fate of his hero more to heart. I say this in the face of many performances in which beautiful actresses were content to present her as insipid. '*Cinthio* affirms that *She was not overcome by a Womanish Appetite, but by the Vertue of the Moor*. It must be a good-natur'd Reader that takes *Cinthio*'s word in this case, tho' in a Novel.' Rymer is here[1], as we shall see in a moment, in touch with the thought of Venice, and as this thought is destined to pass to the foreground, we must give it some attention. But since modern commentators have in their own way thought similar thoughts we must press home the fact, as I take it, that Shakespeare did not create a female monster to match his male. One strand of modern thought is seen in a commentary on these lines:

> That I loue the Moore, to liue with him,
> My downe-right violence, and storme of Fortunes,
> May trumpet to the world. My heart's subdu'd
> Euen to the very quality of my Lord;
> I saw *Othello*'s visage in his mind,
> And to his Honours and his valiant parts,
> Did I my soule and Fortunes consecrate.
> So that (deere Lords) if I be left behind
> A Moth of Peace, and he go to the Warre,
> The Rites for why I loue him, are bereft me: . . .

Mr Ridley wrote[2] in defence of the Quarto reading as follows:

---

[1] *Op. cit.*, p. 89.　　[2] *The Arden Shakespeare: Othello* (1958).

[Desdemona] is saying 'My love for Othello makes me want to live with him; I do not want to be a grass widow, but to live with him in full marital intercourse; and since he is a soldier and now ordered on foreign service, I can do that only by going to the wars with him.' Desdemona, like all Shakespeare's best women, is outspoken, and part of the trouble here is caused by the commentators who boggle at allowing her to mean what she says, prefer *very quality*[1] as more 'maidenly' and want, needlessly and even insultingly, to preserve Desdemona's 'delicacy' by reading 'rights' for *rites* six lines below.

The motives imputed to the commentators are reprehensible: such thoughts are not relevant. Nor, however, it seems to me, are considerations of the normal pleasures of marital intercourse. In saying that the first act is comic I also had in mind that it invites us to accept the marvellous uncritically. Here I suppose rather that Desdemona was thinking throughout of the soldierly virtues and longed to be present when what she had merely heard about came into action. (We could at a pinch press something here out of the lines:

> she wish'd
> That Heauen had made her such a man.)

Her love is as strange and challenging to common sense as Othello's grandeur.

Another representative modern view can be found in Mr Auden's essay:

> Everybody must pity Desdemona, but I cannot bring myself to like her. Her determination to marry Othello—it was she who virtually did the proposing —seems the romantic crush of a silly schoolgirl rather than a mature affection: it is Othello's adventures, so unlike the civilian life she knows, which captivate her rather than Othello as a person.[2]

Once again we note the unsatisfactoriness of the choric verdict:

> I thinke this tale would win my Daughter too . . .

which has the effect of belittling everything and of insulting Brabantio. He, I think, is the point on which we rest, for he has entertained monstrous thoughts about his daughter and nothing he hears makes him change his mind. Yet so great is our bias in favour of lovers that we may never take either his verdict or his grief seriously until we find that Shakespeare requires us to note its effects:

[1] to 'vtmost pleasure'.     [2] *Op. cit.*

> Poore *Desdemon*:
> I am glad thy Father's dead,
> Thy Match was mortall to him: and pure greefe
> Shore his old thred in twaine.

When we begin to see the action through his eyes we may feel that his greatest pain was caused by what Roderigo in all seriousness called *a grosse reuolt*:

> Do not beleeue
> That from the sence of all Ciuilitie,
> I thus would play and trifle with your Reuerence.
> Your Daughter (if you haue not giuen her leaue)
> I say againe, hath made a grosse reuolt,
> Tying her Dutie, Beautie, Wit, and Fortunes
> In an extrauagant, and wheeling Stranger...

This pain may have been aggravated by discovering that he had completely misread her nature. We in fact cannot help wondering whether he is making it up or 'putting it on' when he says that Desdemona was

> a Maid, so tender, Faire, and Happie,
> So opposite to Marriage, that she shun'd
> The wealthy curled Deareling of our Nation...

and

> A Maiden, neuer bold:
> Of Spirit so still, and quiet, that her Motion
> Blush'd at her selfe...

But as with Juliet so here we must allow for the weight given by Shakespeare to the sin of disobedience to parents and add to it our own uneasiness over the degree of deliberate deception inevitably involved. We catch a hint of this perhaps when father and daughter hastily reject the tactless suggestion that Desdemona should go back to her father while her husband was away. Yet the astonishing thing is, when we later discover how scrupulously obedient Desdemona is as a wife, that she had no sense of having behaved shamelessly to her father when before the senators. Shakespeare clearly felt for Brabantio when she so pertly passed over the vulnerable point in contrasting her former duty as an unmarried daughter and her new duties as a wife. But however tactless and heartless the gesture, Desdemona performed it without a pang. The proof is here:

> —Giue me your hand.
> This hand is moist my Lady.
> —It hath felt no age, nor knowne no sorrow.

But to return to the monstrous thought. It is never pushed home in this act and it is only on looking back after we have heard Brabantio's thought in the terms of Iago:

> Not to affect many proposed Matches
> Of her owne Clime, Complexion, and Degree,
> Whereto we see in all things, Nature tends:
> Foh, one may smel in such, a will most ranke,
> Foule disproportions, Thoughts vnnaturall,

that we can justly call it monstrous. The thought, however, is that as Desdemona was going against nature in loving Othello, her love could not have been either pure or noble; there must have been something inherently impure in her nature; in short, she must have been drawn to the Moor in the hope of discovering that he was what Iago had imagined. This thought does not, of course, engage with our Desdemona, but it powerfully predisposes us when Iago and Roderigo are left behind to make us attend to the general tone prevailing in Venice.

That this is the right way to take the remaining portion of the first act I hope will become clear when the design of the whole play is apparent. But that anybody could feel sure of having got this scene right on first acquaintance I very much doubt. I have an awkward feeling of having been much too active and selective in pressing out a significance from these lines. Nor can I altogether dismiss other readings, especially those that describe the main design as being to exhibit Iago's soul in action. Yet I would argue from the very differing reports that are given of that soul not that the commentators are all fools but that Shakespeare has not given us a fully-worked-out piece. If he ever did any part of his playwriting *con amore*, it surely included those comic villains who are given low language but superior idiomatic speech and all the mother wit the author could command. It is when measured by Shakespeare's success with a Falstaff or an Enobarbus that the Iago of this scene must be pronounced a tentative sketch.

Though the function of this scene may well be what I have hinted at, its purpose does not exclude the exhibition of Iago's parts. We are bound to ask ourselves why Iago performs as he does with Roderigo. I find it quite impossible to take the scene straight, as a shrewdly calculated stage in a plot in which every stroke tells. On the contrary, it seems to me from the beginning a purely *buffo* or extravagant performance that reduced Roderigo to a mere puppet, so that we can say no calculating was needed

D

to win *him* over. In fact I would be quite ready to reverse the usual account and say that Roderigo does not lose his honour as a result of any specific devices invented by Iago but is a helpless victim of the general state of the sexual *mores* of Venice. Venice is a world where such things are *generally* credited. After all, Iago is himself a victim of the usual run of thought on sexual matters in Venice:

> . . . it is thought abroad, that 'twixt my sheets
> He ha's done my Office.

Iago knows of no evidence, it is all a matter of dirty surmise. (We learn later that he tried, like Othello, to get proof from his wife.) The interesting point is that such a monstrous rumour could ever be born and propagate. So the interesting thought here is that Venice is a place where a man can so easily step down from honourable love to adultery.

Just as nobody can find a convincing point for Iago's diction in his dialogue, though if we follow the Quarto here he seems to be using some very rare words, so it is hard to believe in the soliloquy as representing Iago's thought. This may be because Shakespeare had not yet worked out his own plot. I say this because if he had already faced in his mind the coming complexities of Short and Long Time he would not have set our minds working the wrong way with

> *After some time*, to abuse *Othello*'s eares,
> That he is too familiar with his wife.

But where above all we need agreement is that as yet Iago does not represent Evil in any serious way. He is so far from associating with graver evil that I don't think anybody pays attention to his mock assumption of the Devil's rôle when he says: 'If Sanctimonie, and a fraile vow, betwixt an erring Barbarian, and super-subtle Venetian be not too hard for my wits, and all the Tribe of hell, thou shalt enioy her'. So for me the last lines of the Act belong to a play not yet in sight, and must therefore make us laugh rather than shudder:

> Hell, and Night,
> Must bring this monstrous Birth, to the worlds light.

This is a remarkable fact: that we have reached the end of the first Act without finding a *donnée*.

The first act is not so much the commencement of the movement as a preparation for it. It is devoted to bringing out the situation of the various parties at the opening of the story. This is just what a classical dramatist, tied by the unities, would merely assume, and bring it out by incidental reference.[1]

We have just enough of a plot to make us mildly curious, but we are merely the slaves or followers of capricious events few of which we can as yet foresee. In a comedy we rather enjoy this, but in a tragedy we like to feel that events are chained together. Hence I am all the more inclined to insist that we withstand the mild temptation to regard as the essence of the play its plot—which is so far only a shadow—and that we take for substance the play of thought aroused by the contrasting views of the worth of love and the power of passion to endure. The fact that the disturbing thoughts are put into the mouth of a morally worthless villain hardly seems to matter, since after they have entered Brabantio's mind we know that they are inescapable.

Thought is a very loose term for what goes on in our minds as we listen to the comic villain teasing his victim. We allow the mind to play round certain areas known previously to be awkward, ambiguous and potentially dangerous. This mental play is gently elastic and will vary in any audience according to temperament and experience. Those who know both their Shakespeare and their Traversi[2] will seize on the word 'blood' and note two associations: first 'the blood, and basenesse of our Natures' and then the claim that love 'is meerly a Lust of the blood. . .'. Vary as we may in our sense of the how much, we all know that *something* is being left out of account here. Similarly, however little we wish to make of it we all know that there is *something* in the analogy between passion and appetite, appetite for love and appetite for other pleasures we quite cheerfully classify as bodily. We all know there is a basis in nature for Iago's humour as for the wit and hyperbole of Donne's 'love' poems. We do not ourselves have to have crept up and down staircases at night before we recognize common humanity in 'If thou canst Cuckold him, thou dost thy selfe a pleasure. . .'. But familiar as this world of common evil is, nothing in Iago's manner makes it more seductive to us. There is something unpleasantly hard in 'But we haue Reason to coole our raging Motions, our carnall Stings, or vnbitted Lusts . . .'. At most we are relieved to think that the threatened couple of noble lovers are sailing out of this atmosphere into (we hope) the clearer air of Cyprus.

[1] R. G. Moulton, *Shakespeare as a dramatic artist*, Third edition, revised and enlarged, 1893. Samuel Johnson: *op. cit.*, p. 473. Had the scene opened in *Cyprus*, and the preceding incidents been occasionally related, there had been little wanting to a drama of the most exact and scrupulous regularity.

[2] *Approach to Shakespeare* (1938).

To leave the theatre at the end of the second Act would strengthen an impression that the first two Acts are strikingly alike in structure and content. This similarity has some point: we must surrender any hopes that the change of scene might mean a change of fortunes and a picture of war; we must resign ourselves to the truth of

caelum non animum mutant qui trans mare currunt.[1]

So once again the peace of the night is broken by the contriving of Iago, once again the love of Othello is presented in contrasting lights. We begin to see that Venice may be everywhere. We observe how easily by the villain's machinations Cassio is made a beast and Othello might be made something more serious than a mere ass. Yet though there are one or two small new developments, there is as yet no sense that Shakespeare has fully opened his mind or imposed on the play any unifying powers to create anything that we could dignify by the name of a general point or *donnée*. Indeed, we might well believe that Shakespeare was playing the first Act over again *because* he had not yet seen what his general point was to be. There are consequently numerous repetitions: some are improvements on what we find in the first Act, others do not advance or intensify what we were there given.

Another impression strengthened by this somewhat artificial method of breaking away at the end of the Act is that so far the play is still a comedy. The man in the theatre notices at once that everything is being made *surprisingly* easy for Iago. I doubt whether anybody has found the Iago of this Act a master-criminal. He is a scoundrel, of course, but our general sense of within what limits is altered in only one particular, which I shall come back to in a moment. We have every reason to go into the foyer at the end of the Act with a confident expectation that the author would soon be redressing the balance he had so arbitrarily tilted in Iago's favour; we should be cheerfully expecting that one set of mild improbabilities was going to be countered by another. What, for instance, is the natural reaction when we first hear this:

Diuinitie of hell,
When diuels will the blackest sinnes put on,
They do suggest at first with heauenly shewes,
As I do now . . .?

Can we take it as gravely as Banquo's warning:

[1] Horace. *Ep.* 1.11.27.

> . . . oftentimes, to winne vs to our harme,
> The Instruments of Darknesse tell vs Truths,
> Winne vs with honest Trifles, to betray's
> In deepest consequence. . .?

Is it not enough to contrast *honest Trifles* and *heauenly shewes* to laugh off all serious comparison of Iago and the Devil? And do we not chuckle to think what a come-uppance Iago is going to get if he carries out his further threats, such as

> Ile powre this pestilence into his eare:
> That she repeales him, for her bodies Lust,
> And by how much she striues to do him good,
> She shall vndo her Credite with the Moore.
> So will I turne her vertue into pitch,
> And out of her owne goodnesse make the Net,
> That shall en-mash them all . . .?

And if we happen to think of Claudius here, do we not reflect that Hamlet's father was *asleep* when the wicked uncle stole up

> And in the Porches of [his] eares did powre
> The leaperous Distilment . . .?

It is probably not a suitable question to ask a mere playgoer whether he at any point in this Act felt that Shakespeare was not gratifying the ear of the spectators with the kind of verse that assures us of the author's firm grasp of his matter. Indeed many students of the play fail to notice inequalities in the verse. 'The storm, within the idealizing mode, is at the other extreme from sentimentality; it serves to bring out the reality of the heroic Othello and what he represents.'[1] There is a judgement which, if we did not listen to the verse, we should not dream of challenging. But if we take the first scene seriously as verse we are bound to notice lines that *undermine* 'the reality of the heroic Othello and what he represents'. For example, if a comparison were made of the conceits of:

> Tempests themselues, high Seas, and howling windes,
> The gutter'd Rockes, and Congregated Sands,
> Traitors ensteep'd, to enclogge the guiltlesse Keele,
> As hauing sence of Beautie, do omit
> Their mortall Natures, letting go safely by
> The Diuine *Desdemona* . . .

and those of:

[1] F. R. Leavis, *op. cit.*, p. 267.

> Purple the Sailes: and so perfumed that
> The Windes were Loue-sicke with them.
> The Owers were Siluer,
> Which to the tune of Flutes kept stroke, and made
> The water which they beate, to follow faster,
> As amorous of their strokes . . .

would it not bring out the frigidity of *the guiltlesse Keele?* Is Cassio any happier here:

> Great Ioue, *Othello* guard,
> And swell his Saile with thine owne powrefull breath,
> That he may blesse this Bay with his tall Ship,
> Make loues quicke pants in *Desdemonaes* Armes,
> Giue renew'd fire to our extincted Spirits,
> And bring all Cypresse comfort . . .?

Othello himself is given Cassio music:

> If after euery Tempest, come such Calmes,
> May the windes blow, till they haue waken'd death:
> And let the labouring Barke climbe hills of Seas
> *Olympus* high: and duck againe as low,
> As hell's from Heauen.

There are two puzzling scenes in this Act, puzzling in that they seem excessive or out of place, so that while living through them a first-nighter would not be able to say what they had been *for.* They have in fact continued to seem unsatisfactory to many students of the play and one of them I have already mentioned among the portions actors are unwilling to perform. My very, very tentative explanation of their presence is that they represent the dawning of a design in Shakespeare's mind. Both scenes may very well be there to make a marked *contrast* with Othello's future conduct. If Shakespeare were a Henry James, if *Othello* were any kind of novel, we should not hesitate to proclaim such a function for them. But with Shakespeare, and in this play, who would dare venture beyond conjecture? Both scenes certainly challenge us to pronounce, and if they have no function they will have to be described as gross faults.

If Shakespeare had had a collaborator—and he could be anybody from the most insignificant scribbler to the most judicious of contemporary dramatists—we can be sure that Desdemona's conversation at the harbour would have been suppressed. At least I can recall no critic who has approved of it; most of them would, for once, agree with Rymer:

Now follows a long rabble of Jack pudden farce betwixt *Jago* and *Desdemona*, that runs on with all the little plays, jingle, and trash below the patience of any Countrey Kitchin-maid with her Sweet-heart. The Venetian *Donna* is hard put to't for pastime! And this is all, when they are newly got on shoar, from a dismal Tempest, and when every moment she might expect to hear her Lord (as she calls him) that she runs so mad after, is arriv'd or lost. And moreover

—*In a Town of War,*
—*The peoples Hearts brimful of fear.*

Never in the World had any Pagan Poet his Brains turn'd at this Monstrous rate. But the ground of all this Bedlam-Buffoonry we saw . . . were Carpenters, Coblers, and illiterate fellows; who found that the Drolls, and Fooleries interlarded by them, brought in the rabble, and lengthened their time, so they got Money by the bargain.[1]

Yet this scene is obviously something Shakespeare wanted: nothing in the action made it absolutely necessary. We ought, therefore, in honour to Shakespeare, to search for its point.

Students of the music and poetry of the early Tudor period have often had occasion to notice how constantly-recurring social situations have favoured the development of art forms that are as much social behaviour as manifestations of the art. If the arts flourished to adorn true leisure hours they were also drawn on to while away enforced leisure, the many inevitable delays for participants in severely formal ceremonial movements. Just as brass bands are now used before football matches, so, I imagine, while Tudors were waiting for some Great One to appear there was a frequent call for entertainment. This would also be an occasion for the Clown, and one form of entertainment in which he would rival the poet would be the impromptu answering of riddles or the composition of witty answers to set themes. In this performance he enjoyed two privileges denied to the poet: he could tell painful truths and he could talk bawdy before the ladies.

If the stage was in this way a mirror of life, much of the odium attaching to Desdemona would be taken off. It would be socially in place for her to initiate themes to test the clown's wit and socially proper to enjoy his jests. At any rate I should like to think that one of the functions of this scene was to illustrate the main theme of the play, that solid virtue is not seriously exposed to temptation by the mere insinuation of base thoughts. They can safely come into the mind because they do not find themselves invited to stay there. On the other hand, there is danger in pushing the

[1] *Op. cit.*, pp. 110–111.

theme of Desdemona's immunity to the ambient evil too far as there is in exaggerating the extent to which Iago is merely witty. Consideration of this scene forces us to recognise two new developments which will become important constituents of the play.

'New' is, perhaps, too strong: they are accessions of greater confidence in 'lines' that were only sketched in the first Act. Both commit the play in the direction of the monstrous and shocking, though in these two Acts we feel only something marvellous and unusually tart. They shew us that the set of the play is not towards the probable and therefore those critics who thought the play was primarily intended to exhibit 'character' got off on the wrong foot. Shakespeare has no plausible explanation for Desdemona's love of Othello. It would have been child's play to provide one: he could have made her slightly anaemic, actually afraid of marrying a young blade of Venice; he might have made her a daughter unconsciously in search of a 'father-substitute'; she might have been represented as hoping that her married life would merely prolong the ecstasies of courtship where she would for ever be sitting as a listener to eternal martial thrills. Instead Shakespeare has taken the daring line of making her unusually well endowed as a woman, so much so that some have found her indecently 'forward'. 'Think what she must have been doing on the trip from Venice', one critic remarked. Those critics who are so anxious to see curtness in her first greeting of Cassio allow absolutely no raw material for Iago's indecent fancy in her subsequent extension of 'courtesy' to Cassio. She seems to me to have carried it as far as Browning's Duchess:

> Sir, 'twas not
> Her husband's presence only, called that spot
> Of joy into the Duchess' cheek: perhaps
> Frà Pandolf chanced to say 'Her mantle laps
> Over my lady's wrist too much', or 'Paint
> Must never hope to reproduce the faint
> Half-flush that dies along her throat': such stuff
> Was courtesy, she thought, and cause enough
> For calling up that spot of joy. She had
> A heart—how shall I say?—too soon made glad,
> Too easily impressed; she liked whate'er
> She looked on, and her looks went everywhere.

But before we can appreciate to what lengths Shakespeare wishes us to go, we must take in the other innovation, which has to do with Iago. Shakespeare's control over this character can be seen to be growing as the act develops. The soliloquies are still uncertain, but when Iago has someone to talk to he now commands an idiom and each of his styles in dialogue is well done. The best is the least conspicuous; the clarity, economy and dispatch of the reports that doom Cassio to loss of office are the work of a master hand. What we relish consciously are the triumphs in the comic manner:

—I cannot beleeue that in her, she's full of most bless'd condition.
—Bless'd figges-end. The Wine she drinkes is made of grapes. If shee had beene bless'd, she would neuer haue lou'd the Moore: Bless'd pudding. Didst thou not see her paddle with the palme of his hand? Didst not marke that?
—Yes, that I did: but that was but curtesie.
—Leacherie by this hand: an Index, and obscure prologue to the History of Lust and foule Thoughts. They met so neere with their lippes, that their breathes embrac'd together. Villanous thoughts *Rodorigo*, when these mutabilities so marshall the way, hard at hand comes the Master, and maine exercise, th' incorporate conclusion: Pish.

This we now realise was what Shakespeare was feeling for in giving Iago so many words of Latin origin in the parallel scene in the first Act. But, as we did there, we take all this as background evil. The innovation is to allow Iago to talk plain sense out of his clown's rôle. This he does in his exchanges with Cassio. The consequence for us is that he becomes the choric voice, our best informant about Desdemona. What Cassio says as a gentleman Iago reinforces and this time, I think, as Shakespeare's spokesman.

Partly, no doubt, because actions speak louder than words and Desdemona's speaking part is itself so reduced in this Act, the critics I have read make very little of the evidence so abundantly provided by the choric commentary. Consequently, they fail to enter fully into Desdemona's situation in the following Acts and do not do justice to some of Othello's suspicions. Two points are made so strongly that we cannot miss the author's intention. The first is that however 'divine' Desdemona may be she is in the fullest sense a woman. The dialogue of praise at the beginning of the third scene supplied a necessary note: that her manner is such as to give rise to two interpretations:

—What an eye she has!
Methinkes it sounds a parley to prouocation.
—An inuiting eye:
And yet me thinkes right modest.

Yet when Iago tries to sum her up he must leave his salacious point:

D 2

She is of so free, so kinde, so apt, so blessed
a disposition . . .
She's fram'd as fruitefull
As the free Elements.

The second point is assurance that what we saw at the harbour may be
taken at face value: Othello is a doting husband, Desdemona has been
given a blank charter:

His Soule is so enfetter'd to her Loue,
That she may make, vnmake, do what she list,
Euen as her Appetite shall play the God,
With his weake Function.

These are lines to bear in mind when we notice in what spirit Desdemona undertakes Cassio's suit.

This excursion was intended to prepare us to understand a surprising
phrase in the conversation at the harbour while Desdemona was waiting
for Othello's ship to come in. If we ask ourselves—supposing ourselves
to be morally neither very pure nor very impure—how we take the whole
conversation, we might answer: 'as Emilia does'. We could do without it;
it is not particularly instructive or pleasing. So we are as surprised as I
presume Desdemona was when she asked: 'How say you (*Cassio*) is he
not a most prophane, and liberall Counsailor?' and got the answer: 'He
speakes home (Madam)'. We may take the remark with some latitude but
we now probably have to accept that in the world of this play

*There's none so foule and foolish thereunto,*
*But do's foule pranks, which faire, and wise-ones do.*

Consequentlywe hear Iago's asidewith more than a superstitious shudder:

Oh you are well tun'd now: But Ile set downe the peggs that make this
Musicke, as honest as I am.

What I have to say about Cassio's self-accusations is so tenuous that it
might almost be tucked away in a note at the end of the book. It is, however, an attempt at explanation, and surely Shakespeare had something
specific in mind in developing the scene as he did? It is given peculiar and
careful emphasis, yet none of this is strictly required by the plot, which
has to make plausible Cassio's reluctance to face Othello and his desire to
appeal to Desdemona for help. What makes me hesitant about my
'explanation' is that what I take to be the point emerges only at the very
end of the play and only then if the spectator feels shocked that when

Othello learns what he has done he is not truly penitent. His is an easy way out; not only does he evade punishment on earth, a fate far worse than death, but he lies in the face of the evidence, not the evidence of Desdemona's innocence, but of his own guilt and degradation. Iago is an all-too-convenient scape-goat to permit Othello the self-indulgence of

> Then must you speake,
> Of one that lou'd not wisely, but too well:
> Of one, not easily Iealious, but being wrought,
> Perplexed in the extreame. . . .

We do not find Othello saying anything like this: 'To be now a sensible man, by and by a Foole, and presently a Beast.' 'Think what Iago could easily have said at the end of the play!' we might counter.

All this will be folly to the reader who has found the end of the play satisfactory, and I must apologise for drawing on views that have yet to be argued for. The same apology is needed for going on to say that there is further point in Cassio's use of expressions like 'It hath pleas'd the diuell drunkennesse, to giue place to the diuell wrath, one vnperfectnesse, shewes me another to make me frankly despise my selfe'. The abundance of references in this play to Heaven and Hell, God and the Devil is such, paradoxically, as to discourage a thought that was never planted during a visit to the theatre and has grown exclusively as a result of excessively close focus on the text, namely, that the play is at its deepest level reliving an account of temptation in Mansoul in which Salvation and Damnation are the opposed issues. What is discouraging is that the references are both so many (when we think of the general reasons why on the Eliza-bethan stage they are so few) and so perfunctory. But suppose this account convincingly made out for Cassio, the difficulty of this interpretation lies once again in the distance between the time when Cassio utters these strange remarks and the moment when we begin to knit them into the play. If we could suppose that Shakespeare had in the vaguest way sensed a specifically Christian theme so early in the composition, what bizarre thoughts we should be led into when we hear the drunken Cassio saying: 'Well: heau'ns aboue all: and there be soules must be saued, and there be soules must not be saued . . . For mine owne part, no offence to the Generall, nor any man of qualitie: I hope to be saued. . .'

Since I cannot believe that Shakespeare went back after completing the play and inserted these features into the Cassio scene, I must leave the point with a sense of curiosity unsatisfied and pass to what may not be a puzzle but only the consequence of hasty writing. Many commentators have noted that Shakespeare has not taken care to define Montano. If so, it is clear that very slight revision was needed to settle him in his place. On the other hand, this could not be done without taking some general decisions about the socio-military-political hierarchy in the play. These decisions would be desirable in the first place to clear up the relations of Iago and Cassio. At first these may seem minor plot troubles but as we explore them they are found to have a bearing on more necessary matters. Everybody I take it has had a shock on hearing Cassio described as *Lord Gouernor* and given the task of finishing off Iago. But it is only a mild shock, since the discrepancy is merely between the drama and the fictional historical background. But if we travel backwards and readjust our relation to Cassio in the light of his final politico-military importance we may come to the beginning of the play and, like Mr Auden, decide that it was quite impossible that the dignitaries of Venice could have thought of Iago rather than Cassio as Othello's immediate *aide*. If so, on revision Shakespeare ought to have let us know that when Iago said

> I know my price, I am worth no worsse a place

he was either lying or deluded. But far more important, we need greater clarity about Othello's relation to him. The play needs rewriting if we are to take as a fact that Othello and Cassio were close friends. For as it stands, Othello is open to a serious charge of preferring to trust Iago long before he can have had his judgement warped by jealousy. We shall in any case have to ask whether Othello knew what trust was. Readers of Professor Leavis's essay will recall a crucial passage that must come up for everybody anxious, like Bradley, to do his best for Othello. Bradley had claimed of Othello that: 'His trust, where he trusts, is absolute.' To which Professor Leavis retorted: 'Othello's trust, then, can never have been in Desdemona'. I would now add to this: 'What became of his trust in Cassio?' Other critics have found fault with Othello's conduct in cashiering Cassio, but have put it down to a momentary loss of self-command, taking their hint from these lines:

> Now by Heauen,
> My blood begins my safer Guides to rule,
> And passion (hauing my best iudgement collied)
> Assaies to leade the way.

I should therefore like to have Othello cleared by having it put beyond doubt that he loved his friend too well to be in earnest and that after a politic period intended to restore him. This is in fact how Emilia puts it:

> The Moore replies,
> That he you hurt is of great Fame in Cyprus,
> And great Affinitie: and that in wholsome Wisedome
> He might not but refuse you. But he protests he loues you
> And needs no other Suitor, but his likings
> To bring you in againe.

This is also how Desdemona sees it:

> you do loue my Lord:
> You haue knowne him long, and be you well assur'd
> He shall in strangenesse stand no farther off,
> Then in a politique distance.

But Othello's behaviour, alas, does not support these accounts, and we shall have to ask minute questions, some of which will turn on the supposed standing of Cassio as an officer and as a friend in comparison with the standing of Iago. For the moment events take a really threatening or sinister turn we cannot any longer view them with the lightness and looseness of comedy. The bother here is retroactive from the later Acts. In the theatre our minds are carried by Cassio's shame into finding the rebuke just and by our sense that for the moment the author has willed that everything Iago has planned is to succeed.

Another retroactive consideration comes if we decide that as a fact of the story Othello committed a dangerous *gaffe* in dismissing Cassio without hearing his defence. For it may then cross our minds that Desdemona may have been wishing to rescue Othello as well as to demonstrate, as she says, that

> If I do vow a friendship, Ile performe it
> To the last Article.

Again we shall not bother about this unless the complete experience of the play makes us want passionately to have a Desdemona less foolish than, as we shall be seeing, the lack of clearness in the writing allows her to appear.

# CHAPTER 3

# The Devil's Own

'FROM the moment when the temptation of the hero begins, the reader's heart and mind are held in a vice, experiencing the extremes of pity and fear, sympathy and repulsion, sickening hope and dreadful expectation.'[1] Especially when we recall Rymer's concession that 'this is the top scene, the Scene that raises *Othello* above all other Tragedies on our Theatres' (p. 118), we may well believe that Bradley has here spoken for all time. The mood of comedy, when we could take everything loosely, departs: from now on every word is *decisive*. The universal acclaim of this scene should mean that its main point is clear and that our sympathies all flow in similar channels. Since it is notorious that they do not, we are bound to ask whether Shakespeare abandoned work on the scene confident that it would be for ever engrossing and indifferent to the possibility that it might be open to widely-contrasting interpretations. We are also bound to ask whether we have refused to face the whole text or imported for its interpretation action and 'business' that do not grow naturally out of the text.

This, then, is one of the crucial moments for the critic who would bring together rather than separate readers, and it is more difficult than usual because on this scene Bradley has not spoken for all time. As we shall be seeing, he has dismissed without argument a view that an eminent predecessor took to be the natural one and has advanced as a 'fact' an interpretation that seems to me to be tenable only so long as certain parts of the text are forgotten or left out of account. It will be my endeavour to make it seem plain that Othello is far more to blame than Bradley allows. I shall try to bring further argument in support of the thesis in Professor Leavis's article: 'Iago's power . . . in the temptation-scene is that he represents something that is in Othello . . . the essential traitor is within the gates'.[2] In doing so I am aware that I shall be removing the grounds on which Bradley rests his claim that *Othello* is a tragedy.[3]

---

[1] *Op. cit.* p. 176.     [2] *Op. cit.*
[3] And perhaps with only a show of resistance from Bradley. He seems to concede a great deal in saying, 'If [Desdemona's] part were acted by an artist equal to Salvini and with a Salvini for Othello, I doubt if the spectacle of the last two Acts would not be pronounced intolerable'.

It seems to me plain, that whatever we find ourselves most concerned about at the end of the play, we begin the third Act with an interest in the quality of the love between Othello and Desdemona. Here the flow of our sympathy is more powerfully directed by what is dramatically shewn to be present and absent than by conjectures about behaviour that is either off-stage or over before the action of the play. I would next argue that the behaviour of Desdemona is presented in this Act in such a way as to force on us a contrast between her trust and Othello's want of trust, that it is through letting ourselves respond to Desdemona that we become aware that all is far from well with Othello as soon as Othello's attention was directed to Cassio. His uneasiness began as he focussed his eyes. There is no need to say what the first second of seeing contained: all that matters is to say what happened to his love in the immediately following seconds. We judge that by his behaviour to Desdemona before he dismisses her.

The next chapter will be largely devoted to exploring what may be called Desdemona's guilt or failure to rise to the demands of the situation. Here, on the contrary, we see her as the perfect lover. The evidence I find above all in the lilt and buoyancy of her tone in assuring Cassio. For me her love is crowned by her ability to joke about her endeavours on his behalf. Her love shines out in her confidence: it is of her not of Othello that we should be saying, 'her trust, where she trusts, is absolute'. The thought that it had been well for her had she entertained human fears (in the Wordsworthian sense) will certainly crop up later, but here her perfect love is shewn in her perfect trust. In the following chapter I shall be urging all that makes it plausible to suppose that in this play Shakespeare was drawing with some immediacy on Christian formulations. For the moment I will anticipate only so much as to say that so far Desdemona's love must be thought of as a human analogue of the perfect love of God, as in *The first epistle of Saint Iohn the Apostle*, The .iiij. Chapter vv. 16–19:

> God is loue, and he that dwelleth in loue,
> dwelleth in God, and God in hym.
> Herein is the loue perfect in vs, that we
> shoulde haue boldnesse in the day of iudgement:
> For as he is, euen so are we in this worlde.
> There is no feare in loue, but perfect loue
> casteth out feare: for feare hath paynefulnesse.
> He that feareth, is not perfect in loue.
> We loue hym, for he loued vs first.

All the dignity and miraculous beauty of her submission to Othello goes if we do not suppose her justified in thinking herself possessed of unlimited rights to drafts on Othello's trust. She is admirable in that she does not doubt that she is granted royal freedom and prerogatives by Othello's love. So that as yet we have no right to murmur, 'a slumber did her spirit seal'.

Another remark that seems to apply more aptly to her than to Othello is

> Then must you speake,
> Of one that lou'd not wisely, but too well. . .

Certainly many readers have put Othello's question: *Are you wise?* to her as early as this scene where she pleads for Cassio. Rymer was quite sure that any husband would have been jealous on the spot! Critics who have judged her to be preeminently *childish* have found this moment typical. Mr. Ridley, who does not think her so, nevertheless writes as follows:[1]

> It is true that she has, in her first pleading for Cassio, a child's innocent, though in the circumstances fatal, persistence, calculated to exasperate a much more slow-tempered man than Othello. In just this way a child tries to pin down a treat. 'Can we go to the zoo this afternoon?' 'No, not this afternoon, dear, I'm busy.' 'Tomorrow morning, then?' 'Well, we'll see, but I think not.' 'Tomorrow afternoon?' 'No dear, I've people coming in to tea.'

This strikes me as wrong-headed and open to a continuation as follows:

> 'Now, mother dear, I don't mean to lecture you; you know I'm not one of those spoilt modern children who regard it as axiomatic that parents should always give way to children's whims. But, my dear, you *have* certain duties as a parent, haven't you? And what prior duty compels you to have a tea party next Wednesday afternoon? You're not a committee woman. All your evenings are free. I never bother you after 7 p.m. And in a week or two I shall be going to school. I don't say a visit to the Zoo is a necessity for my emotional and intellectual development. But it's not like asking for a model Jaguar costing twice the money you spend *per annum* on cosmetics. If I wanted to test whether you really love and respect my childish person, I could put far more stringent demands, and I don't doubt that if you saw that I'm asking for something perfectly proper you wouldn't instantly fix a day. You know that I would easily let you off one of your promises and amuse myself alone for hours if I thought you were ill or had urgent business. But are you being perfectly frank?"

[1] *Op. cit.*, p. lxv.

I hope I am labouring the obvious and Desdemona's language here is sufficient proof of the quality of her love and trust:

> I wonder in my Soule
> What you would aske me, that I should deny,
> Or stand so mam'ring on? What? *Michael Cassio*,
> That came a woing with you? and so many a time
> (When I haue spoke of you dispraisingly)
> Hath tane your part, to haue so much to do
> To bring him in? Trust me, I could do much.
> —Prythee no more: Let him come when he will:
> I will deny thee nothing.
> —Why, this is not a Boone:
> 'Tis as I should entreate you weare your Gloues,
> Or feede on nourishing dishes, or keepe you warme,
> Or sue to you, to do a peculiar profit
> To your owne person. Nay, when I haue a suite
> Wherein I meane to touch your Loue indeed,
> It shall be full of poize, and difficult waight,
> And fearefull to be granted.
> —I will deny thee nothing.
> Whereon, I do beseech thee, grant me this,
> To leaue me but a little to my selfe.
> —Shall I deny you? No: farewell my Lord.
> —Farewell my *Desdemona*, Ile come to thee strait.
> —*Æmilia* come; be as your Fancies teach you:[1]
> What ere you be, I am obedient.

Now let us study Othello's behaviour. I am assuming that the facts are as we have been led to believe, that Cassio's suit has been the subject of friendly debate and that it had been left for Othello to name the day of reconciliation—nothing else was left to ask for. If so, must we not ask whether Othello is being perfectly frank? What does he mean by 'I will deny thee nothing'? Why doesn't he name the day or give his reason for not doing so? Why doesn't he meet frankness with frankness? Everybody could write a frank reply here. Everybody would have felt that to turn off the matter as Othello does would be to snub Desdemona.[2] We are therefore bound to ask: what has happened to Othello's perfect love? And if we look back we see that all that an audience can know is that Othello saw Cassio leaving Desdemona and Emilia with the apparent intention of avoiding

---

[1] Dreadful dramatic irony.
[2] The first snub she had ever received?

an interview with him. True, Othello also heard that his Ancient had volunteered the observation that his superior officer looked guilty. 'What the devil do you mean?', I hear the free, open-souled commander saying. 'Call your superior officer a guilty sneak! Guilty of what? Are you such an ill-bred lower-class upstart that you can't imagine that a decent well-bred man might still be smarting from a sense of lapse and while he could talk about it to my wife, an old trusted friend, he might not want to face me until I had pardoned him. Go away and attend to your professional duties!' (*Non sò io a che mi tenga, che non ti tagli questa lingua, tanto audace, che ha hauuto ardire di dar tale infamia alla Donna mia.*)[1]

What then must we say has clouded Othello's relations with Desdemona? I am bound to think it was a suspicion of her purity or discretion: and not a slight one: in fact, a horrible imagining like that which assailed Macbeth before he met the witches. I can see no alternative: we must argue that either at this point Othello has suspected his wife and grossly, or if this is a *normal* scene between them he never matched her love.[2] And here we must adjust our view to what Desdemona regarded as normal. A phrase that commentators who think of Desdemona as an infatuated schoolgirl overlook is

> and so many a time
> (When I haue spoke of you dispraisingly)
> Hath tane your part. . .

Not many wives would dare tell their husbands that they had *many a time* pointed out their faults to a third person. From this one phrase I argue that Desdemona must have been on the easiest terms with her husband. She must have shewn him that all the usual arguments against him had occurred to her but counted as nothing. It is this independence of spirit that gives value to and shews the seriousness with which she took her marriage vow to obey her husband. If we compare the quality of Desdemona's and Othello's love, ought we not to distinguish Othello's state as sensually drugged but say that until she is wounded Desdemona's vision is unusually clear? In this spirit I should press gently for the concession that she exhibits wonderful tact in refusing to recognize the crude snub she is getting. Instead of accusing Othello of falling below the standard of perfect love she conveys the fine point of reproach in the aristocratic good humour of her balanced mind.

---

[1] Quoted from: *Hecatommithi ouero Cento Nouelle* di Gio. Battista Giraldi, In Venetia M.DC.VIII, Prima Parte, p. 316.

[2] And she had no grounds for her complete trust.

Bradley will have none of this. He has a special note on the temptation scene, which opens with these words:

> One reason why some readers think Othello 'easily jealous' is that they completely misinterpret him in the early part of this scene. They fancy (*sic!*) that he is alarmed and suspicious the moment he hears Iago mutter 'Ha! I like not that', as he sees Cassio leaving Desdemona. But, in fact, (*sic!*) it takes a long time for Iago to excite surprise, curiosity, and then grave concern—by no means yet jealousy—even about Cassio; and it is still longer before Othello understands that Iago is suggesting doubts about Desdemona too.

Now Bradley had the Furness 'New Variorum' edition of the play before him when he composed his lecture and he cannot have missed a long extract printed there from an essay by G. H. Lewes entitled *Foreign Actors on our Stage.*[1] There, if his mind had been open, he could have attended to a passage which he could not easily have passed off as mere fancy. It is a great pleasure to record that the Coleridge line was not the only line known to the nineteenth century.[2] Some of Lewes's incidental remarks have the further interest of shewing how poor ideas in Shakespeare criticism get passed on as well as good. (The actor criticized is Fechter.)

> The second illustration which may be noticed, is the perverse departure from the obvious meaning of the text, which, in his desire for originality and naturalness in the business, makes him destroy the whole art of Shakespeare's preparation, and makes the jealousy of Othello seem preposterous. One defect in the play which has been felt by all critics is the rapidity with which Othello is made to believe in his wife's guilt. Now, allowing for the rapidity which the compression necessary to dramatic art renders almost inevitable, I think Shakespeare has so exhibited the *growth* of the jealousy, that it is only on reflection that the audience becomes aware of the slight grounds on which the Moor is convinced. It is the actor's part to make the audience feel this growth—to make them go along with Othello, sympathising with him, and *believing* with him. Fechter deliberately disregards all the plain meaning of the text, and makes the conviction sudden and preposterous. It is one of his new arrangements that Othello, when the tempter begins his diabolic insinu-

[1] This essay appeared first in *Blackwood's Edinburgh Magazine*, vol. XC, December 1861. It was reprinted with small changes in *On Actors and the Art of Acting* (1875). I have taken all my quotations from this text, pp. 156–173.

[2] The interpretation that Lewes regarded as the obvious one was shared by Allardyce Nicoll, who wrote in *Studies in Shakespeare* (1927): 'To believe that Othello's suspicions were not in embryo before ever Iago spoke is to deny all meaning to Shakespeare's lines'.

ation, shall be seated at a table reading and signing papers. When first I heard of this bit of 'business', it struck me as admirable; and indeed I think so still; although the manner in which Fechter executes it is one of those lamentable examples in which the *dramatic* art is subordinated to serve *theatrical* effect. That Othello should be seated over his papers, and should reply to Iago's questions while continuing his examination, and affixing his signature, is *natural*; but it is not natural—that is, not true to the nature of Othello and the situation—for him to be dead to the dreadful import of Iago's artful suggestions. Let us hear Shakespeare.

Othello and Iago enter as Cassio takes leave of Desdemona; whereupon Iago says, meaning to be heard, 'Ha! I like not that!'

(Lewes then quotes the passage down to 'I shall not dine at home' with the following emphasis:

> I cannot think it,
> That he would *steal away*, so *guilty-like*
> Seeing *your coming*.)

These short evasive sentences are subtly expressive of the state of Othello's mind; but Fechter misrepresents them by making Othello free from all misgiving. He 'toys with her curls', and treats her as a father might treat a child who was asking some favour which could not be granted yet which called for no explicit refusal. If the scene stood alone, I should read it differently; but standing as it does between the two attempts of Iago to fill Othello's mind with suspicion, the meaning is plain enough. He has been made uneasy by Iago's remarks; very naturally, his bearing towards his wife reveals that uneasiness. A *vague* feeling, which he dares not shape into a suspicion, disturbs him.

Just as no textual emendation can be accepted until an explanation has been found to account for the fault arising in the text, so in disputes there can be no satisfactory conclusion unless a plausible account is offered of how eminently sensible men came to hold such perverse views. Professor Leavis's case is not weakened but its persuasive power is much lessened by the implied slur on Bradley's *general* ability as a reader of Shakespeare. I can, however, only guess that, in addition to a perhaps unconscious dread of damaging Othello's purity of soul if he allowed the evidence of the early part of this scene to get through to his mind, Bradley also brought a positive assumption that Shakespeare intended to make the onset of jealousy in some way justifiable. I am convinced of the contrary: I think that Shakespeare had deeply pondered this very question of how jealousy can take hold of a mind without apparent cause, and had maturely decided it was a mystery, and part of a general mystery. But if wonder is the ground note:

> Can such things be,
> And ouercome vs like a Summers Clowd,
> Without our speciall wonder? . . .

the main note is of *monstrosity*. What heightens our interest is the horrible revelation that Othello is, first, unable to fight back when the unexpected visitor makes itself felt in his soul, and, second, brings out from that soul such streaks of evil that we must long for his removal from our sight. Jealousy, then, is a minor thing; the major interest is the triumph of evil; *Othello* is much more like *Macbeth* than any other play, the main difference being the want in *Othello* of a steadying confidence in the possible goodness in the world. *Othello* is consequently sickening and unbearable. *Macbeth* is . . . but that is another story and the point needed here is merely that in *Macbeth* horrors are tolerable, pain has different dimensions.

I have several times been tempted to strike out the above paragraph since it is far too cut-and-dried. The points are never so plainly made out in this play that we can accept such a summary account. I let it stand only to force the reader to ask himself what he is assuming about the general set or drift of the play. (Just as we find extraordinary gleams of penetration in Rymer, so, I think, we ought to see something in Stoll.) I also let it stand to usher in a plea that we give more weight to certain passages than they usually get. One of these always gets some attention, but I would ask for more. In its due place I shall be arguing that Shakespeare was deliberately using *Emilia* as a mouthpiece. Not that even so Shakespeare meant us to surrender our dramatic interest in judging how much authority to attach to her words. Yet that she is in general intended to guide us will be one of my main contentions. Therefore I suggest that we should give deciding weight to her account of jealousy:

> —          Pray heauen it bee
> State matters, as you thinke, and no Conception,
> Nor no Iealious Toy concerning you.
> —Alas the day, I neuer gaue him cause.
> —But Iealious soules will not be answer'd so;
> They are not euer iealious for the cause,
> But iealious for they're iealious. It is a Monster
> Begot vpon it selfe, borne on it selfe.
> —Heauen keepe that Monster from *Othello*'s mind.

The passage that seems to me to come straight out of Shakespeare's deepest thought is put into the mouth of Iago:

> As where's that Palace, whereinto foule things
> Sometimes intrude not? Who has a breast so pure,
> But some vncleanly Apprehensions
> Keepe Leetes, and Law-dayes, and in Session sit
> With meditations lawfull?[1]

There, if I mistake not, we have an instance of the powerful application of Shakespeare's thought to Christian commonplace. That it was Shakespeare's thought is suggested by its recurring in this form in *Macbeth*:

> Mercifull Powers, restraine in me the cursed thoughts
> That Nature giues way to in repose.

All this, however, would be a scandalous digression if its purpose were not to send us back to the theatre ready to hang on every word and if every word were not decisive. Minute attention is needed to prevent our going badly, irrevocably astray, but we must experience everything with the dizzy speed at which Othello's evil is now growing from a shapeless nothing to a full-blown and damning *prise de conscience*. It is essential to grasp the real dynamism of this scene. Why is Othello in such a hurry to get rid of his wife? Not, surely, to enjoy a disgusting and degrading interview with a subordinate, but to enjoy, if I may put it in such a ghastly way, the growth in his own mind of a toad that with every mental breath is growing into a monster. Iago does not have to work to set Othello's mind working. He is merely echoing, putting into words what Othello is thinking and feeling. It is only because if Iago has the words Othello has the thoughts and is totally absorbed by them that he does not expostulate in some such way as I imagined. The absence of this or any protest is the most frightening thing in the play so far. We know that horror must be on the way as soon as we notice the absence of the normal active resistance to evil that would occur in a lover even if he had the most palpable evidence of infidelity before his eyes. In asking for *Macbeth* to be kept in mind as we go over this temptation scene I do not lose the sense that *Troylus and Cressida* is always close to us:

—Al's done my Lord.

—It is.

—Why stay we then?

[1] Cf. Milton: *Paradise Lost*, v. 117–119. Evil into the mind of God or Man / May come and go, so unapprov'd, and leave / No spot or blame behind.

—To make a recordation to my soule
Of euery syllable that here was spoke:
But if I tell how these two did coact,
Shall I not lye, in publishing a truth?
Sith yet there is a credence in my heart,
An esperance so obstinately strong,
That doth inuert that test of eyes and eares,
As if those organs had deceptious functions,
Created onely to calumniate.
Was *Cressed* here?
—I cannot coniure Troian.
—She was not sure.
—Most sure she was.

When we look over the dialogue we see that Iago is not really leading
Othello, but Othello Iago. In particular we see that Othello is using Iago
to give himself permission to go even lower in his suspicions, to encourage what is so rapidly expanding inside him. That Othello is leading Iago
is seen clearly here:

> By heauen he ecchoes me
> As if there were some Monster in his thought
> Too hideous to be shewne.

Why else does he jump to *Monster*? Surely with the plot as it stands nobody but Othello could forget the cold facts of probability: it is the wed-
ding-morn. No genuine thought about adultery in these circumstances
could arise, nothing save a monster, something quite unconnected with
reality. It is Othello reading himself and wanting to hear his own thought
back who supposes Iago's contracted brows suggested in his mind *Some
horrible Conceite*. That Othello is in the lead is further seen when he
challenges Iago like Macbeth when he is about to make his own contact
with evil:

> I will to morrow
> (And betimes I will) to the weyard Sisters.
> More shall they speake: for now I am bent to know
> By the worst meanes, the worst. . .

Do we not catch a similar accent here:

> I prythee speake to me, as to thy thinkings,
> As thou dost ruminate, and giue thy worst of thoughts
> The worst of words . . . ?

The reader will be, I hope, as glad as I was to find Lewes continuing as follows:

If this be the state of mind in which the great scene begins, it is obviously a serious mistake in Fechter to sit down to his papers, perfectly calm, free from all idea whatever of what Iago has suggested; and answering Iago's insidious questions as if he did not divine their import. So clearly does Othello divine their import, that it is *he*, and not Iago, who expresses in words their meaning. It is one of the artifices of Iago to make his victim draw every conclusion from premises which are put before him, so that, in the event of detection, he can say, 'I said nothing, I made no accusation.' All he does is to lead the thoughts of Othello to the conclusion desired. The scene thus begins:

IAGO. My noble Lord—
OTHELLO. What dost thou say, Iago?
IAGO. Did Michael Cassio, when you wooed my lady,
    Know of your love?

Now Iago perfectly well knew this, for he had heard Desdemona say so just the minute before.

OTHELLO. He did from first to last: Why dost thou ask?
IAGO. But for the satisfaction of my thought;
    *No further harm.*

Properly, Iago's answer should end at the word thought; that is the answer to the question; but he artfully adds the suggestion of harm, which falls like a spark on the inflammable mind of his victim, who eagerly asks, 'Why of thy thought, Iago?'

IAGO. I did not think he had been acquainted with her.
OTHELLO. Oh yes; and went between us very oft.
IAGO. Indeed?
OTHELLO. Indeed? Ay, Indeed: Discern'st thou aught in that?

Is he not honest?

IAGO. Honest, my lord?
OTHELLO. Honest? ay, honest?
IAGO. My lord, for aught I know.
OTHELLO. What dost thou think?
IAGO. Think, my lord?

It is difficult to comprehend how anyone should fail to interpret this dialogue, every word of which is an increase of the slowly growing suspicion. If the scene ended here, there might indeed be a defence set up for Fechter's notion that Othello should reply to the insinuation in a careless manner, 'playing

with his pen as he speaks'; but no defence is permissible for one moment
when we know how the scene proceeds.

OTHELLO. Think, my lord? By heaven he echoes me!
　　　　As if there were *some monster* in his thought
　　　　*Too hideous* to be shown. Thou *dost mean something*;
　　　　I heard thee say but now, thou lik'dst not that
　　　　When Cassio left my wife: what didst not like?
　　　　And when I told thee he was of my counsel
　　　　In my whole course of wooing, thou cry'dst, Indeed?
　　　　*And didst contract and purse thy brow together,*
　　　　*As if thou then hadst shut up in thy brain*
　　　　*Some horrible conceit.* If thou dost love me
　　　　Show me thy thought.

Fechter would perhaps urge that this language is not to be understood
seriously, but as the banter of Othello at seeing Iago purse his brow and look
mysterious about trifles. It is in this sense that he plays the part. But how
widely he errs, and how seriously Othello is disturbed, may be read in his
next speech:—

　　　　I know thou'rt full of love and honesty,
　　　　And weigh'st thy words before thou giv'st them breath,
　　　　Therefore these stops of thine *fright me the more*;
　　　　For such things in a *false disloyal knave*
　　　　Are tricks of custom; but in a man that's just
　　　　They're close denotements, working from the heart
　　　　That passion cannot rule.

Is this banter? and when he bids Iago

　　　　　　　Speak to me as to thy thinkings,
　　　　As thou dost ruminate; and give thy *worst of thoughts*
　　　　*The worst of words,*

it is impossible to suppose that his mind has not already shaped the worst
suspicions which he wishes Iago to confirm.

The reader with the play before him will note that the commentary on
this scene has not extended beyond line 137 of the Arden edition. We
have still to hear the following:

—Ile know thy Thoughts.
—You cannot, if my heart were in your hand,
　Nor shall not, whil'st 'tis in my custodie.
—Ha?
—Oh, beware my Lord, of iealousie,

It is the greene-ey'd Monster, which doth mocke
The meate it feeds on. That Cuckold liues in blisse,
Who certaine of his Fate, loues not his wronger:
But oh, what damned minutes tels he ore,
Who dotes, yet doubts: Suspects, yet fondly loues?     [*Folio:* soundly]
—O miserie.

On this Bradley, in the note referred to above, comments:

Nor, even at 171, is the exclamation 'O misery' meant for an expression of
Othello's own present feelings; as his next speech clearly shows, [it expresses
an *imagined* feeling, as also the speech which elicits it professes to do (for][1]
Iago would not have dared here to apply the term 'cuckold' to Othello). In
fact it is not until Iago hints that Othello, as a foreigner, might easily be
deceived, that he is seriously disturbed about Desdemona.

Salvini played this passage, as might be expected, with entire understand-
ing. Nor have I ever seen it seriously misinterpreted on the stage. I gather
from the Furness Variorum that Fechter and Edwin Booth took the same
view as Salvini. Actors have to ask themselves what was the precise state of
mind expressed by the words they have to repeat. But many readers never
think of asking such a question.

In view of this reference to actors it will be appropriate to give Fechter's
critic the last word:

Here, I affirm, the plain sense of Shakespeare is not only too clearly indicated to admit of the most ingenious reading in another sense, but any other
reading would destroy the dramatic art with which the scene is conducted,
because it would destroy those indications of the *growth* of the feeling, which
feeling, being really founded on Iago's suggestions and the smallest possible
external evidence, becomes preposterous when the evidence alone is appealed
to. Now, Fechter so little understands this, as not only to miss such broadly
marked indications, but to commit the absurdity of making Othello *suddenly*
convinced, and by what? by the *argument* of Iago, that Desdemona deceived
her father, and may therefore deceive her husband! But *that* argument (setting aside the notion of a character like Othello being moved by merely
intellectual considerations) had already been forcibly presented to his mind
by her father:—

[1] The passage in square brackets is an after-thought appearing first in the second
edition (1905) as a substitute for 'it is as general as the words that elicit it (and how
general they are may be seen from the use of 'cuckold', which . . .'.

Look to her, Moor, have a quick eye to see:
She did deceive her father, and may thee.

Whereupon he replies, 'My life upon her faith'. And so he would reply to
Iago, had not his mind already been filled with distrust. Fechter makes him
careless, confident, unsuspicious, until Iago suggests her deception of her
father, and then *at once* credulous and overcome. This may be the art of the
Porte St. Martin, or the Variétés; it is not the art of Shakespeare.

The reader who has noticed that I have made no attempt to adjust my
account to fit this admirable piece of Victorian good sense may have
wondered why, since I was willing to chop up things so fine, I did not go
on to argue the points of difference that emerged. The minuteness of
treatment that I found necessary here is foreign to my plan and would in
fact destroy my plan if pushed to extremes. A common reading in any
large community must make allowances for variations in detail. I would
even claim that close friends must resign themselves to permanent dis-
agreements over lesser aspects. When an old man looks back over the
period of his maturity he must notice how often he has changed his mind
about things in the play with and without external assistance. I stooped to
detail here because without agreement over the main point there could be
little interest in continuing. But my object must be to tackle only the
largest questions: what sort of a play is *Othello*? and, has it a general point?
and, is it significantly designed? I am not alone in finding any sort of
conviction that there is a design dawning very late, for me in the 'undressing scene' before Desdemona is murdered. On the other hand, I can
discern a scheme in the presentation of Othello which begins to emerge
in the third Act. The belief that such a scheme is really there and not invented depends in turn on the conviction that the play has to do essentially with mystery and monstrosity and culminates in a *monstrous Acte*,
and is not essentially described in some such phrase as, 'now that the
mechanism of Othello's character is laid bare the play is done.' The stress
on 'essentially' is a confession that incidentally so many other things are
going on and so powerfully that it may require some especially strong
pleading to allow the main emphasis to lie where I shall declare I found
it! For the fact remains that *Othello* is the one play of Shakespeare's with
some serious plot-interest; it is equally true that Othello's behaviour can
be analysed and that the analysis gives pleasure. It is also true that *Othello*
is a play of a strange kind of poetry, as described by Professor Knight,[1]

[1] *Op. cit.*

and to dwell on its strangeness is to move towards the heart of the play.

What troubles me is that, comparatively speaking, all these three aspects, 'plot, 'character', 'music' are both powerful and plain, whereas what I am about in my next chapter to describe as the underlying design is faint and questionable. My only consolation is that this unifying interest does draw on and is served by what appear in my argument as three subordinate aspects. But as regards Othello, I would suggest that the ground-plan of the design is given by Cassio in the passage already discussed: 'To be now a sensible man, by and by a Foole, and presently a Beast'. In the first two Acts Othello has been the sensible man: we now see him becoming a fool and then becoming a beast. I shall then argue that he descends even lower and in his worst stage becomes a devil. This downward progression is also in the direction of greater dramatic intensity. That is why I deprecated dwelling too much on the first stage, where Othello is still some sort of man. The chief danger in this scheme is that our interest in a man will normally be greater than that we can take in a human being transformed into a beast or a devil. This downward progression is, too, an exploration of the unbearable. Shakespeare has helped us at the end by restoring the old Othello to share the soul of the Othello-devil but I cannot join with those readers who would say of Othello what we find in Stoll: 'he keeps our sympathy and admiration to the end . . .',[1] though I hope here to perform a minor mediating task.

Since, when I come to the 'undressing' scene, I shall be making so much of *intelligence about life* as Shakespeare's chief concern, it may seem odd to relegate the question of Othello's intelligence to second or third place. Alas, the text is here plain: Othello is not merely a gull, he is shewn at the end to be an ignorant fool.[2] We may begin then with Emilia's choric pronouncements:

> Oh Gull, oh dolt,
> As ignorant as durt . . .
> Oh thou dull Moore . . .
> . . . . what should such a Foole
> Do with so good a wife?

but only because they sum up what we have seen to be the chief fact about Othello. Poor man, he knew nothing about life and proved incapable of learning. (I think we must face this: it will not do to say he had no opportunity to learn about life because he had spent all his time in the

[1] *Art and Artifice in Shakespeare* (1933), p. 43.
[2] Othello's last words before his dramatic self-dismissal from life were:
O Foole, foole, foole!

army.) Shakespeare, we may think, was *too seuere a Moraller* in forcing us to see the ignorance as culpable. He makes it the consequence of an excessive preoccupation with self and an admiring self-contemplation. At this point I could wish the reader to possess every word of Professor Leavis's analysis and synthesis of Othello's character, especially where he traces everything back to Othello's self-regard. For Shakespeare is doing what is there alleged, and once the reader gets the tips he has no trouble in applying them. Once it is pointed out how Othello's nobility becomes 'the disguise of an obtuse and brutal egotism' we can make sense of another remark: 'Self-pride becomes stupidity'. Two other happy phrases to be exploited are: '. . . a habit of approving self-dramatization is an essential element in Othello's make-up, and remains so at the very end . . .' and 'Contemplating the spectacle of himself, Othello is overcome with the pathos of it'.

At this point of transition to the theme of Othello as beast I was about to dismiss the topic of Othello as fool with the remark that Professor Leavis never paid so great a tribute to Bradley (by treating *Othello* as a character-study) as in this essay in which Bradley is held up for scorn, when my eye fell on the following sentences, which in power and economy I cannot hope to equal[1]:

> Such jealousy as Othello's converts human nature into chaos, and liberates the beast in man; and it does this in relation to one of the most intense and also the most ideal of human feelings. What spectacle can be more painful than that of this feeling turned into a tortured mixture of longing and loathing, the 'golden purity' of passion split by poison into fragments, the animal in man forcing itself into his consciousness in naked grossness, and he writhing before it but powerless to deny it entrance, gasping inarticulate images of pollution, and finding relief only in a bestial thirst for blood? This is what we have to witness in one who was indeed 'great of heart' and no less pure and tender than he was great.

Yet admirable as this is, it suffers from the gravest of the defects in Bradley's lectures on *Othello*. Here, it seems to me, there is no appeal from the verdict delivered by Professor Leavis, and what was said of Bradley must be true of many other and many living critics. Bradley's Othello is Othello's Othello and a sentimental version at that. He focussed excessively and he focussed narrowly on the hero in such a way that he *had* to create an almost superhuman villain to carry off the evil he could not bear to see attaching itself to Othello. This is a critical crime:

[1] *Shakespearean Tragedy*, p. 178.

the play is always the thing, and Shakespeare always, in every play (yes, even in *Hamlet*) invites us to see larger than his largest figure.

Students have told me that while reading the play they thought of the author as a dentist who had forgotten to use an anaesthetic or no longer remembered how much drilling hurts. Shakespeare, it seems to me, is not so inconsiderate, and I take it to be part of his design to *detach* us from his hero by making him repellent as well as attractive and at the same time inviting us to see a general problem just where the particular case becomes too appalling to dwell on. *Facilis descensus Auerno*,[1] and if we could add 'speedy' to 'easy', would be a fair summing up of much Elizabethan and Jacobean rumination on the nature of sin and temptation. If I am right in thinking the play culminates in spiritual death and damnation, there would be great point in the violation of psychological probability in Othello's sudden collapse. But as long as we are looking for 'character-study' in the play we are bound to work on the principle

*nemo repente fuit turpissimus*[2]

and search for the distant origins of the catastrophe. Now the play as constructed cannot supply us with what we would need. The early history of Othello and Desdemona, the actual progress of the courtship— these are things we must pass lightly over: these, we may say, are matters reserved for the *novel*.

The play is now so rich that the word 'beast' must cover many things. The meaning that knits the play together is the sense that Othello has succumbed to that general evil of the Venetian world I touched on earlier. We thought Othello was remote from such filth and in a moment we see it as part of his inmost being. Never once after his fall does he speak as if he knew the meaning of language such as the Senator put to him:

such faire question
As soule to soule affordeth . . .

nor does he ever suppose such language could have had any meaning for Desdemona. His drop from the human to the bestial has two stages: the reduction of love to lust, the degradation of sensuality to bestiality. Both stages were presented to us together in the expository Acts, but in tracing the loss of humanity, the fall into the pit, we should notice that Shakespeare makes a distinction which we feel strongly as we contrast the

[1]          The Gates of Hell are open Night and day;
          Smooth the Descent, and easie is the Way:
*Virgil's Æneis, The Sixth Book*, lines 192–3, translated by John Dryden (1697).
   [2] Juvenal, 2.83 (For none becomes at once completely vile).

heroic level with the normal, Othello with Cassio and Desdemona with Emilia, yet which dwindles to nothing when we contrast these two normal characters with what Othello finally becomes.

As I shall be making much, later on, of Emilia as our norm, I will here take Cassio as the normal figure by which to judge the human standards Othello falls below. I am sorry that, for the sake of the gross eavesdropping scene Shakespeare puts certain alien touches into his picture of Cassio's affair with Bianca, for it otherwise has a consistency strong enough to make it into a norm. A man, in Shakespeare's scheme of things, is not normally totally absorbed by his relations with women. In so far as Othello is wholly dependent on his love he is to be pitied and . . . condemned as a dotard. Loose sexual morals are compatible with a delicate conscience in all other matters. In short, we are to take it that Iago's verdict is a reasonable guide in summing up what Cassio represents:

> He hath a dayly beauty in his life,
> That makes me vgly . . .

There is consequently a border territory marching with the soiled area, but people living on the wholesome side know where they are and how they differ from their neighbours on the Iago side of the fence. Sir Thomas Wyatt the poet provides a notable instance from 1541 when he was defending himself against the accusation made by Bishop Bonner that while he was in Spain he used to live viciously among the nuns of Barcelona:

> Come on now my Lorde of London, what is my abhominable and viciouse lyvinge? Do ye knowe yt, or haue ye hard yt? J graunte J doo not profess chastytye, but yet J vse not abhomynation. Yf ye knowe yt tell yt here with whome and when, yf ye harde yt who is *your* Aucthor? Haue you sene me have anye harlott in my howse, whylest ye were in my Companye? Did you ever see woman somuche as dyne or supp at my table? None but for *your* pleasure the woman that was in the Gallie, wich J assure you maie be well sene, for byfore you came neyther she nor anye other came above the maste . . .[1]

Nothing that Cassio does with Bianca troubles his vision of sexual purity. He knows what it is and salutes it when he sees it.

Similarly some of Iago's insinuations come from near the border. We saw a piece, as it were, of overlapping territory when Cassio jokingly supported Iago's remarks at the harbour. So we may say that many of his insinuations to Othello cannot have been even *news*. It seems preposterous

[1] Taken from a manuscript in the British Museum, Yelverton Papers, vol. xxi, fo: 171 *verso*.

to suppose that army life does not throw up as fair a picture of mankind's sexual proclivities as any city-state. In fact we can distinguish the wholesome and the depraved mind by saying that the former thinks sexual malpractice widespread, the latter, universal. It was therefore something far worse than ignorance in Othello that made him unable to resist falling into universal doubt. Since we cannot understand Iago's reputation for honesty, we must take it that what we are allowed to know as spectators could not be known to the actors. But Othello knew Desdemona better than any spectator and all the actors. By comparison Brabantio and Roderigo were going on surmise when it came to the fact of her sexual nature. So we need a word for his loss of hold on the evidence for thinking that Desdemona had a soul as well as a body and that soul was of miraculous purity. Moral imbecility is not enough: it is hard to keep out of our minds the thought that the lower view of human nature must have had some extraordinary *attractive* power over Othello.

This stage has been artificially marked out by me, it was not a historical step. I have resorted to this artifice to prepare the way for a justification of our loathing as we come to understand Othello's mind. I suppose that if we can say that '*any* husband would have been troubled by [Iago's warnings]' (which I deny), we can say with greater assurance that any man who imagines himself married to Desdemona could furnish material for resistance to them. Must we not then conclude that Othello was unfit to be a husband to Desdemona from the moment when he came to think her no better than many another fine lady of Venice, and that it was nauseating that he was even allowed to speak to her after he had consented to give house room to such thoughts? But in history what sprang into being as Othello spied Cassio leaving Desdemona was a *monstrous Birth*; it contained worse horrors than those I have treated as the first stage long before Othello had the words ready for uttering them. As we see his thoughts growing we join up with the opening of the play. When Iago says to Othello

> Looke to your wife

we remember that he had said to Brabantio

> Looke to your house, your daughter . . .

and the degraded sensuality of Iago's foul language returns to us as we see Othello matching and outdoing the foulest expressions.

'Degraded sensuality' calls for some definition. One instance, however, will put the matter before us and spare us painful analysis. It is no doubt a discovery of the study but once discovered it becomes part of our theatre experience. (Its creation is to my mind one of the strongest clues to the author's inner life.) Iago has been rather scornfully protesting that the supposed adulterers could not be spied on *flagrante delicto*:

> It is impossible you should see this,
> Were they as prime as Goates, as hot as Monkeyes . . .

This was the very food Othello was craving: soon he saw nothing else but human beings turned into animals in rut. This rioting imagery is still with him when he gives his wife a public blow and when he plays on the word 'turne':

> . . . you did wish, that I would make her turne:
> Sir, she can turne, and turne: and yet go on
> And turne againe.

Now we can see that it is Othello not Roderigo

> Whom Loue hath turn'd almost the wrong side out.

Now Othello has only the seamy side. Shakespeare makes it very plain that sensuality has gone wrong in him. But I should like to protest in passing that there was nothing repellent in the aroused sensuality in itself. That he found his wife a *sweet Body* was natural: that he could find her nothing else is degrading. His notion of possession almost itself generates the stream of vile thoughts that come over him as he dreads loss of possession. Once again one striking example will serve for all. On an earlier page I tried to fix the quality of Juliet's love by dwelling on the bird imagery she used:

> O for a Falkners voice,
> To lure this Tassell gentle backe againe. . .

She was there remembering an every-day experience in the use of male hawks as hunters. Othello goes to the same source: he thinks of himself as the falconer taming his bird and of the short straps on the hawk's legs by which it was fastened to the leash. A well-trained hawk when allowed to fly made only for the prey the falconer wished to have for his dinner, his master's dinner or the market. A badly-trained hawk, a haggard, when unleashed would fly at every bird it saw. As such a bird was not worth the cost of training or keeping, it was allowed to return to the state of nature. So Othello says:

> If I do proue her Haggard,
> Though that her Iesses were my deere heart-strings,

E

> I'ld whistle her off, and let her downe the winde
> To prey at Fortune.

I have selected this passage because of something nasty and cold in the sensuality. Although the natural end for the beast is, as Bradley saw, in images of hot blood, the most repellent thing in Othello is a certain coldness in his sensuality. So, to have done with this side of the play once and for all, I should like to juxtapose two passages, one near the beginning and one near the climax of this degraded sensuality in Othello. The first in fact is a continuation from the bird passage:

> O Curse of Marriage!
> That we can call these delicate Creatures ours,
> And not their Appetites? I had rather be a Toad,
> And liue vpon the vapour of a Dungeon,
> Then keepe a corner in the thing I loue
> For others vses.

The Toad returns in the passage where Othello speaks from his inmost heart:

> But there where I haue garnerd vp my heart,
> Where either I must liue, or beare no life,
> The Fountaine from the which my currant runnes,
> Or else dries vp: to be discarded thence,
> Or keepe it as a Cesterne, for foule Toades
> To knot and gender in.

The word 'devil' is even more ambiguous than the word 'beast'. Once again we may start by taking Emilia as the choric voice, which would give us an unambiguous sense:

—'Twas I that kill'd her.
—Oh the more Angell she, and you the blacker Diuell.
—She turn'd to folly: and she was a whore.
—Thou dost bely her, and thou art a diuell.

Othello grants part of her case (that he is damned), first hypothetically:

> O, I were damn'd beneath all depth in hell:
> But that I did proceed vpon iust grounds
> To this extremity. . .

and when he sees (if he does) that he had no just grounds, he invites damnation:

> Whip me ye Diuels,
> From the possession of this Heauenly sight:
> Blow me about in windes, roast me in Sulphure,
> Wash me in steepe-downe gulfes of Liquid fire.

On the other hand, Othello does not seem to be feeling genuinely in-
wardly damned, as we see at once immediately after this. When *Lodouico*
asks:

> Where is this rash, and most vnfortunate man?

he replies at once:

> That's he that was *Othello*: heere I am.

This could be dismissed as one more in the long tale of self-deceptions of
a very puddled spirit and a much perplexed mind. I think, however, that
every fair-minded theatre-goer would have to confess to a sense of strain
at the end of the play between the spectator's verdict on Othello and the
'public' verdict on the stage, which seems to support Othello in his deluded account of himself. *Macbeth* ends on a very different note. The
hero, called a *Hell-hound* and a

> bloodier Villaine
> Then tearmes can giue thee out . . . ,

has his severed head produced and pronounced 'cursed', and he himself
is then described as a *dead Butcher*. *Lodouico* treats Othello as a criminal
but his tone on arresting him is courteous:

> You shall close Prisoner rest,
> Till that the Nature of your fault be knowne
> To the Venetian State . . .

and his behaviour is not compatible with the view that Othello has be-
come a monster. The text is quite against the creation of *two* villains.[1]
*Lodouico* and Othello agree here: the fault is all Iago's: *he* is the *demy-
Diuell*. We get

> Where is that Viper?
> Bringe the Villaine forth . . .

and

> Falne in the practise of a cursed Slaue

---

[1] See p. 140 and p. 150 for Emilia's disagreement.

which is very like

> ... he hath ... ensnar'd my Soule and Body.

We may smile at the conceit of Iago supposing that his 'medicine' was
working, but *Lodouico* supports him:

> Oh Sparton Dogge:
> More fell then Anguish, Hunger, or the Sea:
> Looke on the Tragicke Loading of this bed:
> This is thy worke. . .

And the text gives us as we leave the theatre the *contrast* between Othello
as 'great of heart' and Iago as 'hellish villaine'.

At this point, when we are seeking to separate what is attractive in
Othello from what is repellent, the reader must put himself through an
examination. Many critics write as if they had only heard of jealousy, and
the degrading consequences we meet with in this play were matters they
could only match from observing other people. Such critics have nothing
of value to offer in the present task. At the other extreme are those who
are so ashamed of their own behaviour while suffering from fits of jealousy
that being unable to bear the reminder they project their abhorrence on to
Othello. I am convinced that as human beings if we merely consider
Othello as a fellow-consciousness we can travel sympathetically with him
lower and lower to the very gates of hell. Indeed it is there that I came
upon the clue that helped me to understand what had happened to him.
The scene where the extremes of sympathy and loathing occur is the
murder of Desdemona. There Othello is struggling with (for me) the
fiction of caring for Desdemona's soul while 'sacrificing' her body, and a
truth bursts from him that helps me to share his plight:

> Sweet Soule, take heed, take heed of Periury,
> Thou art on thy death-bed.
> —I, but not yet to dye.
> —Presently.
> Therefore confesse thee freely of thy sinne:
> For to deny each Article with Oath,
> Cannot remoue, nor choake the strong Conception
> That I do grone withall.

The *Conception* is the *conceit* of the Quarto, the *horrible Conceite* that
fastened on Othello and grew so rapidly from almost a chance visitor to a
permanent inmate. After we have apportioned the responsibility of
Othello in not taking immediate action while the conception was still

withoutwords, and of Iago in dangling the thing before him in such a way
that it could only grow and attach itself tighter, we must allow for the
possibility suggested by Emilia when she said,

> It is a Monster
> Begot vpon it selfe, borne on it selfe . . . ,

that is something that grew greater by its own inner power. Well, the
thought intrudes here and turns what (for me) would be a moment of
supreme loathing into one of compassion and fellow-feeling.

But Othello is not the only moral centre in the play: there is also Desdemona.[1] As soon as we look at the play from that centre, behaviour that
seemed all-too-human and even perhaps pardonable in Othello becomes a
nauseating offence. This will in fact become the issue in the following
chapter. But even here it may be noted that there is some doubt whether
Shakespeare consistently saw the play as a whole from a centre including
Desdemona. There is a marked lack of chivalrous feeling among the
critics: can Shakespeare himself be accused of want of decent feeling?
Was Rymer right in finding *Lodouico* far too feeble when Othello strikes
Desdemona?

> My Lord, this would not be beleeu'd in Venice,
> Though I should sweare I saw't. 'Tis very much,
> Make her amends: she weepes . . . . .

Is there not a shrewd hit underneath Rymer's coarse, derisive tone?

> The Moor has no body to take his part, no body of his Colour: *Ludovico* has
> the new Governour *Cassio*, and all his Countrymen Venetians about him.
> What Poet wou'd give a villanous Black-amoor this Ascendant? What
> Tramontain could fancy the Venetians so low, so despicable, or so patient?
> this outrage to an injur'd Lady, the *Divine Desdemona*, might in a colder
> Climate have provoked some body to be her Champion: but the Italians may
> well conclude we have a strange Genius for Poetry.[2]

(Once again we may reflect how important for righting our judgement is
the voice of Emilia.)

I come now to a second *crux* for the would-be *Versöhnender*. I was going

---

[1] I am dismayed to find that Mr Traversi does not consider her worthy of discussion
in the twenty-odd pages he allots to the play in the second edition (1957) of *An
Approach to Shakespeare*.
[2] *Op. cit.* p. 130.

to advance with great confidence that there is one strain of loathsomeness
in Othello that cannot be disputed; that when Othello assumes that he has
God with him in his evil thoughts and deeds, then we must withdraw our
sympathy since there we have a fixed principle behind which Shakespeare
never goes. Yet Bradley stands across my path and his language has
captured so many hearts that it would be an illusion of progress to pass
his words by without comment:

> The Othello who enters the bed-chamber with the words,
>
>> It is the cause, it is the cause, my soul,
>
> is not the man of the Fourth Act. The deed he is bound to do is no murder,
> but a sacrifice. He is to save Desdemona from herself, not in hate but in
> honour; in honour, and also in love. His anger has passed; a boundless
> sorrow has taken its place; and
>
>> this sorrow's heavenly:
>> It strikes where it doth love.
>
> Even when, at the sight of her apparent obduracy, and at the hearing of words
> which by a crowning fatality can only reconvince him of her guilt, these
> feelings give way to others, it is to righteous indignation they give way, not to
> rage; and, terribly painful as this scene is, there is almost nothing here to
> diminish the admiration and love which heighten pity.[1]

What is to be done in the face of this? The general form of the counter-
argument must be that Shakespeare is inviting us to see a discrepancy
between what Othello thinks is happening and what is really happening.
To this we must come, but it may help to go back and say that if Othello
here is not the man of the Fourth Act he is in essence the man of the
third scene of the Third Act, and that if we can trace back the actions that
culminate in the following words we shall have prepared ourselves to see
what Shakespeare is shewing us in the murder scene:

> —Damne her lewde Minx:
>    O damne her, damne her.
>    Come go with me apart, I will withdraw
>    To furnish me with some swift meanes of death
>    For the faire Diuell.
>    Now art thou my Lieutenant.
> —I am your owne for euer.

As long as no agreement is in sight we must be prepared to let many

[1] *Op. cit.*, pp. 197–198.

things lie in favour of the one thing that might produce general conviction. So here, as long as we are dealing only with *horrible Imaginings* and thought

> whose Murther yet is but fantasticall

(to borrow the language of *Macbeth*) we may let the view of Othello going to the devil drop temporarily out of sight in favour of a more palpable fact, that he is hopelessly at sea, that his language and his thoughts cannot be brought together. The only real thing about him is his inability to be *dans le vrai*. If we could see him as grotesque, bordering on farce in fact, in a kind of nasty play, evading by clownish means the things he cannot face, then we might be able to bear the monstrosity of his transference of his own diabolical guilt to Desdemona and the assumption of her angelic purity to himself. Unlike Macbeth, Othello is not a serious character. The very lines which for some people are the height of pathos and the perfection of noble tragedy may be taken to distinguish the histrionic from the real:

> Oh now, for euer
> Farewell the Tranquill minde; farewell Content;
> Farewell the plumed Troopes, and the bigge Warres,
> That makes Ambition, Vertue! Oh farewell,
> Farewell the neighing Steed, and the shrill Trumpe,
> The Spirit-stirring Drum, th'Eare-piercing Fife,
> The Royall Banner, and all Qualitie,
> Pride, Pompe, and Circumstance of glorious Warre:
> And O you mortall Engines, whose rude throates
> Th' immortall Ioues dread Clamours, counterfet,
> Farewell: *Othello's* Occupation's gone.

To estimate the extent to which Othello is playing before himself as audience we have only to place alongside these lines the passages where Macbeth realises that *his* occupation's gone:

> I haue liu'd long enough, my way of life
> Is falne into the Seare, the yellow Leafe,
> And that which should accompany Old-Age,
> As Honor, Loue, Obedience, Troopes of Friends,
> I must not looke to haue: but in their steed,
> Curses, not lowd but deepe, Mouth-honor, breath
> Which the poore heart would faine deny, and dare not . . .

and

To morrow, and to morrow, and to morrow,
Creepes in this petty pace from day to day,
To the last Syllable of Recorded time:
And all our yesterdayes, haue lighted Fooles
The way to dusty death. Out, out, breefe Candle,
Life's but a walking Shadow, a poore Player,
That struts and frets his houre vpon the Stage,
And then is heard no more. It is a Tale
Told by an Ideot, full of sound and fury
Signifying nothing.

Here, we feel, Macbeth is grasping something and is hardly aware of himself as he faces reality: his own feelings are lost in the confrontation of the facts. It may be a low suspicion of mine that the male part of Shakespeare's audience was too horn-mad to burst into laughter at some of Othello's antics, yet I do think that occasionally we come near to having a *bloody Farce* on our hands, and that Rymer's case—'. . . the Jealous Booby has his Brains turn'd . . .'[1]—is well supported by Shakespeare's text. (Think how very objectionable Othello's love affair with Iago would be if it were not merely ludicrous or sickening!)

There is a marked swing in the action as soon as it becomes apparent that Othello does not know his own mind and what is going on but Iago does. For then Iago takes the lead and does not lose it even when Othello threatens to kill him. This inversion of rôles emphasizes the unreality of Othello, and Shakespeare marks the point:

The Moore already changes with my poyson . . .

But both characters have their first lapse into ludicrous unreality here, where Othello's thought first struggles for the meaning of damnation:

—If thou dost slander her, and torture me,
Neuer pray more: Abandon all remorse
On Horrors head, Horrors accumulate:
Do deeds to make Heauen weepe, all Earth amaz'd;
For nothing canst thou to damnation adde,
Greater then that.
—O Grace! O Heauen forgiue me!
Are you a Man? Haue you a Soule? or Sense?
God buy you: take mine Office. Oh wretched Foole,
That lou'st to make thine Honesty, a Vice!
Oh monstrous world! Take note, take note (O World)

[1] *Op. cit.*, p. 128.

To be direct and honest, is not safe.
I thanke you for this profit, and from hence
Ile loue no Friend, sith Loue breeds such offence.

It is true that, in American phrase, they immediately snap out of such
tushery, and Iago rises to some mastery and even inspiration as he mimics
the very filthiness of Othello's imagination:

And then (Sir) would he gripe, and wring my hand:
Cry, oh sweet Creature: then kisse me hard,
As if he pluckt vp kisses by the rootes,
That grew vpon my lippes, laid his Leg ore my Thigh,
And sigh'd and kiss'd and then cried cursed Fate
That gaue thee to the Moore.
—O monstrous! monstrous!

Yet Othello is back again into the ludicrous with

Arise blacke vengeance, from the [hole of] hell,
Yeeld vp (O Loue) thy Crowne, and hearted Throne
To tyrannous Hate. Swell bosome with thy fraught,
For 'tis of Aspickes tongues. . .

I have as much difficulty in taking this seriously as I had in Iago's efforts
to personate the devil. I hope the Quarto gives us Shakespeare's text here
in order to get the point of passing at once from

Oh blood, blood, blood. . .

to

Now by yond Marble Heauen,
In the due reuerence of a Sacred vow
I heere engage my words.

Of course, if Othello meant it, he would be damned. But it is too absurd
to think that in a Christian context these words could apply to anything,
and we find Iago mimicking the action by joining Othello on his knees and
invoking what Othello will later call *you chaste Starres*. Othello's is the
action of a booby, and the result is that we do not believe the naughty
boys when they promise to commit two murders. The scene formally
closes in an embrace. Othello's mind is apparently unified in terms of
evil, yet we are more convinced of his play-acting than of his real self-
damnation.

E 2

For the hero the loss of *dignity* is irreparable. Fortunately, we do not need to argue here since any doubt on this point is extinguished when Othello is finally humiliated by Iago, who now towers over his master:

> Thus credulous Fooles are caught. . .

and, (in the crude scene with Cassio)

> As he shall smile, *Othello* shall go mad. . .

We must take this almost literally, since Shakespeare has inserted the following exchange:

—He is much chang'd.
—Are his wits safe? Is he not light of Braine?

But now, in his much lowered condition, Othello is really dangerous. His hate is murderous, but his thought about Desdemona as a devil still sounds fantastic rather than blasphemous, although his cry of *Hence, auaunt* in the presence of *Lodouico* and his greeting of Emilia as

> You Mistris,
> That haue the office opposite to Saint *Peter*,
> And keepes the gate of helle

shew that the idea of Desdemona as a white devil was a fixed delusion. We carry forward to the murder scene two moments that will find their counter-parts there. One is the desire to destroy Desdemona's soul:

—Come sweare it: damne thy selfe, least being
like one of Heauen, the diuells themselues
should feare to ceaze thee. Therefore be
double damn'd: sweare thou art honest.
—Heauen doth truely know it.
—Heauen  truely knowes, that thou art false as hell.

Yet, once again, we are more certain of what Desdemona calls the *Fury* than of the blasphemy. The second is the bloody war-cry:

> Strumpet I come

(I cannot credit Shakespeare with the couplet:

> For of my heart, those Charmes thine Eyes, are blotted.
> Thy Bed lust-stain'd, shall with Lusts blood bee spotted.

which I hope some inferior hand concocted out of Iago's

strangle her in her bed,
Euen the bed she hath contaminated.)

Now I suggest we see how to take the whole murder scene once we note
that Othello kills his wife with

Downe Strumpet

and after professing to want to spare her soul, kills her in haste:

Kill me to morrow, let me liue to night . . .
But halfe an houre . . .
But while I say one prayer.
—It is too late.          *Smothers her.*

The full enormity of the act comes out only when Desdemona cries out
and Othello exclaims:

She's like a Liar gone to burning hell . . .

so that we may say, if he at the end thought Iago had damned him, body
and soul, he had first done his best to procure the same end for Desdemona. This helps us to see as the most serious fate for Othello that he has
inverted truth and lies, and has therefore become incapable of remorse.

For nought I did in hate

is a plain untruth if not a deliberate lie.

It is a strange fact that one of the finest pieces of writing, where
Shakespeare develops his full powers, occurs in a scene impossible to
read or see without pain.

The Obiect poysons Sight,
Let it be hid.

If we suspect ourselves of being unable to face things in the play which
ought to be faced, in the murder scene we have a pain that ought not to
have been inflicted on us. Just as the act itself was monstrous, the agent
becomes a monster—or so I should have said. And I should have turned
to the voice of normality quietly speaking a grave judgement and Othello's
complete inability to listen or comprehend. Othello thinks he knows
what a spectacle he is offering, but he doesn't:

—I know this acte shewes horrible and grim.
—Poore *Desdemon*:
I am glad thy Father's dead. . .
Did he liue now,

This sight would make him do a desperate turne:
Yea, curse his better Angell from his side,
And fall to Reprobation.
—'Tis pittifull: but yet *Iago* knowes. . .

But in the effort to meet the many readers who love and pity Othello all
through the scene, let us briefly dismiss the facts that strike the spectator
who is detached from Othello, and do what they are doing and see the
action only through Othello's eyes. One of these facts, Othello's cruelty,
he does not feel in the least ashamed of mentioning, although that alone
would, on a normal scale, count as damnable. The other is his sensuality.
After what we have seen of the inside of his mind, his kissing and pawing
and smelling and savouring the externals of the sleeping body—well, if
Emilia could speak of 'a lady in Venice who would have walked barefoot
to Palestine for a touch of [*Lodouicos*] nether lip', we may be pardoned if
we think that if another lady had known her husband as we know him she
might have killed herself rather than continue to be contaminated by his
lust. But the form of question we require here is: can we detect in any of
these expressions of satisfaction to his senses that Othello's mind has
undergone a profound change since the last time he gave vent to his
degraded sensuality? Let us try

> Oh thou weed:
> Who art so louely faire, and smell'st so sweete,
> That the Sense akes at thee,
> Would thou had'st neuer bin borne.

Is there a cleaner imagination at work here?

> When I haue pluck'd thy Rose,
> I cannot giue it vitall growth againe,
> It needs must wither. Ile smell thee on the Tree.
> Oh Balmy breath, that dost almost perswade
> Iustice to breake her Sword. One more, one more:
> Be thus when thou art dead, and I will kill thee,
> And loue thee after.

We may now consider Coleridge's argument:

Othello's *belief* not jealousy; forced upon him by Iago, and such as any man
would and must feel who had believed of Iago as Othello. His great mistake
that *we* know Iago for a villain from the first moment. Proofs of the contrary
character in Othello. [But in considering the essence of the Shakespearian

Othello we must perseveringly place ourselves in his situation, and under his circumstances.][1]

Let us go further in imagination and suppose we know that Desdemona miraculously contrived to commit adultery. Would this make Othello a hero or any less of a moral desperado? Let me continue Othello's soliloquy:

> One more, and that's the last.
> So sweet, was ne're so fatall. I must weepe,
> But they are cruell Teares: This sorrow's heauenly,
> It strikes, where it doth loue,

The blasphemous reference does not shock us directly; it is only when we become Othello that we must suffer from sharing a consciousness which can have self-approval on such terms. And as we share in the vileness of his pretence to be treating Desdemona like a confessing priest and as he dares to invoke Heaven:

> I would not kill thy vnprepared Spirit,
> No, Heauens forfend, I would not kill thy Soule . . . ,

it is with immense relief that we snatch at the external evidence proving his mind does not go with his words, and we believe with Desdemona

> Some bloody passion shakes your very Frame.

At this point it will be well to return and take a fresh look at Bradley's words. They are odd. 'He is to save Desdemona from herself. . . .' (Nothing in the text justifies this. The best reason Othello can find for murdering his wife is the lame one

> . . . she must dye, else shee'l betray more men.)

'His anger has passed; a boundless sorrow has taken its place. . . .' (This is the *heauenly* feeling that *whom the Lord loveth he chasteneth*, a text which does not include killing even when God himself and not a self-appointed minister (*honourable Murderer*) is dealing with sinners.) 'Even when, at the sight of her apparent obduracy . . . these feelings give way to others, it is to righteous indignation they give way, not to rage.' Firstly, are *these* the marks of righteous indignation?

> you're fatall then
> When your eyes rowle so. . .
> Alas, why gnaw you so your nether-lip?

[1] *Coleridge's Shakespearean Criticism*, edited by T. M. Raysor (1930), Vol. I, p. 125. The portion in square brackets is from *Literary Remains* edited by H. N. Coleridge.

Secondly, all this happens before there has been any 'apparent obduracy'.
This is what happens the moment these words have been exchanged:

—Talke you of killing?
—I, I do.
—Then Heauen haue mercy on mee.
—Amen, with all my heart.
—If you say so, I hope you will not kill me.
—Humh.

Immediately after the murder Othello loses all sense of being God's
henchman, and is still sufficiently bloody-minded to comment

> Not *Cassio* kill'd? Then Murther's out of tune,
> And sweet Reuenge growes harsh.

Would there be *nothing* in all this to diminish one's admiration and love
for an Othello who was a genuine cuckold? Perhaps Professor Leavis was
too kind in not condemning even more severely this unhealthy streak in
Bradley. Surely Bradley ought to have felt the whole picture he was
building up was smashed for ever by two blows from Emilia:

> She was too fond of her most filthy Bargaine . . .

and

> This deede of thine is no more worthy Heauen,
> Then thou wast worthy her.

My conclusion is that somewhere along the line Othello did go to the
devil in the sense that his moral coherence disintegrated beyond the
possibility of restoration. After hearing Emilia he still has sufficient
mental powers to recognise that he has been tricked into believing untruth about his wife. But there is no sign that he recovers a feeling of what
it must have been like for Desdemona to hear him pouring out his filthy
accusations, nor indeed does he seem to be aware of his own spiritual degradation. He is incapable of remorse. But the chief question to be decided is whether he was meant to stand before us as a man doomed to
eternal punishment. The thought of damnation has been ringing in our
ears throughout the play. And once again Emilia comes to mind:

> If he say so, may his pernicious Soule
> Rot halfe a graine a day . . .

and, in a very significant context,

> A halter pardon him:
> And hell gnaw his bones.

This, not mere extinction of life, was the goal of Iago's devilish plan.

Yet at first sight Othello's final speech seems to be intended to make us forget

> Oh ill-starr'd wench,
> Pale as thy Smocke: when we shall meete at compt,
> This looke of thine will hurle my Soule from Heauen,
> And Fiends will snatch at it.

Placed where it is, and with the form and content it has, it would be quite extraordinary if Shakespeare had not used this speech to bring out a main point about the hero and perhaps about the play. There have been two chief views: one, that it restores the hero to all that he had lost under Iago's influence, the other that it exhibits more strikingly than ever the hero's principal weakness; and it is hard to find anybody holding an intermediate view. But before sampling this opposition I should like to look at what follows upon the death blow. Some critics have spoken as though this suicide were an act we are called on to admire. Cassio certainly thought so, but two other voices do not agree:

> LOD. Oh bloody period.
> GRA. All that is spoke, is marr'd.

and in the last line of the play it is called *This heauie Act*. There is therefore no external *necessity* to believe that the speech was intended to change the view prevailing about Othello once all the facts were known. For many readers such an appeal is otiose since Othello's final words speak for themselves. A great many people, I imagine, who might have abandoned Bradley in his attempt to make Coleridge's not-too-easily-jealous Othello plausible, rejoin him when he speaks of the close:

> And pity itself vanishes, and love and admiration alone remain, in the majestic dignity and sovereign ascendency of the close. Chaos has come and gone; and the Othello of the Council-chamber and the quay of Cyprus has returned, or a greater and nobler Othello still. As he speaks those final words in which all the glory and agony of his life—long ago in India and Arabia and Aleppo, and afterwards in Venice, and now in Cyprus—seem to pass before us, like the pictures that flash before the eyes of a drowning man, a triumphant scorn for the fetters of the flesh and the littleness of all the lives that must

survive him sweeps our grief away, and when he dies upon a kiss the most
painful of all tragedies leaves us for the moment free from pain, and exulting
in the power of 'love and man's unconquerable mind'.[1]

On the other side, Eliot's account has received much praise but its implications have been felt to be far too drastic, at least for those who claim
that the play has a tragic end:

> I have always felt that I have never read a more terrible exposure of human
> weakness—of universal human weakness—than the last great speech of
> Othello. I am ignorant whether anyone else has ever adopted this view, and it
> may appear subjective and fantastic in the extreme. It is usually taken on its
> face value, as expressing the greatness in defeat of a noble but erring
> nature. . . What Othello seems to me to be doing in making this speech is
> *cheering himself up*. He is endeavouring to escape reality, he has ceased to
> think about Desdemona, and is thinking about himself. Humility is the most
> difficult of all virtues to achieve; nothing dies harder than the desire to think
> well of oneself. Othello succeeds in turning himself into a pathetic figure, by
> adopting an *aesthetic* rather than a moral attitude, dramatizing himself
> against his environment. He takes in the spectator, but the human motive is
> primarily to take in himself. I do not believe that any writer has ever exposed
> this *bovarysme*, the human will to see things as they are not, more clearly than
> Shakespeare.[2]

Professor Leavis is one of those who have praised this passage, but his
own account is different, and brings us closer to the text. One of his
services is to force us to see the speech as having three distinct moments[3]:
'The quiet beginning gives us the man of action with his habit of effort-
less authority.' This is in fact the Old Moor, and in these lines we do
recover the accent of the speech before the Senate. 'Othello really is, we
cannot doubt, the stoic-captain whose few words know their full suffici-
ency: up to this point we cannot say he dramatizes himself, he simply *is*.'

> Soft you; a word or two before you goe:
> I haue done the State some seruice, and they know't:
> No more of that. I pray you in your Letters,
> When you shall these vnluckie deeds relate,
> Speake of me, as I am. Nothing extenuate,
> Nor set downe ought in malice.

---

[1] *Op. cit.*, p. 198.
[2] Quoted from 'Shakespeare and the Stoicism of Seneca' in *Selected Esssays* (1932).
[3] *Op. cit.*

But now comes the first critical tug. These first lines come from a mind fully composed. What will Othello—the returned Old Othello—have to say about the monsters he harboured in his mind and allowed to govern his actions? Surely to mention them now will shake him even more than it shook us to hear and see them? And how can he now bear to think of Desdemona? Professor Leavis continues:

> But then, in a marvellous way (if we consider Shakespeare's art), the emotion works itself up until in less than half-a-dozen lines the stoic of few words is eloquently weeping. With
>
> > then must you speak
> > Of one that loved not wisely but too well,
>
> the epigrammatic terseness of the dispatch, the dictated dispatch, begins to quiver. Then, with a rising emotional swell, description becomes unmistakably self-dramatization—self-dramatization as un-self-comprehending as before . . .

Here the reader must ask whether he can accept Othello's account as the truth, and if he believes that Shakespeare has been shewing us other things about Othello, he cannot continue to say that he is hearing the accent of the Old Moor, since when Othello was addressing the Senate he was very largely telling the truth, and part of his dignity was due to his truthfulness.

Professor Leavis sees Othello's *coup de grâce* as 'a superb *coup de théâtre*', but before continuing with his justification, I should like to interpose some remarks from Professor Knight that seem to me to help the case since they start from an uncommitted examination of the poetry. He has just been contrasting the way Othello and Lear address the heavens[1]:

> Lear thus identifies himself in kind with the heavens to which he addresses himself directly: Othello speaks of 'yon marble heaven', in the third person, and swears by it, does not pray to it. It is conceived as outside his interests.
>
> Now this detached style, most excellent in point of clarity and stateliness, tends also to lose something in respect of power. At moments of great tension, the Othello style fails of a supreme effect. Capable of fine things quite unmatched in their particular quality in any other play, it nevertheless sinks sometimes to a studied artificiality, nerveless and without force. For example, Othello thinks of himself as:

[1] *Op. cit.*, p. III.

> ... one whose subdued eyes,
> Albeit unused to the melting mood,
> Drop tears as fast as the Arabian trees
> Their medicinal gum.                                    (v. 11. 348)

Beside this we might place Macduff's

> O I could play the woman with mine eyes
> And braggart with my tongue! But, gentle heavens,
> Cut short all intermission. . .                        (iv. iii. 230)

Now Othello's lines here have a certain restrained, melodic beauty, like the 'Pontic sea' passage; both speeches use the typical Othello picturesque image or word; both compare, by simile, the passion of man with some picture delightful in itself, which is developed for its own sake, slightly over-developed—so that the final result makes us forget the emotion in contemplation of the image. Beauty has been imposed on human sorrow, rather than shown to be intrinsic therein. But Macduff's passionate utterance has not time to paint word pictures of 'yon marble heaven', or to search for abstruse geographical images of the Hellespont, or Arabia. There is more force in his first line than all Othello's slightly over-strained phraseology of 'subdued eyes' and 'melting mood'.

This shift from power to beauty, which forces us to become aware of the conceit in 'melting', though slight, ought, I think, to undermine the reader's confidence that Shakespeare was himself taken in by Othello's explanations.

It is only a moment, of course, and Othello quickly recovers. As Professor Leavis says: 'But this is not the part to die in: drawing himself proudly up, he speaks his last words as the stern fighting man who has done the state some service. . .'. And here, surprising to me, comes his verdict:

As, with that double force, a *coup de théâtre*, it is a peculiarly right ending to the tragedy of Othello. The theme of the tragedy is concentrated in it—concentrated in the final speech and action as it could not have been had Othello 'learnt through suffering'. That he should die acting his ideal part is all in the part: the part is manifested here in its rightness and solidity, and the actor as inseparably the man of action. The final blow is as real as the blow it re-enacts, and the histrionic intent symbolically affirms the reality: Othello dies belonging to the world of action in which his true part lay.

A play cannot end on a trick and command our deep approval. (*Hamlet* has a similarly unsatisfactory catastrophe.) The play ought to have a

THE DEVIL'S OWN 135

dramatic rather than a theatrical close. The story needed rounding out
with a return to Venice and a sentence of banishment. Othello was
*rightly* killed in Cinthio's tale by the kinsmen of Desdemona. Keeping to
the play, we may be sorry that Gratiano does not catch Emilia's fire and
hold a moral mirror up to Othello giving him one last chance to see himself as he was. As things are, starting perhaps from the apparent absurdity
of

> Where a malignant, and a Turbond-Turke

or the brutality of

> the circumcised Dogge

one may allow oneself to wonder whether the murder in Aleppo was not
one more rash and inconsiderate act, and the Venetian perhaps deserved
his beating. Certainly we relish the Ruffian here more than the General.
Such thoughts make the actual end—where Professor Leavis has no
comment—more difficult to bear.

> I kist thee, ere I kill'd thee: No way but this,
> Killing my selfe, to dye vpon a kisse.                    *Dyes*

But the nerve of nausea has ceased to throb.

# CHAPTER 4

# Intelligence about Life

T HE reader of the preceding chapter could complain with reason that no vestige of a general point emerges out of my survey of the action from the moment of temptation to the dispersal of the actors on the death of Othello. The normal consequence, when re-living a Shakespeare play, of taking trouble to get the particulars right is that general considerations look after themselves. (One consequence that, I trust, has emerged is that the design of the play now appears such as to compel attention for Othello and to make the reader who has been in the habit of elaborating on the rôle of Iago begin to wonder whether that habit was forced on him by the text. On the other hand, if, in the thirty years of life that Professor Leavis's article has enjoyed, the board has not been swept clear of Iago-mongering, if in fact, as we have seen, and could easily confirm by taking sample opinion polls, Iago is still felt by most readers to be a fascinating mystery, I cannot believe that anything written by me will do more towards righting the proportions. But once the proper subordination is accepted, I would not wish to prescribe the bounds of an interest in Iago over and above the interest of his various functions. All that I would deny is that such an interest in Iago is *central* to the play. Othello naturally wonders why Iago behaved as he did; nobody else appears to share his curiosity. Most readers, I think, finish this part of the story off in their own minds with Iago dying under torture without any comment on or explanation of his actions emerging from those closed lips.) Yet if I have been unable to make out what in the largest sense this action was all for or to give any hint that the play is more than a well-worked-out intrigue or to arouse an interest in the personages that extended beyond each as an individual, I have not suffered a peculiar fate, for nobody has been able to find and put into plain words any convincing main point. I think it was this inability that Rymer wittily seized on when he offered his version:[1]

> What ever rubs or difficulty may stick on the Bark, the Moral, sure, of this Fable is very instructive.
> 1. First, This may be a caution to all Maidens of Quality how, without their Parents consent, they run away with Black-amoors...

[1] *Op. cit.*, p. 89.

Secondly, This may be a warning to all good Wives, that they look well to their Linnen.

Thirdly, This may be a lesson to Husbands, that before their Jealousie be Tragical, the proofs may be Mathematical.

The best thing Bradley said about the play is, by common consent, contained in the passage I quoted on p. 71 where he gives his reasons for placing *Othello* a little lower than the other three tragedies and brings out an affinity with *Troylus and Cressida*. His central finding of 'an intense intellectual activity, but at the same time a certain coldness and hardness, as though some power in his soul, at once the highest and the sweetest, were for a time in abeyance' has received both a wonderful confirmation and an unexpected extension in Professor Knight's essay: *The Othello Music*. These seem to me the places to return to when attempting to say firmly what one finally thinks of the play. But before opening the question of what sort of activity play-writing was in Shakespeare's hands, I should like to dismiss one sentence from Bradley's passage, where he gives his opinion that the suppression of this power in Othello 'seems . . . to follow simply from the design of a play on a contemporary and wholly mundane subject'. 'Contemporary' I think we can dismiss at once since Shakespeare does not make us feel that the action was near him in time. And 'wholly mundane' we know is an anachronistic expression. The 'world' for Shakespeare and all men of his time was so interpenetrated with spirituality that no human relation could ever be free from its divine or diabolical aspect.

The reader who would accept this at once might nevertheless be inclined to agree with Bradley when he says[1]:

> . . . although this or that *dramatis persona* may speak of gods or of God, of evil spirits or of Satan, of heaven and of hell, and although the poet may show us ghosts from another world, these ideas do not materially influence his representation of life, nor are they used to throw light on the mystery of its tragedy. The Elizabethan drama was almost wholly secular; and while Shakespeare was writing he practically confined his view to the world of non-theological observation and thought. . .

It is a law of Shakespeare's and perhaps of all great art that everything must be subject to the maker, must pass through his mind and re-emerge as part of that mind. Hence the absence of many matters from the plays that could not be so assimilated and reproduced. But wise as Bradley's reminder is when we are thinking of religious *dogma*, it would be blinkering Shakespeare to suppose him incapable of re-thinking and making his own the great facts of religious *experience*. (Though when Shakespeare has thoroughly digested such facts there is no point in reversing the process and abstracting from the play a mere Christian commonplace.) It may be that it is because *Othello* was never thoroughly thought through that partly assimilated Christian thinking can be detected. Tempting as it is to play at reconstructing Shakespeare's experience, I put forward a 'religious' significance as something we find only when we ask whether the play has any obvious point. If it has such a significance, it may be that the play started from meditation on facts of religious experience, but the play bears no marks of having been designed to illustrate those facts.

We should therefore do well to cling to the substance—the human facts charged with all the significance the author could see in them—and treat as mere aids to grasping that significance any relations we may think we find with common religious experience. In this spirit we may say that the play is concerned with souls rather than minds and extends into the religious sphere only so much as the word 'soul' extends compared with 'mind'. Similarly we may say that the play is concerned with conditions leading to the eternal destruction of the soul's healthy state rather than with mental disorder. What may be adventuring beyond the facts is to treat the very human particulars which destroy Othello as *exemplary*, as standing for 'evil' and 'sin' generally and to claim that the *mystery of temptation* is the underlying point of reference for the whole play. We could use as our basic formula this portion of *The Epistle of Saint James*, The First Chapter, vv. 13-15:

> Let no man say when he is tempted, I am tempted of God, for God can not be tempted with euyl, neither tempteth he any man: But euery man is tempted, when he is drawen away, & entised of his owne concupiscence. Then, when lust hath conceaued, it bryngeth foorth sinne: and sinne when it is finished, bryngeth foorth death.

That Shakespeare was fascinated by the mystery is proved by the wonderful passage I have already quoted once:

> As where's that Palace, whereinto foule things
> Sometimes intrude not? Who has a breast so pure,
> But some vncleanly Apprehensions
> Keepe Leetes, and Law-dayes, and in Session sit
> With meditations lawfull?

In the context of *Othello* the *vncleanly Apprehensions* are those that cluster round the blessed facts of sex. Sexual life is marked by an unusual discrepancy between what is overt and what is hidden, and carries with it the stinging judgement: (*The Gospell by Saint Matthaewe*, The .v. Chapter, vv. 27-28):

> Ye haue hearde, that it was sayde vnto them of olde tyme: Thou shalt not commit adultry: But I say vnto you, that whosoeuer loketh on a woman, to luste after her, hath committed adultry with her alredy, in his heart.

Othello was as exposed to the atmosphere of Venice as was Desdemona. We cannot understand his fall when tempted without some sort of norm. None of his faults of *character* has any effect for good or ill on the power of evil thought to stick and then to breed so monstrously. Shakespeare does not know why one pure soul catches the contamination; but he needs another to shew that our world is not fantastically frightening. The heart of the play has nothing to do with character and morals: it is concerned with a problem of metaphysics and religion. The first stage in my argument, then, is that to understand the significance of Othello's fall we must appreciate what James meant by (The first Chapter v.27): 'Pure deuotion and vndefyled before God and the father, is this . . . to kepe hymselfe vnspotted of the worlde'; and to do this we must treat Desdemona as an independent moral centre.

I have already suggested that if we do this consistently we shall find that we have abandoned Shakespeare and the play and have gone in for a literary love affair with the heroine. At times Desdemona *is* what many critics dismiss as not worthy of discussion, a passive and submissive creature. But fair-minded critics who take her father's view of her character note that her behaviour is not consistent. Indeed if we go over the text carefully we find that Shakespeare has created if not a monster yet a being very difficult to face: an angel with a moist palm. The point is made too sharply to be overlooked or mistaken:

> —Giue me your hand.
> This hand is moist, my Lady.
> —It hath felt no age, nor knowne no sorrow.
> —This argues fruitfulnesse, and a liberall heart:
> Hot, hot, and moyst. This hand of yours requires
> A sequester from Liberty: Fasting, and Prayer,
> Much Castigation, Exercise deuout,
> For heere's a yong, and sweating Diuell heere
> That commonly rebels: 'Tis a good hand,
> A franke one.
> —You may (indeed) say so:
> For 'twas that hand that gaue away my heart. . .

This reminder of Iago's

> She's fram'd as fruitefull
> As the free Elements

forces us to have many a hard thought about the delusions Othello must have been suffering from in regard to Desdemona's love. But it also commands us to supply from our imagination as deep a response to that *sootie bosome* as would surpass what magic might perform or the dirty thought of Rymer could suppose. And all this from an angel.

To discover what is meant by Shakespeare's insistence on the word 'angel' will be as difficult as it was to fix the word 'devil' on Othello. But whereas Shakespeare refused to make a general polar equation of the two characters, he did regularly oppose the *fallen* Othello and the intact Desdemona. We have to determine whether it is one more of his lapses into easy antithesis or whether it contains any deep dramatic thought. Our method may for the same reason be the same as when characterising Othello. Let us see first how the 'choric' Emilia speaks to Othello:

> —She's like a Liar gone to burning hell,
>   'Twas I that kill'd her.
> —Oh the more Angell she, and you the blacker Diuell.
> —She turn'd to folly: and she was a whore.
> —Thou dost bely her, and thou art a diuell.
> —She was false as water.
> —Thou art rash as fire to say
>   That she was false. Oh she was heauenly true.

And a little later she tells him:

> Nay, lay thee downe, and roare:
> For thou hast kill'd the sweetest innocent,
> That ere did lift vp eye.

I take it that this last phrase suggests *prayer*, for if we look back through the play we note how often a slight or great stress is laid on Desdemona as a Christian and how often she relates herself to heaven.

The specifically Christian note is naturally most obtrusive when Othello is accusing Desdemona of being a devil and claiming that it is he who is in touch with heaven. No playgoer can forget what passes between them while Othello is acting out his travesty of the brothel, especially where Desdemona goes on her knees:

> —Why? What art thou?

—Your wife, my Lord: your true and loyall wife.

—Come sweare it: damne thy selfe, least being like one of Heauen, the diuells themselues should feare to ceaze thee. Therefore be double damn'd: sweare thou art honest.

—Heauen doth truely know it.

—Heauen truely knowes, that thou art false as hell.

Then more emphatically:

—What committed, impudent strumpet?

—By Heauen you do me wrong.

—Are you not a Strumpet?

—No, as I am a Christian.
   If to preserue this vessell for my Lord,
   From any other foule vnlawfull touch
   Be not to be a Strumpet, I am none.

—What, not a Whore?

—No, as I shall be sau'd.

—Is't possible?

—Oh Heauen forgive vs.

When a little later she again goes on her knees before Iago and Emilia, we cannot escape the parallel and contrast when Othello knelt

In the due reuerence of a Sacred vow. . . .

The following, I take it, was a wholly Christian act:

Heere I kneele:
If ere my will did trespasse 'gainst his Loue,
Either in discourse of thought, or actuall deed,
Or that mine Eyes, mine Eares, or any Sence
Delighted them in any other Forme,
Or that I do not yet, and euer did,
And euer will, (though he do shake me off
To beggerly diuorcement) Loue him deerely,
Comfort forsweare me.

I conclude from this that we are intended to take Desdemona as representing Christian Agape in human form (*The first Epistle to the Corinthians*, The .xiij. Chapter, vv. 4–7):

Loue suffreth long, and is curteous: Loue enuieth not, loue doth not frowardely, swelleth not, Dealeth not dishonestlie, seeketh not her owne, is not prouoked to anger, thynketh none euyll, Reioyceth not in iniquitie: but reioyceth in the trueth: Suffreth all thynges, beleueth all thynges, hopeth all thynges, endureth all thynges.

It may therefore sound as if I were accusing Shakespeare of blasphemy in saying that he has shewn this love to be defective and has raised the question whether Desdemona is not guilty in all her innocence. It is time now to examine the claim made earlier that the description:

... one that lou'd not wisely, but too well ...

applies more aptly to her than to Othello, and to weigh the choric ejaculation:

She was too fond of her most filthy Bargaine.

(Before settling down to judge this case there are two historical considerations to be raised and dismissed. One is that from our point of view (and Rymer's) Desdemona's obedience to her Lord goes beyond what we should approve in a self-respecting wife. I take it that Shakespeare did not regard Desdemona's wifely obedience as a fault but as Christian conscientiousness. The other is that in Shakespeare's days married people were always being warned against loving too much. Although it is a thought constantly in the filthy minds of the play, Shakespeare nowhere asks us to have it about our heroic couple.)

But there is something false in thus putting Desdemona on trial. That is not how we feel when we are in and near the play. There would be no point in this examination if we did not feel obscurely at first but with growing sadness that Shakespeare was not going to do something that we had, we see as the play developed, been dimly hoping for. From the moment that we sense something defective in Othello's way of loving we long for a contrast from Desdemona. (The reader may recall that I earlier threw out a feeler.) As soon as we see that Othello is blind and ignorant we hope that Desdemona will be able to save him by a love both clairvoyant and active. We are consequently appalled to find her with her warm-blooded nature, in matters of intelligence about life so cold, inert, and self-contained. We feel that something that ought to have been outgoing in her is dammed up:

... shut vp
In measurelesse content ... ,

to borrow a phrase from an ominous context (*Macbeth*, Act II, *Scena Prima*). The play thus draws out of us a definition of the love we want and the intelligence life requires. As it cannot be the same for each of us I do not apologise for putting it forward in personal terms. When I used the word 'outgoing' I was thinking of true love as an army commanded by a vigilant general, who keeps an advanced line of scouts constantly far out. Their duty is to pick up intelligence of things before they happen. Wordsworth's phrase 'I had no human fears' records the fatal slumber of those scouts or their failure to pass the vital advance news to the central intelligence. So the price of true love, the possibility of its continuance, is *eternal vigilance*. For human existence in time—quite apart from malice —is an unbroken cold war on true love. To declare that the world is in a state of universal peace because one is happily in love is to fall into dangerous complacency and to substitute a delightful delusion for the waking state.

In a play which is anyhow difficult to bear it adds excessively to our pain to find Desdemona as much a failure as Othello when it comes to using her intelligence. What can we cling to when in the chaos to which we surrender in the theatre we find everything human so vulnerable and incapable of righting itself, when there is no equivalent of Christian grace and heaven's influence for good is never once felt? It is in this agitation that we feel the deficiency in Desdemona and it is this agitation we recall in going back over the items. Our response to them must therefore be treated as flickerings of the mind: the question they arouse is 'I wonder?' and the temporary answer is 'wait and see'. For Desdemona's behaviour is only in one scene, to which I am coming, the centre of attention. Only once are we given time to ponder over what we see her experiencing. So here we should give each other plenty of sea-room and not try to thrust interpretations down each other's throats. In this spirit I should like to reply to those critics who exonerate Desdemona by supposing her ignorant and ignorant in a way no girls ever have been in the closest convent, ignorant, I mean, with the extravagant, impossible ignorance found only in Victorian fiction and the trashy novelettes printed for maidservants that I used to steal when I was a little boy. The one consistent point in my reading of Shakespeare's intent is that in making Desdemona out to be pure in the spirit of James, he thought of her soul as of stainless steel: it came into contact with the universal taint but could not be corroded. So we must not suppose in Act III, scene iii that Desdemona was ever as ignorant as we were in our schooldays of the significance of a man's reference to his forehead. In Shakespeare's day cuckolds and horns could be named in common conversation; they were not matters of whispered bawdry. So, I would argue, we must see here an occluding power blocking the passage of a vital message. If this fancy sticks, we may see more and guess that what was blinding Desdemona was a disagreeable self-confidence of the type that makes us say 'hen-sure is worse than cocksure'. When Desdemona hears her husband complain, she has all the un-pleasant briskness of a calloused hospital nurse. Was it likely that a pro-fessional soldier would get a head-ache from loss of sleep? When I recall this exchange:

> —Why do you speake so faintly?
> Are you not well?
> —I haue a paine vpon my Forehead, heere.
> —Why that's with watching, 'twill away againe.
> Let me but binde it hard, within this houre
> It will be well. . .

I am reminded of my tone when I comfort small children whose head-aches I suspect are appeals for attention rather than genuine *migraine*!

Can we speak of culpable self-confidence now when, after the first snub she received when pressing Cassio's suit, she remains as hopeful of getting her way? According to my impression of that snub, Othello was acting in a manner quite unusual for him. The audience, of course, by now knows much more than Desdemona can about Othello's mind, but do we not murmur *quem deus vult perdere dementat prius* when we hear her passing over what might have been a saving moment of doubt with such glib confidence of knowing her husband's mind?

> —Beleeue me, I had rather haue lost my purse
> Full of Cruzadoes. And but my Noble Moore
> Is true of minde, and made of no such basenesse,
> As iealious Creatures are, it were enough
> To put him to ill-thinking.
> —Is he not iealious?
> —Who, he? I thinke the Sun where he was borne,
> Drew all such humors from him.

Yet, as we hear this incidental proof that for her the black man was the soul of goodness, we are just as likely to reflect that if she was blind it was with the blindness of virtue to vice, the exact opposite of Iago's supposed blindness to virtue. She did not recognize the symptoms of incipient jealousy because she had never herself been assailed.

But before the two sides of the mind can develop the debate a crucial instance occurs.

What would 'any wife' think if her husband abruptly took to making remarks on her over-abundant sexuality and suggested that there was something devilish, nay, *a yong and sweating Diuell* in her palm? Would she not, like Desdemona, remind him that however warm her temperament and however dangerous such a temperament might be in a wanton woman, she had vowed it all at the altar in the service of matrimony? But what would any wife feel if this rebuke made no impression on her husband and he continued with his dark hints? Would she continue as briskly, as blindly, and at bottom so complacently contemptuous of all the signals as this?

> I cannot speake of this:
> Come, now your promise.

I do not mean that if all had been well Desdemona was not right to appeal for Cassio since I take it that on every ground Othello ought to have given way. But ought she not to have worried more when she suspected—as I think she did, and we should—that Othello, if not exactly lying, was 'stretching' the truth or 'piling it on' as we say, about the handkerchief? Where were the delicate feelers of her tact in this over-brisk insistence?

> —This is a tricke to put me from my suite,
> Pray you let *Cassio* be receiu'd againe.
> —Fetch me the Handkerchiefe,
> My minde mis-giues.
> —Come, come: you'l neuer meete a more sufficient man.
> —The Handkerchiefe.
> —A man that all his time
> Hath founded his good Fortunes on your loue;
> Shar'd dangers with you.
> —The Handkerchiefe.
> —Insooth, you are too blame.
> —Zouns.                                                    *Exit Othello.*

Do we not get the impression that Desdemona is living in a water-tight compartment, a self-created paradise of one, rather than in the sensitive give-and-take of a human partnership?
  True, she can say

> I neu'r saw this before

and it is equally true that she now begins to wake up. She is markedly more vigorous and alert than Ophelia, as we may see by contrasting

> O what a Noble minde is heere o're-throwne?
> The Courtiers, Soldiers, Schollers: Eye, tongue, sword,
> Th'expectansie and Rose of the faire State,
> The glasse of Fashion, and the mould of Forme,
> Th'obseru'd of all Obseruers, quite, quite downe.
> And I of Ladies most deiect and wretched,

That suck'd the Honie of his Musicke Vowes:
Now see that Noble, and most Soueraigne Reason,
Like sweet Bels iangled out of tune, and harsh,
That vnmatch'd Forme and Feature of blowne youth,
Blasted with extasie. Oh woe is me,
T'haue seene what I haue seene: see what I see.

with

     Something sure of State,
Either from Venice, or some vnhatch'd practise
Made demonstrable heere in Cyprus, to him,
Hath pudled his cleare Spirit: and in such cases,
Mens Natures wrangle with inferiour things,
Though great ones are their obiect. 'Tis euen so.
For let our finger ake, and it endues
Our other healthfull members, euen to a sense
Of paine. Nay, we must thinke men are not Gods,
Nor of them looke for such obseruancie
As fits the Bridall.

A novelist could do much with this: such intelligence, so easily misled!
That she both has the required intelligence and yet hasn't enough is seen
when she returns with *Lodouico* and tells him

Cozen, there's falne betweene him, & my Lord,
An vnkind breach: but you shall make all well . . .

and yet does not divine that somehow Cassio is a sore point concerning
Othello and *herself*. She is consequently not wholly in the right when she
exclaims on being struck:

    I haue not deseru'd this.

She may ask

    Alas, what ignorant sin haue I committed?

but she never finds out.

 It is obviously a delicate matter to use the word 'guilty' for Desdemona's guiltlessness. But we can say that she falls short in two respects of
being the human symbol of divinity. She is too self-confined, when it be-
hoved her to forget herself and understand Othello, to go out and meet
him in his trouble. Her admirable forthrightness is speaking for Cassio
deserts her when she has to battle with the mystery of Othello's demonic

possession. Instead she is too like the fascinated victim of a sorcerer. It was not enough to fall back on repeated protestations of her technical innocence. But the damage to her symbolic value is greater when we see her passively *leaving everything to Heaven*. She ought in a sense to have *embodied* Heaven, given us a human equivalent that would 'make sense' of Heaven. For this task she had the wrong sort of purity. She needed the intelligence that could descend into and comprehend the hell in Othello's heart. She fails because she cannot in any sense become continuous with Othello's sensual delusions. She refers everything to a remote Heaven:

> Heauen keepe that Monster from *Othello*'s mind . . .

but she is not in touch with that Heaven. So we find ourselves having to say of Desdemona what Professor Knight remarked of Othello contrasted with Lear.

> Now Othello's prayer, with its 'marble heaven', is most typical and illustrative. One watches the figure of Othello silhouetted against a flat, solid, moveless sky: there is a plastic, static suggestion about the image. Compare it with a similar Lear-prayer:

> > O heavens,
> > If you do love old men, if your sweet sway
> > Allow obedience, if yourselves are old,
> > Make it your cause; send down and take my part!
> >
> > (II. iv. 192)

> Here we do not watch Lear: 'We are Lear'. There is no visual effect, no rigid subject-object relation between Lear and 'the heavens', nor any contrast, but an absolute unspatial unity of spirit. The heavens blend with Lear's prayer, each is part of the other. There is an intimate interdependence, not a mere juxtaposition. Lear thus identifies himself in kind with the heavens to which he addresses himself directly: Othello speaks of 'yon marble heaven', in the third person, and swears by it, does not pray to it.[1]

Desdemona's helpless relation to the central mystery of the play is flashed on the spectator in one moment where the design appears in concentrated miniature:

> —Hath she forsooke so many Noble Matches?
> Her Father? And her Country? And her Friends?
> To be call'd Whore? Would it not make one weepe?
> —It is my wretched Fortune.
> —Beshrew him for't:

[1] *Op. cit.*, pp. 110–111.

How comes this Tricke vpon him?
—Nay, Heauen doth know.
—I will be hang'd, if some eternall Villaine,
   Some busie and insinuating Rogue,
   Some cogging, cozening Slaue, to get some Office,
   Haue not deuis'd this Slander: I will be hang'd else.
—Fie, there is no such man: it is impossible.
—If any such there be, Heauen pardon him.
—A halter pardon him:
   And hell gnaw his bones.

Emilia's superior force of mind and clairvoyance are hints that we shall
not be able to progress further with Desdemona without making out the
rôle of Emilia in the play.


Another strong argument against thinking that Shakespeare read
*Othello* through twice is the treatment of Emilia. I cannot believe that
Shakespeare began the play with anything in his mind more than to
create an attractive wife for Iago and *confidante* for Desdemona. He then
decided to make her an innocent accomplice over the handkerchief and
only later on found for her the important part she ends with. So I think
it most unlikely that Shakespeare first introduced Emilia with the intention of creating dramatic irony:

—Sir, would she giue you so much of her lippes,
   As of her tongue she oft bestowes on me,
   You would haue enough.
—Alas: she has no speech.
—Infaith too much.

I cannot think that we or Iago are meant to recall these words at the end of
the play when he says:

> Go too, charme your tongue

and Emilia replies:

> I will not charme my Tongue;
> I am bound to speake. . .

One of the clumsiest contrivances in the play is to make Emilia so empty,
so unintelligent about the handkerchief, first in contemplating handing it
over to Iago:

what he will do with it
Heauen knowes, not I:
I nothing, but to please his Fantasie . . .

which gives us a foretaste of the witless side of Desdemona, and, secondly
in not confessing her deed when she heard and saw how distressed Desdemona was. It does not seem to be a point in the play that she was, as it
were, on Iago's side in anything that concerned her mistress. She becomes
morally worthless in our eyes from the moment she fails to take Desdemona up when she says:

> Sure, there's some wonder in this Handkerchiefe,
> I am most vnhappy in the losse of it.

The failure comes very awkwardly because it is at this point that
Shakespeare apparently decided to provide a badly-needed centre to the
play. As Iago ceases to be the dominating power Emilia is brought forward and gives us the positive proof of which Desdemona has shewn only
the negative. Emilia, who can stomach all the hard facts about human
nature that might so easily lead one to become callous, resigned, or cyni-
cal, has the moral force to care passionately for the right. Shakespeare
uses her to give us our first tragic moment, where we see what it is to be
damned:

> I durst (my Lord) to wager, she is honest:
> Lay downe my Soule at stake: If you thinke other,
> Remoue your thought. It doth abuse your bosome.
> If any wretch haue put this in your head,
> Let Heauen requit it with the Serpents curse,
> For if she be not honest, chaste, and true,
> There's no man happy. The purest of their Wiues
> Is foule as Slander.

It was not Iago who put the suspicion into Othello's mind that Emilia had
connived at the adultery. Hers is not the language of a *simple Baud* lying
her mistress out of trouble. It has a moral force that obliterates social dis-
tinctions. Because Emilia is dramatically credible in these scenes, we can
tolerate the device by which she is later made to serve as Shakespeare's
mouth-piece. It is easier to believe here that Shakespeare was looking
ahead and had planned to exploit this scene when Emilia dies:

> Moore, she was chaste: She lou'd thee, cruell Moore,
> So come my Soule to blisse, as I speake true.

STL F

Bradley has felt her and her function admirably[1]: 'She is the only person who utters for us the violent common emotions which we feel . . . [she] says what we long to say, and helps us.' She draws us safely *down* to a 'popular' morality.

One of the grandest moments in the play, which recalls in *Lear*

> A pezant stand vp thus?

is that when Emilia rises to her full height and calls Othello *this Villaine* to his face and names the whole transaction *villany*. But though her voice comes across direct to us and to Othello and makes an impression like Desdemona's 'posthumous' explanations, the other actors on the stage are mute and, as I said earlier, carry on as if there were only one villain, and thus rob the ending of its proper dignity and power. (I cannot attribute to Shakespeare the nauseating falsity of Emilia's dying *in Musicke*. That is a vicious attempt to make the audience do something the play should be doing by itself and it is a bullying attempt to make us remember now something that we ought to be allowed to bring in as for each of us the significance of the women's love comes swimming back. That it is quite out of character is a minor matter. The major matter is the desubstantialising of all the choric weight this play so badly needs. Since I cannot suppose that Shakespeare would deliberately 'dish' his own conception, I conjecture that for some performances *two* boy singers were available.)

I have unnaturally held up until both women were introduced—and we must not forget Bianca either—a consideration that may have occurred at once to anybody searching for a profound interest in *Othello*. I will bring it in by way of the charming reply Ophelia made to her brother, who had been displaying fraternal solicitude about her virtue:

> I shall th'effect of this good Lesson keepe,
> As watchman to my heart: but good my Brother
> Doe not as some vngracious Pastors doe,
> Shew me the steepe and thorny way to Heauen;
> Whilst like a puft and recklesse Libertine
> Himselfe the Primrose path of dalliance treads,
> And reaks not his owne reade.

The reader may recall in the discussion of *Romeo and Juliet* the argument that if it were a tragedy it could only be so in a limited sense, since the human predicament was taken in such a limited way. The major preoccupation was with *young* lovers, and with the onset of love rather than with its fulfilment in an extended life either in the persons of lovers

[1] *Op. cit.*, p. 241.

growing to their maturity or in the whole fabric of society. Similarly *Othello* is limited by being too exclusively a man's view of a matter that requires to be seen also as women see it. This is not the place to defend the thesis that all profound works of art have more than one moral centre. But most people notice a lack of complexity in *Othello* and some deplore the lack. On the other hand, to argue that the women in the play bring a possibility of seeing all round is not to argue for a play called *Othello and Desdemona*, but to claim that through Desdemona and Emilia we can see further into the state which is at the heart of the play.

I should not have ventured the *mystery of temptation* as something on which the play turns if I had only one very suggestive passage to go on. I don't think I could take any claims to centrality very seriously if what is claimed as central was not the principal concern of some scene that nobody could omit in a brief summary of the play. Dramatic art has its simplicities as well as its complexities, and once an author knows what he is up to he will find himself almost automatically embodying his deepest thought in a *strikingly* dramatic way. Many people, however, have regarded the scene in which Desdemona chats with Emilia before going to bed as a 'dead' moment in the play. They say that nothing happens in it and suppose it was put into the play to make time before the real 'business' of the last act gets under way. The view I shall be defending is that this scene is the pivot of the whole play; that the point of the play is here made clear; that this is one of the moments when we look before and after and gain our sense of what kind of whole we are being offered. (As a point of interest I would claim for this scene a marked similarity to a scene of *Macbeth*, which used to be omitted in all stage performances, was regarded as padding by armchair critics, and is now seen to be the turning point of the whole play. I am referring to the scene in which Malcolm and Macduff tempt or test each other. Both scenes close the Fourth Act and usher in the Fifth.)

The 'willow' scene does not have the disadvantage of having been for long overlooked. Indeed its very beauty has disarmed some people and blinded them to its function and significance. Whether or not it has the special features I am claiming for it, everybody will see at once that it is taking us to a level or taking us in a direction that we have been longing for, and once we have read *Macbeth*, that we painfully miss. For what makes the damnation and degradation of Macbeth bearable is that he has the words that enable us to be inward with his state. What makes Othello an intolerable spectacle is the collapse of his power to tell us or himself what is going on. We have to stand outside him when he is beside himself:

Lye with her? lye on her? We say lye on her, when they be-lye-her. Lye with her: that's fullsome: Handkerchiefe: Confessions: Handkerchiefe. To confesse, and be hang'd for his labour. First to be hang'd, and then to confesse: I tremble at it. Nature would not inuest her selfe in such shadowing passion, without some Instruction. It is not words that shakes me thus, (pish) Noses, Eares, and Lippes: is't possible. Confesse? Handkerchiefe? O diuell. *Falls in a Traunce.*

'No hint of this trash in the 1st edit.', was Pope's comment.[1] In Othello we have all the ugliness of the hurt mind, in Desdemona, all the beauty.

What makes us feel for the first time in the play that we have broken through the hard surface that keeps the inward movements of the soul at arm's length is the co-presence of levels of consciousness.

—How do you Madam? how do you my good Lady?
—Faith, halfe a sleepe.

The conditions are at work that issue in good or evil thoughts and acts. The evil is lodged in the mind and the breached mind is like a city with the walls down. Uninvited thoughts come in and out with light movement and while the deeper thoughts are known only indirectly there is conscious reflection on the central topic in the dialogue with Emilia. Yet though the scene is highly charged and very much more *real* than anything else in the play, it marks a sad limitation. The two women in their different ways read so much less into their situation than they might. Desdemona's rôle is too like that of the *deranged* figures of Ophelia and Lady Macbeth. She has no healing restoring natural contacts such as Cordelia felt she could call on. Though she triumphs both in conquering the desire to think evil of her husband and in failing to conceive the evil imputed to her, she is impotent and quite helpless in her sense of imminent fate. We are therefore bound to see a resemblance between her state and that of Othello just after he has killed her, and to recall Professor Knight's general formula of an excess of beauty marking a failure of power. The difference is that while Desdemona overwhelms us with the presence of spirituality, so that we feel we are *in* a soul, Othello banishes it from the universe. His beauty of phrase is maddeningly irrelevant to any mental or soul state:

Oh insupportable! Oh heauy houre!
Me thinkes, it should be now a huge Eclipse
Of Sunne, and Moone; and that th'affrighted Globe
Did yawne at Alteration.

[1] *The Works of Mr William Shakespeare*, Volume the Sixth (1723), p. 551.

Of what can Othello be said to be conscious here?

> It is the very error of the Moone,
> She comes more neerer Earth then she was wont,
> And makes men mad.

The different styles are wonderfully adapted to their different purposes. Our sympathies are withdrawing from Othello at astronomical
speed: we are drawn to Desdemona by every token that tells of her failure.
She is now a wounded creature seeking mental cover. From the departure
of Othello she is in a dazed state: even when she speaks 'practically' it is
from force of habit. Her mind is elsewhere. She has retreated from the
stress of reality into simpler attitudes. And in this semi-slumber many
thoughts wander in and out of her mind without asking permission of the
waking self. What she really thinks comes out in apparent foolishness, as
here:

> good Father, how foolish are our minds?
> If I do die before, prythee shrow'd me
> In one of these same Sheetes.

But the greatest device for regression to simplicity is the bringing in of the
song. It has not the poignancy of Ophelia's songs because Desdemona's
waking mind is not so deeply asleep. But it helps her out with the unconscious thought, 'my husband is coming in in a moment to murder me
and I want to be a victim'.

Some people wish to take away from Desdemona the apparently pointless reference to *Lodouico*:

> This *Lodouico* is a proper man.

Others wish to interpret it too easily as an unconscious desire to have
made the expected marriage:

> Though her relation with Cassio is perfectly innocent, one cannot but share
> Iago's doubts as to the durability of the marriage. It is worth noting that,
> in the willow-song scene with Emilia, she speaks with admiration of Ludo-
> vico and then turns to the topic of adultery. Of course, she discusses this in
> general terms and is shocked by Emilia's attitude, but she does discuss the
> subject and she does listen to what Emilia has to say about husbands and
> wives. It is as if she had suddenly realised that she had made a mésalliance
> and that the sort of man she ought to have married was someone of her own
> class and colour like Ludovico. Given a few more years of Othello and of
> Emilia's influence and she might well, one feels, have taken a lover.[1]

[1] W. H. Auden, *op. cit.*

I find it more poignant for it to be dreamy gossip; it is part of the pretence that this is an ordinary night and that there will be no sudden knock of fate.

Finally, a touch that might easily have come from a Freudian case-book occurs when we think Desdemona completely absorbed in 'being' poor Barbary and enjoying, we may almost say, the vicarious sorrow, and we hear her suddenly substituting her own thoughts for the words of the song:

*Let no body blame him, his scorne I approue...*

But she then catches herself up and breaks off with a shudder:

— Nay that's not next. Harke, who is't that knocks?
— It is the wind.

We now enter a piece of cross-play. Desdemona is thinking her own thoughts but she uses words which allow Emilia to become the waking consciousness. That is to say, while Desdemona is brooding on the horror that has benumbed her and can only think of dying, Emilia comes in to remind us that bad as adultery is, taken in itself, it is a venial sin, one that a body may repent of and purge in Purgatory. Some have called her tone coarse and vulgar, and, like Mr Auden, have even described her as im-moral. I don't think they have appreciated either her humour or what she is actually saying. The price of her virtue was a good deal higher than what is normally required for seducing respectable women! And surely we should look on her formula from the other end, as putting Desde-mona's virtue on the heroic shelf and her own on the normal level. How she regards herself when she is not joking we can tell from the exchange with Bianca in the next scene:

— O fie vpon thee Strumpet.
— I am no Strumpet, but of life as honest,
   As you that thus abuse me.
— As I? Fie vpon thee.

I think, on the contrary, we are meant to see a saving health in Emilia's jokes. They shew that goodness can co-exist with evil. It seems appro-priate to recall a remark of Tawney's here: 'Commonsense and a respect for realities are not less graces of the spirit than moral zeal'. The tiniest particle of Emilia's spirit might have released Othello from becoming a murderer and a suicide. A little more of it and a great deal of the pother in Othello's mind would come to seem petty and absurd.

But Emilia is side-tracked into a flat tit-for-tat, the parallel to what we get in the song:

*If I court mo women, you'le couch with mo men.*

But what the play needs is not the obverse of the man's world but a view embracing and transcending both. Instead Emilia speaks with as one-sided a voice as Shylock:

Hath not a *Iew* eyes? hath not a *Iew* hands, organs, dementions, sences, affections, passions, fed with the same foode, hurt with the same weapons, subiect to the same diseases, healed by the same meanes, warmed and cooled by the same Winter and Sommer as a Christian is: if you pricke vs doe we not bleede? if you tickle vs, doe we not laugh? if you poison vs doe we not die? and if you wrong vs shall we not reuenge? if we are like you in the rest, we will resemble you in that. . . .

> Why we haue galles: and though we haue some Grace,
> Yet haue we some Reuenge. Let Husbands know,
> Their wiues haue sense like them: They see, and smell,
> And haue their Palats both for sweet, and sowre,
> As Husbands haue. What is it that they do,
> When they change vs for others? Is it Sport?
> I thinke it is: and doth Affection breed it?
> I thinke it doth. Is't Frailty that thus erres?
> It is so too. And haue not we Affections?
> Desires for Sport? and Frailty, as men haue?
> Then let them vse vs well: else let them know,
> The illes we do, their illes instruct vs so.

But Desdemona gets the last word:

> God me such vses send,
> Not to picke bad, from bad; but by bad, mend.

If she had as a human being been able to personate redeeming grace, we might have had an ending like that of *Macbeth*; but Shakespeare's mind in this play could not create the embodiment of grace in the face of the evil in the world. He merely *posits* it in Desdemona.

The kindest remark I might expect to hear on this sketch of a central point is that I had perfectly anticipated the inevitable comment in calling it, if it is the main design, something adumbrated by Shakespeare rather than fully drawn. It is not a magic formula which once pronounced instantly compels every episode to fall into a conforming shape. It is not that towards which everything is running as mountain rivulets hurrying in many directions but all down to some central tarn or torrent. A comment I might wish for is: would that it were! since I should like to sketch a hypothesis that has little interest unless the absence of a deep centre embodying wisdom about life is felt as both distressing and requiring explanation. It will be a fanciful way of dealing with that disappointment since the comparative success of *Macbeth* does not *prove* that if Shakespeare had taken time off to brood over *Othello* he would have supplied something that is now felt to be missing.

The resort to fancy is a desperate measure and is a sign that I have reached the limits of my powers in suggesting the lines of a common reading. It would not normally figure in a book like this. But the reflections I am about to touch on arise equally naturally from the treatment of the play by Bradley and Professor Knight. When we find the latter summing up his description like this[1]:

> In this essay I have attempted to expose the underlying thought of the play. Interpretation here is not easy, nor wholly satisfactory. As all within *Othello* —save the Iago-theme—is separated, differentiated, solidified, so the play itself seems at first to be divorced from wider issues, a lone thing of meaningless beauty in the Shakespearian universe, solitary, separate, unyielding and chaste as the moon. It is unapproachable, yields itself to no easy mating with our minds. Its thought does not readily mesh with our thought. We can visualize it, admire its concrete felicities of phrase and image, the mosaic of its language, the sculptural outline of its effects, the precision and chastity of its form. But one cannot be lost in it, subdued to it, enveloped by it, as one is drenched and refreshed by the elemental cataracts of *Lear*; one cannot be intoxicated by it as by the rich wine of *Antony and Cleopatra*. *Othello* is essentially outside us, beautiful with a lustrous, planetary beauty. . . .

we are bound to wonder what correspondingly powerful shock it was that drove Shakespeare so far out of his orbit. Is it merely fanciful to ask whether there might not have been something that Shakespeare could not face which he ran into these uncharacteristic extremes to avoid? If so, it can hardly have been the gross facts of our bawdy planet:

> I know our Country disposition well:
> In Venice, they do let Heauen see the prankes
> They dare not shew their Husbands.

[1] *Op. cit.*, pp. 130–131.

> Their best Conscience,
> Is not to leave't vndone, but keepe't vnknowne. . .
> . . . . . There's Millions now aliue,
> That nightly lye in those vnproper beds,
> Which they dare sweare peculiar . . .

observations I would rank with those of Emilia, such as:

> 'Tis not a yeare or two shewes vs a man:
> They are all but Stomackes, and we all but Food,
> They eate vs hungerly, and when they are full
> They belch vs.

It is more likely to have been the *Dangerous conceites* Iago spoke of:

> Dangerous conceites, are in their Natures poysons,
> Which at the first are scarse found to distaste:
> But with a little acte vpon the blood,
> Burne like the Mines of Sulphure.

Since the plot raises the whole edifice of suspicion on a foundation of impossibility, Shakespeare's interest was clearly rather in the creative work of the diseased imagination than in the moralist's observation of ideals desecrated and God mocked. There is no need to force on the reader of this play the prominence and significance of *monster* in all its different forms. We may therefore speculate whether Shakespeare was lending Othello part of himself here:

> Committed? Oh, thou publicke Commoner,
> I should make very Forges of my cheekes,
> That would to Cynders burne vp Modestie,
> Did I but speake thy deedes. What committed?
> Heauen stoppes the Nose at it, and the Moone winks:
> The baudy winde that kisses all it meetes,
> Is hush'd within the hollow Myne of Earth
> And will not hear't.

Nobody will deny that the characteristic movement of Othello's mind is from extreme to extreme and that

> Trifles light as ayre,
> Are to the iealious, confirmations strong,
> As proofes of holy Writ

sums up his predicament. So here the horrifying thing is the limitless
STL F 2

extension of fancies, dreadful possibilities of evil which are not deduc-
tions from what may be called 'objective facts', the *données* about human
nature, but come from sightless substances, floating horrors of the imagination which our nature generates round the blessed facts of sex, in-
distinguishable at first from the grosser conceptions that express current
practice, but capable of monstrous growth until the very possibility of
blessedness is obliterated. That we are liable to succumb to forces which
we cannot place satisfactorily as either external to us or as essentially inherent to our nature is made to appear an ever-present and inescapable
condition of being alive.

But Shakespeare is a dramatist and a comprehensive soul. He could
lend from his imagination as well as from his substance. A more convincing explanation rests on the *absence* rather than the presence of
Shakespearian features. This was what Bradley felt so strongly: somewhere in Shakespeare the leading faculty was dammed up. For this
reason we may prefer as the most personal note in the play these lines:

> But there where I haue garnerd vp my heart,
> Where either I must liue, or beare no life,
> The Fountaine from the which my currant runnes,
> Or else dries vp: to be discarded thence,
> Or keepe it as a Cesterne, for foule Toades
> To knot and gender in . . .

and, responding to the Biblical overtones of the passage, conjecture that
horror froze the genial current of the soul and prevented Shakespeare
from seeing his chosen situation with the counterbalancing sanity of a
man who had an assured meaning for such phrases as (*The Gospell by
Saint Iohn*, The .vij. Chapter, v.38): 'He that beleueth on me, as saith the
scripture, out of his belly shall flowe ryuers of water of lyfe . . .' and (The
.iv. Chapter, v. 14): '. . . the water that I shall geue him, shalbe in him a
well of water, spryngyng vp into euerlasting lyfe'.

Perhaps it is more important to be clear about the central defect of the
play than to conjecture causes for the failure. Essentially it is a want of
*balance*; with the consequence that the play is excruciating rather than
deeply moving. As Shakespeare does not believe deeply enough in the
*genial wonders* in the play, the *monstrosity* is felt too prominently. Much
could have been done for the play by a more deeply-felt Desdemona, but
what the play needed even more was to *establish* Othello before demolish-
ing him. Something, it seems to me, was preventing Shakespeare from
endowing him with the necessary substance. Take away two or three
pieces of convincing drama, such as

Keepe vp your bright Swords, for the dew will rust them . . .

and

> For Christian shame, put by this barbarous Brawle:
> He that stirs next, to carue for his owne rage,
> Holds his soule light: He dies vpon his Motion . . .

where we are convinced that a man is speaking, and what have we left? A great deal of vague suggestion, an aura rather than a substantial creature: many passages of 'poetry' where we are more aware of beauty than power. The balance of the play requires maximum substantiation of Othello as a figure of nobility. What I am suggesting is that corroding doubts about the fragility of the possibility of living out the romantic ideal of nobility have worked on Shakespeare's imagination and, as it were, eaten out the core of the ideal. What we are left with is a beautiful outer shell.

The various forms of objection I have been tentatively putting can be unified in a vocabulary which even if it does not make them more plausible may make a general discussion possible. It is to say that in so far as *Othello* fails it does so because of a failure to function of the specific form of *intelligence* for which we value Shakespeare. Many features of this intelligence have been incidentally touched on in defining the want of intelligence shewn by Othello and Desdemona. I would rather call the claim one of *vocabulary* in order to avoid apparent clashes with the psychologist, but I believe this use of the word points to realities, and, more important, enables us to rescue ourselves from some unreal problems. I have several times in this chapter slipped into language that might be misleading in suggesting that what Shakespeare was and ought to have been grappling with was the subject matter of psychology, theology, philosophy or medicine. In real life a 'case' like Othello's could be profitably examined by experts in all these branches of knowledge. (I exclude the sociologist only because I do not think that Shakespeare was interested in what has become our principal interest, but I would not maintain the exclusion if a plausible claim were put forward.) But Shakespeare's study is never more or less than human life, and success in a play must always be the successful application of an intelligence adapted to the needs of that raw material. Yet in asking for the use of the word 'intelligence' I wish to appeal to our common experience, to what everybody would agree to be there when asked what it is that brings off the very finest things we can imagine occurring in a play. I assume that we are all aware of coming up against mysteries as soon as we focus our minds on the topic. My vocabulary is not intended to solve any riddles.

*Othello* makes us highly conscious of what is *not* the supreme thing. I we go over Professor Knight's essay and note how he rings the changes on the word 'separate' we have our primary negative definition. This is the first thing to seize on: Shakespeare's intelligence is quite unlike the intelligence that stands off from all the other activities of man. It is characteristically a unifying power and it distinguishes only to unify. It was not a mere aesthetic dislike that made me pitch on the characteristic exaggerated splitting up into their opposites of the various matters in the play. The great Shakespeare is somehow able to transcend his antitheses —not in any Hegelian way—but by supplying a tie and a means of passage between them. When his touch is right we feel that all things are connected, that there is a human nature that connects. If we are to think of the various forms of mental play he exhibits as like organs functioning together, we can find their *antithesis* in Iago's account:

> Our Bodies are our Gardens, to the which, our Wills are Gardiners. So that if we will plant Nettels, or sowe Lettice: Set Hisope, and weede vp Time: Supplie it with one gender of Hearbes, or distract it with many: either to haue it sterrill with idlenesse, or manured with Industry, why the power and Corrigeable authoritie of this lies in our Wills. If the beame of our liues had not one Scale of Reason, to poize another of Sensualitie, the blood, and basenesse of our Natures would conduct vs to most prepostrous Conclusions. But we haue Reason to coole our raging Motions, our carnall Stings, or vnbitted Lusts: whereof I take this, that you call Loue, to be a Sect, or Seyen.

Shakespeare's intelligence is the whole beam and runs back and forth from scale to scale and causes reason to be interpenetrated with feeling and feeling with reason.

We can therefore say that in *Othello* his lovers are lesser figures than he meant them to be. If he could have brought his whole intelligence to bear on his concepts of 'holy' and 'noble', we should not have had what can now in retrospect be seen to be the tell-tale bombast of the description of their arrival in port. But to grasp this intelligence in its most vital rôle we must return to the image of the fountain of living waters welling up from a mysterious source and continuously irrigating and refreshing the soul. Then tragedy can be black without the play degenerating into a *pièce noire*. It will be for the reader to decide whether he wishes to continue to class *Othello* among Shakespeare's tragedies, but I can offer a touchstone to help us feel the difference between the many confrontations of 'devil' and 'angel' in *Othello* and a real apprehension of these linked opposites. It is the celebrated passage where Duncan stands before Macbeth's castle:

—This Castle hath a pleasant seat,
   The ayre nimbly and sweetly recommends it selfe
   Vnto our gentle sences.
—This Guest of Summer,
   The Temple-haunting Martlet does approue,
   By his lou'd Mansonry, that the Heauens breath
   Smells wooingly here: no Iutty frieze,
   Buttrice, nor Coigne of Vantage, but this Bird
   Hath made his pendant Bed, and procreant Cradle:
   Where they most breed, and haunt, I haue obseru'd
   The ayre is delicate.
—See, see, our honor'd Hostesse. . .

# King Lear

# CHAPTER 1

# The Central Stream

'We wish that we could pass this play over, and say nothing about it. All that we can say must fall far short of the subject; or even of what we ourselves conceive of it. To attempt to give a description of the play itself or of its effect upon the mind, is mere impertinence: yet we must say something.' So wrote Hazlitt in 1817, and so (if it can be managed without cant) must I. When the reader's evidence is all of pain and difficulty overcome and none of visible undergoing and suffering, it may seem gratuitous to harp on the reluctance with which these chapters were embarked on, save that when I have completed my say it will be found that my 'something' is as nothing compared with what I am unable to face and grapple with. Yet even the reader who derives comfort from the play will concede that pain is at least one of the consequences of confronting some of the scenes. It is hard to imagine a man who had sat through *King Lear* during the afternoon queuing up for the evening performance. 'That straine agen' is what we don't ask for when Lear utters his five-fold *never*. Few, I imagine, will think the worse of him when they find Samuel Johnson remarking: 'that I was many years ago so shocked by Cordelia's death that I know not whether I ever endured to read again the last scenes of the play till I undertook to revise them as an editor'.

The reader, however, will have even less patience and indulgence with *my* taking over the plea 'yet we must say something' and none at all when I add 'and once again we must build up the play from the beginning and take nothing for granted'. 'Nothing!', he might well retort, 'does the experience of mankind count for so little with you? Hazlitt went on to say that is was "the best of all Shakespear's plays" and since his day *King Lear* has if anything risen in general esteem. It is commonly regarded as one of the supreme Western masterpieces. And what becomes of your pretended search for a common reading if you begin by turning your back on the universal voice I can't imagine!' To this I can reply in good faith that I never expected or wanted to be in this position and that when I set myself seriously to ask what kind of tragedy this play was I began by assuming it was the supreme example of the kind. I am still shocked at what I shall have to report as my reading of the play and have therefore refrained from pushing my conclusions home until I find by trying it out

whether I have any right to call it a common reading. And if the imputa-
tion then is that however good the faith there must have been some
natural impercipience and incapacity, I might in rebuttal begin by saying
that the universal choir of praise has *not* been joined by some men of undoubted depth and capacity. I shall not assert that Tolstoy was right in
his essay, *Shakespeare and the Drama* and the generality of critics wrong,
since almost all Tolstoy's objections have been met and met brilliantly in
our day, notably by Professor G. Wilson Knight.[1] But Tolstoy's essay
contains one challenging objection that might persuade the reader to re-
open this *res iudicata*. One of the firmest modern convictions is that *King
Lear* is a religious play, religious in spirit if not in its conclusions. Yet
Tolstoy condemned it in the name of religious drama. His formulation is
weighty and impressive:

> By 'the religious essence of art' . . . I mean not an external inculcation of
> any religious truth in artistic guise, and not an allegorical representation of
> those truths, but the expression of a definite view of life corresponding to the
> highest religious understanding of a given period: an outlook which, serving
> as the impelling motive for the composition of the drama, permeates the
> whole work though the author be unconscious of it. So it has always been
> with true art, and so it is with every true artist in general and with dramatists
> especially. Hence, as happened when the drama was a serious thing, and as
> should be according to the essence of the matter, he alone can write a drama
> who has something to say to men—something highly important for them—
> about man's relation to God, to the universe, to all that is infinite and un-
> ending.[2]

I need not, however, have resorted to this off-putting opening, since I
believe there are other good grounds for saying that something radical
must be done. Although the critics by and large agree on a high estimate

[1] *Shakespeare and Tolstoy*, The English Association, Pamphlet No. 88, 1934.
[2] This was, at any rate, sufficiently impressive for me to recall it when reading the
conclusion of a recent book on *King Lear*:
> To me, certainly, the clairvoyance of *King Lear* is hardly distinguishable from
> religious insight. It is not only our profoundest tragedy; it is also our profoundest
> expression of an essentially Christian comment on man's world and his society,
> using the terms and benefitting (*sic*) by the formulations of the Christian tradition.
> This might well justify the reflection that the play will appear a very different thing
> to the man who finds Shakespeare merely echoing the great commonplaces of
> Christianity and to the man who if he wants to use the term 'religious' defines it in
> terms of this play and refuses to identify the terms Shakespeare uses and the same
> words as used by orthodox Christians. And bound up with this reflection is another:
> that the man who automatically identifies the terms without examining the contexts is
> not exposing himself to Shakespeare but accommodating Shakespeare to a precon-
> ceived view.

of the play, they agree on nothing else. There is therefore a task of
mediating and searching for a reading that will command wider assent
than any so far obtained. The worst crimes against criticism are not those
committed by cranks whose emergence into print is barely noticed outside the 'industrial' press but the errors of our most admired pundits,
those whose views have formed our own opinions. If these critics have
been unable to agree over *King Lear* it is plausible to suppose that there
must be special difficulties in addition to the general difficulty of steering
a straight critical course and that an examination of these may help us to
find a remedy. One such special difficulty is that we tend to over-colla-
borate with the author. Of course, all participation by the world in the
work of artists is a form of collaboration: the artist has laboured first that
we might labour successfully after him. But in *King Lear* what the play
makes us do is more important than what is done on the stage. At crucial
moments we are required not merely to take in what the actors are saying
and doing but to represent to ourselves what it means for the consciousness that this or that be said or done. This meaning cannot be said to lie on
the page; it is released in us by the action. Now where this happens there
is a danger of a split in our minds. I am thinking of the duality of approach
that very much lessens the value of Bradley's lectures on the play:

> When I read *King Lear* two impressions are left on my mind. . . . *King
> Lear* seems to me Shakespeare's greatest achievement, but it seems to me
> *not* his best play. And I find that I tend to consider it from two rather differ-
> ent points of view. When I regard it strictly as a drama, it appears to me,
> though in certain parts overwhelming, decidedly inferior as a whole to
> *Hamlet, Othello* and *Macbeth*. When I am feeling that it is greater than any of
> these, and the fullest revelation of Shakespeare's power, I find I am not
> regarding it simply as a drama, but am grouping it in my mind with works
> like the *Prometheus Vinctus* and the *Divine Comedy*, and even with the great-
> est symphonies of Beethoven and the statues in the Medici Chapel.[1]

Here, it seems to me, we have a split that ought to be spliced.

I say this the more firmly in that since Bradley the dangers of seeing
*King Lear* as more than a play have grown plainer, especially when what
Shakespeare wrote has been treated as matter for edification. It seems to
me a crime against criticism to confuse the activity which is the end-product of an experience of the play and that which is a mere by-product.
However difficult it may be to draw up the terms, we must distinguish a
utilitarian from an intrinsic value of *King Lear*. We may go from the play
and, inspired by it, re-examine some or all of our private preoccupations,

[1] *Shakespearean Tragedy*, p. 244.

but this is not necessarily the function of the play. Shakespeare undoubt-
edly can be made to serve successfully the purposes of edification, but I
must confess that I think some coarsening of the mind occurs when this
habit sets in. As a possible instance we might take an essay reprinted by
Professor L. C. Knights in *Some Shakespearean Themes* in which he tells
us that the play reveals something to him which he summarises as
follows:

> love is that without which life is a meaningless chaos of competing egotisms;
> it is the condition of intellectual clarity, the energizing centre from which
> personality may grow unhampered by the need for self-assertion or evasive
> subterfuge; it is the sole ground of a genuinely self-affirming life and energy.

The question to be put here is: is this a by-product or an end-product, is
this matter for edification or does it represent insight into a particular
play? If it is an end-product, has something happened to the reading of
the play, and is that something a process of wilful abstraction, the result
of a deliberate search for edifying matter? If we are to extract a moral from
a play, couldn't this moral of Professor Knights' come equally well from
the version of the play so popular from the days of Tate, in which Lear
and Cordelia *live happily ever after*? This at first sight may look damning
for Professor Knights, but he might reply that for him nothing matters
once Lear and Cordelia are re-united. In his essay by a subtle *escamotage*
the end of the play is whisked away. He recognises that for Lear the death
of Cordelia does matter, but leaves us on this note:

> But the question, ultimately, is not what Lear sees but what Shakespeare
> sees. . . . At the end . . . we are still concerned with nothing less than the
> inclusive vision of the whole; and it is that which justifies us in asserting that
> the mind, the imagination, so revealed is directed towards affirmation *in spite
> of everything*.

This will not do. To remove the suspicion that he had made up that
'whole' before he came to the end, or that he wanted at all costs to be able
to conclude, 'for what takes place in *King Lear* we can find no other word
than renewal', a detailed account of his reading of the end of the play was
a necessity. But all he says is, 'The scene of Lear's final anguish is so painful that criticism hesitates to fumble with it'. What we need if we are to
take the play in this sense is to get rid of the feeling that the end of the play
brings us closer to reality than we have been before and that we learn
reality in the face of the several *deaths*.

> The waight of this sad time we must obey,
> Speake what we feele, not what we ought to say.

(Of course, if we feel like this we should then have to say with Kent

All's cheerlesse, darke and deadly

but this does not involve us in abject pessimism. It is still heroic to have patience unto death, to see this great world wear out to nought, and especially heroic when all Christian consolation is absent.)

As for a possible remedy, I see a chance by taking Samuel Johnson at a tangent. His description of what it feels like to read the play has always been admired:

> There is perhaps no play which keeps the attention so strongly fixed; which so much agitates our passions and interests our curiosity. The artful involutions of distinct interests, the striking opposition of contrary characters, the sudden changes of fortune, and the quick succession of events, fill the mind with a perpetual tumult of indignation, pity, and hope. There is no scene which does not contribute to the aggravation of the distress or conduct of the action, and scarce a line which does not conduce to the progress of the scene. So powerful is the current of the poet's imagination, that the mind, which once ventures within it, is hurried irresistibly along.[1]

From this I should like to take the image of a powerful current but to suggest that, if the play is like a river, the part we should concentrate on is the central stream, for if we miss this we easily find ourselves in eddies or backwater. If we don't find what at each moment is driving the play along, what we are left with is a bore, for the central interest is not spread over the whole matter. Some critics who would concede that there is a central area of intense interest would go on to assert that besides this the play gives the impression of presenting a vast world. Lear's England seems to me very empty in every sense. I don't point this out as a fault but as a fact and as a reminder that there is not much marginal interest in this play; it has far less of it than *Macbeth*.

More than this, there is an unusual contrast between the places where Shakespeare was interested and where his interest lapsed. To clear our minds we must distinguish the very good from the very bad in this play. In this attempt, here as in other plays, the difficulty is to determine whether sheer carelessness and haste account for what we dislike or whether Shakespeare's judgement was at fault. If we think that in any place Shakespeare was not bothering, that is usually a tip to us not to bother too much either. For instance, the many minor inconsistencies in the plot tell us that plot-consistency is not very important for this play. What trouble us more are the clear cases of wilful contrivance. Nobody,

[1] *The Plays of William Shakespeare*, Volume the Sixth (1765), p. 158.

for instance, can really believe that Shakespeare *forgot* to give the Fool a significant departure from the play. Nobody can think the want of plausibility in the opening of the play an instance of neglect. In these cases we should first look for a compensating or over-riding advantage and, if we do not find one, we should say so. On this question of faults my general hypothesis is that Shakespeare always had one or two great things he felt sure of, enough, that is, to secure the worldly success of each play, and I suppose that he said to himself, 'If I can get these across I don't care very much about incidental faults'.

This image of a central stream has a further felicity for me, which was brought out by Johnson's phrase 'the mind . . . is hurried irresistibly along'. Shakespeare is, as it were, always saying, 'don't stop, don't linger, follow me to the end'. It is natural for us to stop and do sums but the play is always asking us to carry forward and perhaps to let some early interests drop away altogether. I think this is above all true of remarks with a theological bearing. All sorts of things get said about the gods but the play does not end with clarification of all or any of the incidental observations. Therefore it seems to me an unnatural attempt to try to extract doctrines from this play or to get by short cuts to universals such as 'man'. I suspect that Shakespeare was not 'universalizing' in the way so many critics want; that he was not trying to tell us what man is but what can be learned from intimate concern with the doings and sufferings of a few old men. His point is not bound up with fathers in general but with very old fathers and foolish old fathers and wise children—but even here the stress is not on the whole complex of duties and obligations but on *selected* goods and ills.

The path of critical sanity seems to me to lie in following the details of the play and never drowning the particular. If Johnson's account of the play is correct we should be *unable* to do anything else. When Lear says

Looke there, looke there

we have no option. If we say, 'Very sorry, your Majesty, but I am attending to the vision of the whole', I think we miss the play altogether. Of course, Shakespeare does provide us in this play with resting places and opportunities to stand back, but on the whole we must always be moving on with the central stream. We must become fluid so that the play can take us out of ordinary comfortable ways of thinking and feeling, seduce us into leaving both common sense and cleverness behind and make us enter into combinations that had never before presented themselves to anyone but Shakespeare. This can only happen if we give our whole attention to each striking particular and 'look there' whenever Shakespeare invites. But since Shakespeare's intelligence is a feeling intelligence and his mental progress shows itself by exposure to feelings, we must be ready constantly to 'feel there' and to refuse to be diverted by over-intellectualised speculations.

This critical procedure is bound to appear lax, dangerously undisciplined. It must begin by being studiously unemphatic and accepting all the disadvantages of the first night. The reading under discussion is primarily of a series of 'visits to the play'. No doubt greater depth comes when the temporal tyranny is relaxed, but until there is some consensus about what happens to us, to our sympathies, as we go through the play as presented, our considered reflections on the play as a whole are not likely to engage with the deeper thoughts of others. Although we make progress by repeating our visits to the play we must take care not to obliterate the original experience, which is in a sense the master experience. There is a danger, if each time we read back into the play all that we have accumulated about the chief personage, of missing something that the text clearly wants: a gradual shift in our feelings towards the chief personage (as the play develops) from something fairly hostile to something profoundly sympathetic. Nothing beyond a remark or two in the preceding scene has happened to the Lear who first appears on the stage. He must be carrying himself as if he thought himself every inch a King, but we judge as we find. I hope I shall be representing the feelings of those who have no conscious or unconscious desires to kill or get rid of their own fathers in recording some hostile moments and some strong adverse judgements as given by the text. Similarly, we must not decide too soon that the play is to be unified by referring *all* actions to the central figure. We must record what happens and search for the central stream wherever it seems to flow, regardless of *a priori* views. Ideally, we should record all expectations that are aroused in us but never fulfilled, that is to say, we should bear in mind that the domination of the most rapt spectator takes time. A state of partial and diminishing irrelevance is a necessary part of our response to a play. These, however, are features of our private response. What we want to bring to a common market are the upshots, the temporary accumulations of verdicts that we find on looking back have made us take a firm line when talking about the whole. These are what we must present to each other if there is ever to be a common pursuit of true judgement.

Every alert spectator probably says to himself that it cannot be for nothing that the first scene turns at once from politics to a presentation and discussion of a father-son relation and that, as Coleridge says, Edmund 'hears his mother and the circumstances of his birth spoken of with a most degrading and licentious levity'. Humanity requires that our attitude to the father be one of mixed feelings. It is something, we feel, that he has regarded the relation to his child as constituting a bond, and it is something that he once used to blush over it. He is made to speak improperly of it, yet it appears that after the original misconduct he has done everything he should: acknowledged his paternity, bred the boy up, and since he could not legally (I suppose) give him a share in the paternal acres, found him honourable employment abroad. More than all this, he has loved him as much as his legitimate son—which makes it very odd, and therefore very striking, that such a father should present the story so unfeelingly or worse, with such coarse relish. For even if Edmund is to be thought of as standing apart and so, like Hamlet in his first scene, offering himself to our curiosity as a well-built young man of the world, there is the absent mother to be thought of. Why, we may wonder, does Gloucester in his old age have only these lights on his youthful behaviour? There are many possible reflections—the worst being that he was an unrepentant lecher, one simply happy to have missed being a lover. Behind this, however, there may lie an appeal to the thoughts taken up by Edmund, that everything was done *properly*, *i.e.* so as to produce the most proper man. As Kent says 'I cannot wish the fault vndone, the issue of it, being so proper'. Perhaps we should allow some scope in our minds for that area where popular superstitions about love-children met the kind of Renaissance thinking to be found in Rabelais, since the irony on this plane is going to be perfect when Edmund turns out to be a proper executioner. Nobody, however, would think of doing a sum yet and our thoughts carry naturally forward the observation that this Gloucester does not intervene in the following scene when Lear goes wrong in *his* relation to his children.

We don't begin to attend to this scene with the verdict that many people have passed on it, that it is as unreal as a fairy story. We may on quitting it decide that during it Lear was speaking like a character from a much earlier play by Shakespeare, but on entering it we are bound to judge that the King's initial act was on the face of it sensible, since he felt he was too old to carry on the business of ruling the state. We note in passing that, while he has the prospect of death in mind, he is not proposing to prepare himself for death as a Christian might, on the lines of the Great Abdicator of Shakespeare's era, the emperor Charles, but speaks neutrally:

> while we
> Vnburthen'd crawle toward death.

Though the expression is a trifle ego-centric, it would not prevent our thinking that he was acting with the welfare of Britain at heart.

Lear's request to his daughters comes as both a surprise and a shock. We had understood from Gloucester and Lear himself that the division between Albany and Cornwall was into equal shares already stipulated. Nobody on the stage could therefore make out exactly what Lear meant by

> Which of you shall we say doth loue vs most,
> That we, our largest bountie may extend
> Where Nature doth with merit challenge.

Critics may say they understand these lines, but no hearers could. Yet Goneril seems to have done the right thing, for Lear does not wait to hear what the other sisters can say. He gives her, I suppose, what he has determined on and published beforehand. In a sense she plays up to the old man and is as insincere as he is—it's all a courteous game. He in a sense no more listens than she speaks: he is not testing her words any more than he was testing his own. Both thereby are bringing a serious matter into contempt—not unlike Gloucester. We find the emptiness on both sides exemplified in the line:

> As much as Childe ere lou'd, or Father found.

It sounds like a protestation from a weak sonnet.

Then we suddenly learn that one of the hearers is taking the situation as real and refusing to play the game. How are we meant to feel about this? Of course, if the other daughters have been already reduced to caricature (and Lear thereby made more of a simpleton than the text requires) we have no choice but to give blank approval to Cordelia. At this stage in the play there is not enough matter to work much in, but can we say, if we should always be adversely critical of anyone who asked such a question as Lear's, yet if Cordelia were an *ideal* figure, that she would have said here rather 'Poore father' than 'poore Cordelia'? Was it the perfect answer to say to a father, 'Nothing'? Or, if we accept the propriety of

> I loue your Maiesty
> According to my bond . . .

need she have added, we may wonder,

> no more nor lesse . . . ?

Once we become free souls in relation to Cordelia, we notice that she is not genuinely tongue-tied by reverence, but damnably explicit. She is scoring off her sisters rather than speaking sincerely. And here, it turns out, we have stumbled on something that is going to crop up again and again in the play: reasons for considering the ambiguities that always surround 'plain' speech. We shall more than once draw on the common experience about people who pride themselves on using plain speech, that it hurts them less to speak it than it hurts us to hear a home truth. We need to have Cordelia expounding the filial bond—and to-day, of course, the young are astounded to learn that honour and obedience were once thought due even to an Aged P., a *croulant* or a doddering old man—yet a point is made and Shakespeare chalks it up in the exchange:

—So young, and so vntender?
—So young, my Lord, and true.

Cordelia is not so tart as the fool, but we may feel an affinity here.

We get a second surprise and shock in the rant that then follows. Lear's oratory is a most unmannerly breach. The language is unreal—though we may not feel it as such until later, when we have some real language to compare it with in those passages where Lear seems to get almost in touch with real powers of nature. But just when we might be about to withdraw all sympathy from the King, he lets out something which must touch us: he had not thought of crawling towards death in solitude but

to set my rest
On her kind nursery.

Because of the taunts that are to come about a man making his daughters his mothers, we must appreciate the extent to which this is the chief way left to both parties to fulfil their bond. We may also say that we now begin to know that there is something real in Lear that can be hurt. Nevertheless the principal fact established is that Lear is an impotent old fool. Some actors have wished us to see him as a terrible awesome Dragon, but he resembles rather the King in *Alice in Wonderland*: he says,

Hence and avoid my sight

but Cordelia stands her ground just as Kent does when Lear says,

Out of my sight.

It is curious to note how the psychological unreality is linked with the political. Lear no more severs himself from his daughter than from his kingdom. You cannot suddenly disclaim paternal care, propinquity and property of blood or give a father's heart away. You can, of course, re-

nounce the kingship, but Lear clings to the name and all the addition. So
everybody present on the stage and in the audience would feel (however
dimly) that Lear was here breaking the laws of common sense. Yet once
again in all this nonsense Lear strikes home with

> pride, which she cals plainnesse.

The central current, however, bears us past this to the disinheritance.
Kent now steps in to introduce the second main bond: that of master and
servant. The element of 'game' is over and we now begin to see the operation of true values. Kent introduces a brand of plainness different from
Cordelia's but above all a sacred note which Shakespeare is anxious we
should not miss:

> Royall *Lear*,
> Whom I haue euer honor'd as my King,
> Lou'd as my Father, as my Master follow'd,
> As my great Patron thought on in my praiers.

That 'Patron' coming on the wave of the culminating line bears the suggestion of the classical *patronus* and the Christian Patron Saint. At the
very least we feel that such a person as Kent had a claim on Lear, that he
ought to have been listened to. I would go further and say that here Kent's
function is to tell us where we stand. Lear is mad, a fool, and has made
two mistakes due to hideous rashness. But Lear is not only the old blind
fool, the crazy fool, of the ballad: the final point comes when Kent says,

> Ile tell thee thou dost euill.

Lear's exchanges with France and Burgundy might have come from
one of Shakespeare's worst history plays. Cordelia has no real relations to
either suitor. But what she says is of the centre of the play. A full character
sketch could be written out of one speech:

> I yet beseech your Maiesty.
> If for I want that glib and oylie Art,
> To speake and purpose not, since what I will intend,
> Ile do't before I speake, that you make knowne
> It is no vicious blot, murther, or foulenesse,
> No vnchaste action or dishonoured step
> That hath depriu'd me of your Grace and fauour,
> But euen for want of that, for which I am richer,
> A still soliciting eye, and such a tongue,

> That I am glad I haue not, though not to haue it,
> Hath lost me in your liking.

There's Lear's daughter, and could she have hit her father harder by saying outright what is implied in this speech? There is more than proper pride here, there is the passion that gave her phrases such as

> that glib and oylie Art,

and

> A still soliciting eye.

She is unrepentant, too, or blind to the necessities of the moment, and her temper is up when she replies to Burgundy,

> Peace be with *Burgundie*,
> Since that respect and Fortunes are his loue,
> I shall not be his wife.

She is conscious of her own worth when she takes a bitter farewell of her sisters. We do not condemn her, I suppose, for allowing herself a moment it would be very hard to deny oneself in such a situation:

> The Iewels of our Father, with wash'd eies
> *Cordelia* leaues you, I know you what you are,
> And like a Sister am most loth to call
> Your faults as they are named.

The drop into prose when the two sisters are left alone on the stage is very effective in bringing us down to the cold facts. Though we may wonder how or when the lodging arrangements were made, we must, I think, take those children's cold observations as facts. Lear, we shall eventually see, has other sides to his nature, but *so far* this is what we must take as the truth:

> You see how full of changes his age is, the obseruation we haue made of it hath beene little; he alwaies lou'd our Sister most, and with what poore iudgement he hath now cast her off, appeares too grossely. 'Tis the infirmity of his age, yet he hath euer but slenderly knowne himselfe. The best and soundest of his time hath bin but rash, then must we looke from his age, to receiue not alone the imperfections of long ingraffed condition, but there-withall the vnruly waywardnesse, that infirme and cholericke yeares bring with them.

\* \* \*

My first impression is of the great *definiteness* of the next scene. It is
sharply cut off at both ends. Though it has been admirably prepared for
both by the as-it-were prologue appearance of Edmund at the beginning
and by the theme-aspect of the preceding Lear scene, Edmund now
enters so decisively that he might be speaking the opening lines of the play.
The end tidily reminds us of what we were presented with at its beginning:

> I see the businesse,
> Let me, if not by birth, haue lands by wit,
> All with me's meete, that I can fashion fit.

Edmund, we find, exhibits himself primarily as a possessor of wit and
invention. We may say that, in a sense, he sees further than others. But
our first impression in time is something sharper: he is the second *character* in the play whose mind works on and produces language to match it.
Hence he is more direct, immediate, than anybody save Cordelia who has
yet appeared on the stage. Because of this we might almost class him
among the plain speakers, but his plainness has a different cause. If his
special plain naked way of speaking comes out here

> Well then,
> Legitimate *Edgar*, I must haue your land . . .

it is plain because his thought is plain. He seems to have no conflict, no
lingering remains of decent feeling. He has his own legitimacy to set over
against that of society. In his own eyes he is a fine fellow. We might care to
enquire further into his morality and ask him to defend himself by
reasons and in particular to say in what sense he thinks his mind as
*generous* as honest madam's issue. But then, we reflect, he is clearly not on
show just now for that purpose. He is confined to the single purpose of
the scene, which is to show him triumphantly practising on the weak-
nesses of his nearest blood relations.

Hence we may also call this scene definite in that it is strictly limited in
function. The light is clear, hard, never shimmering: the verse is of a
peculiarly hard stamp. It has among other things the effect of driving
home the first news we had of Edmund and of arousing us to greater
attention, as we may see if we compare 'I haue a Sonne, Sir, by order of
Law, some yeere elder then this' with

> For that I am some twelue or fourteene Moonshines
> Lag of a Brother

or 'I cannot wish the fault vndone, the issue of it, being so proper' with

> When my Dimensions are as well compact,
> My minde as generous, and my shape as true
> As honest Madams issue

or 'though this Knaue came somthing sawcily to the world before he was sent for: yet was his Mother fayre, there was good sport at his making' with

> Who in the lustie stealth of Nature, take
> More composition, and fierce qualitie,
> Then doth within a dull stale tyred bed
> Goe to th' creating a whole tribe of Fops
> Got 'tweene a sleepe, and wake . . . ,

to which we may add 'My father compounded with my mother vnder the Dragons taile.'

Consequently we build up the idea of the nature that justifies or stands up for Edmund by taking the feel of this verse and by watching the invention of his mother wit. Nature is not to be seen as standing off as an abstraction: 'the lustie stealth of Nature' is the two copulating adults as much as the fierce composition that ensues in the mother's womb. We are, I suppose, to assume there was as little regard for the rights of others in this copulation as Edmund now shows toward his brother and his father. His parents then defied custom and the curiosity of nations with as much apparent triumph as Edmund now enjoys in securing his ends. (The thought that will outcrop later in *Let Copulation thriue* is here in germ.) The same quality of forward thrust down a definite line marks the exchange with Gloucester. The movement of the passage containing the disclosures of the letter is so sure that no spectator could have stopped to find the device far-fetched or improbable. Even the slow Gloucester is quickened into more than usually vigorous expression:

> No? what needed then that terrible dispatch of it into your Pocket? The quality of nothing, hath not such neede to hide it selfe. Let's see: come, if it bee nothing, I shall not neede Spectacles.

\*          \*          \*

Although we need all this plotting to trace Edmund's wit in action, the serious part of our mind engages rather with the background than with the immediate details of the plot. We cannot help moving away from the special aspect of Nature to which Edmund has appealed and seeing more than Edmund does in the supposed plot he attributes to his half-brother. We find ourselves entertaining wider considerations of the rights and

duties of youth and age. One of the advantages of the theatre as Shakespeare made it was the ease with which the particular could suggest the
general. Yet though we must give Shakespeare much of the credit for this
facility in turning bare particulars into significant particulars, it was a
habit in his society. It would be too much to say that a sparrow could not
fall in Jacobean England without somebody foretelling a calamity, but
the activity that fashioned proverbs out of the details of experience was an
old one and far from being worn out. It is one of the ways of making sense
of life and ought to be distinguished from the logical habit, the kind of
conceptual thinking implied in my language, which has been referring to
the single event as a particular and speaking of generalising as the group-
ing of single events into classes of events, etc., etc. And I judge of the importance of making this distinction by the conviction that here is one of
the places in the play where if we generalise in one manner we lose the
play and if we generalise in the other we may find it. One way of generalising ends in dissolving away the particular, the other heightens our sense
of the particular, and the latter is Shakespeare's way. It is more a way of
feeling than thinking since it is more obviously allied to our behaviour in
fear and superstition than to the simpler processes of logic. But *le cœur a
ses raisons, que la raison ne connoist pas* and I do not suppose that Shakespeare would blush to have the phrase applied to his thinking. We can
easily go wrong if we suppose that Shakespeare would have preferred the
mental habits that produced French tragedy or even the good sense behind Samuel Johnson's phrase, 'the grandeur of generality'. This cling-
ing to the particular is not a relic of 'primitive' thinking in Shakespeare.
If he had a philosophy, this retention of the particular is an essential part.
At any rate I would throw out the suggestion that here we have the central
thing to lay hold of in experiencing the play. I shall proceed at once to
give an instance from the present scene, and in their proper place adduce
even more striking cases, and it will be in terms of this special form of
thinking with its own cogency that I shall discuss the apprehension of
reality that we have as the play ends.

On the other hand, I should be sorry to appear to be offering such a
blind reading of the play as would issue in the claim that we move to
wider considerations *solely* because of the offered particulars. The immediate occasion of these remarks, the forged letter, shows that here we
attend to Shakespeare's general statements because of the sharpness of
the particular phrasing:

> This policie, and reuerence of Age, makes the world bitter to the best of our
> times: keepes our Fortunes from vs, till our oldnesse cannot rellish them. I

> begin to finde an idle and fond bondage in the oppression of aged tyranny, who swayes not as it hath power, but as it is suffer'd. Come to me, that of this I may speake more. If our Father would sleepe till I wak'd him, you should enioy halfe his Reuennew for euer, and liue the beloued of your Brother.

It is not only Gloucester who feels the bite in the last sentence. The general remarks are reinforced by it.

Nevertheless we have other reasons for attending to these generalities. The preceding Lear scene has given them a special bearing. We cannot refuse the debate between bond and bondage as it has been so far set up, if only to tell ourselves what constitutes a fair demand by each of the parties and what is the conduct of a *monster*. Yet it would be unreal to expect us to limit ourselves to the amount of *dramatic* treatment the topic has received. We must give way to our sense—a sense we surely share with Shakespeare and all members of civilised communities—that this is one of the central questions for any reflecting man (regardless of the *degree* of stress and pain of the perpetual conflict that the obligations of civilisation impose on the 'natural' man in each of us[1]). At this point in the play we merely let in our sense of the atmospheric pressure on us of an insoluble conflict. The tensions set up by a hereditary monarchy in Tudor times were inevitable. It would be clear to all that if historical necessities justified the retention of a father as wielder of power, governor for life, other interests suffered when that parent's child became an adult and wrong occurred when the parent became unfit for office and the child became obviously the fitter of the two.

This known and felt fact about civilisation (of which kingly power is the paradigm) is not at the centre of the play. Nor is Shakespeare's conviction that however burdensome the bondage it cannot dissolve the bond. We cannot name the central stream until we have digested the degree of sense in Gloucester's superstitious meanderings:

> Loue cooles, friendship falls off, Brothers diuide. In Cities, mutinies; in Countries, discord; in Pallaces, Treason; and the Bond crack'd 'twixt Sonne and Father . . . the King fals from byas of Nature, there's Father against Childe. We haue seene the best of our time. Machinations, hollownesse, treacherie, and all ruinous disorders follow vs disquietly to our Graues . . . and the Noble & true-harted Kent banish'd; his offence, honesty. 'Tis strange.

There we have the counterstatement to Edmund's, the opposite view of what is natural. But the interesting problem is what causes the bond to

[1] This theme was notably treated by Freud in *Das Unbehagen in der Kultur* (1930).

fail, and men to fall 'from byas of Nature'. If not influence from the stars, then what? Here we have the *donnée* of the play. But it is not a problem, it is a mystery. The existence of Edmund is an appalling fact and remains a fact when the play is over. That the voice of naked power thinking was never silenced in Shakespeare's heart we know from the especial brilliance of the following passage from *The Tempest*, which can do more than any commentary to place us well in the central stream:

—            Say, this were death
    That now hath seiz'd them, why they were no worse
    Then now they are: There be that can rule *Naples*
    As well as he that sleepes: Lords, that can prate
    As amply, and vnnecessarily
    As this *Gonzallo*: I my selfe could make
    A Chough of as deepe chat: O, that you bore
    The minde that I do; what a sleepe were this
    For your aduancement? Do you vnderstand me?
—Me thinkes I do
—And how do's your content
    Tender your owne good fortune?
—            I remember
    You did supplant your Brother *Prospero*.
—            True;
    And looke how well my Garments fit vpon me,
    Much feater then before: My Brothers seruants
    Were then my fellowes, now they are my men.
—But for your conscience.
—I Sir: where lies that? If 'twere a kybe
    'Twould put me to my slipper: But I feele not
    This Deity in my bosome: 'Twentie consciences
    That stand 'twixt me, and *Millaine*, candied be they,
    And melt ere they mollest: Heere lies your Brother,
    No better then the earth he lies vpon,
    If he were that which now hee's like (that's dead)
    Whom I with this obedient steele (three inches of it)
    Can lay to bed for euer: whiles you doing thus,
    To the perpetuall winke for aye might put
    This ancient morsell: this Sir Prudence, who
    Should not vpbraid our course: for all the rest
    They'l take suggestion, as a Cat laps milke,
    They'l tell the clocke, to any businesse that

STL G

We say befits the houre.
—                    Thy case, deere Friend
Shall be my president: As thou got'st *Millaine*,
I'le come by *Naples*: Draw thy sword, one stroke
Shall free thee from the tribute which thou paiest,
And I the King shall loue thee . . .

It will always be well to remember this sinister pair when we are tempted
to think of Shakespeare as having harmonised his experience. This want
of conscience, I take it, continued to appal Shakespeare to the end. The
appalling of Edgar's imagination is the final twist to complete the opening
of the play: 'I haue told you what I haue seene, and heard: But faintly.
Nothing like the image, and horror of it.' The prospect held out here will
be fully viewed when we hear these words:

—Is this the promis'd end?
—Or image of that horror.
—Fall and cease.

*                    *                    *

If we grant that this or something like this is how our minds work as we
take in the opening of the play, we must at the same time note that Shakespeare does not go to work at once on the great questions he has put before us. If we survey the action down to the thunderclap, which marks the
first great division of the play, we are bound to say that what the central
current flows out of is the contradiction internal and external of Lear's
self-chosen disinheritance. And if we examine this contradiction carefully in all its aspects we notice that some of them are not the consequence
of want of filial love. This is noticeable when we examine some of Lear's
exclamations against his daughters. What enrages Lear is that he is not
getting an impossibility—it is almost incidental that filial relations are
being flouted. Again, if the point we must grasp is that Lear is a vicious
fool who is going to be hurt by his folly, we must attend carefully to define
his errors and look to the distribution of our sympathies. In this attempt
some of the difficulties we encounter are due to the limitations of drama.
Lear is not continuously present and is never present as a whole. A
novelist would have made everything clear. I am not yet saying that the
want of clarity is a fault, but that several questions that naturally occur to
us get no answers. We must therefore look hard at the *focus* of Shakespeare's interest to discover whether it matters that at the edges some
quite serious questions are left obscure.

The main contradiction might be called political, though it could be discussed in family terms: that a king and a father cannot continue as head man if he surrenders power to his children. Shakespeare has dwelt on one aspect, that bound up with the knights, and left us in doubt about another. What was this life that Lear hoped to keep up in his retirement? Who has not raised an eyebrow when he saw a man on the very verge of life and death so active on the hunting field and with so hearty an appetite for food? We thought Lear was crawling toward death and we find him indulging in a round of pleasures. Everything we hear jars with the thought Lear had earlier thrown out of his looking to his daughter for *nursing*. But nothing obscures the central point that Lear had clearly not thought out the nature of his *duties* to his daughters once he ceased to be king in anything but name. This is flashed upon us in the opening sentence of our *Scena Tertia*: 'Did my Father strike my Gentleman for chiding of his Foole?' We shall have to wait to learn what the Fool may have done or said to provoke chiding, but we know at once that Lear has overstepped the limit in striking a gentleman, or at the very least, he has resumed a right that was no longer his. No household could be run on such conditions. We can easily imagine the effect of Lear's bad example on his knights, and are therefore inclined to go some way with Goneril when she says, 'You strike my people, and your disorder'd rable, make Seruants of their Betters'.

Although Shakespeare lets us know at once that the first division of the play will come with a contrived 'show-down' to settle the question of power, the power-debate allows incidental development to the questions of the good and bad servant and the riddles of truth, truth salutary and truth harmful. As for service, the daughter scants it and Kent offers it. Goneril belongs to the new order of things, Kent to the old. For him Lear is still king, for her Lear is a childish old man. Kent, though, might almost be called a bad influence. A little more of this sort of thing and Lear will become more wilful than he already is:

—What art thou?
—A very honest hearted Fellow, and as poore as the King.
—If thou be'st as poore for a subiect, as hee's for a king, thou art poore enough. What wouldst thou?
—Seruice.
—Who wouldst thou serue?
—You.
—Do'st thou know me fellow?
—No Sir, but you haue that in your countenance, which I would faine call Master.

—What's that?

—Authority.

Yet the 'notion' of service persists since Kent, apart from some poor jokes, is very much a function and very little a character. As such, he serves as a foil to the Bad Servant. Whether Shakespeare wanted us to see something equivocal in Kent's goodness cannot be made out, since hereabouts everything that is done and said is said and done in reference to Lear alone. Kent is at any rate a *loving* servant and the relation of duty to feeling is brought home in the knight's complaint: 'Your Highnesse is not entertain'd with that Ceremonious affection as you were wont, theres a great abatement of kindnesse . . .'.

The same necessity of applying everything to Lear affects our ability to get the Fool right, though here we may eventually lay some of the blame for our difficulty on Shakespeare. It is far less easy to label him a mere function, although I think he is continually serving almost as an allegory. In a general way he stands for the Truth, the truth it will pain Lear to recognize, but we shall not see him properly if we cannot see him literally. First and foremost, he is a *royal* privilege, the king's special fool. Lear's maintaining him when no longer king is a further mark of his unwillingness to learn the new duties imposed by abdication. The Fool, I imagine, has been addressing the courtiers as if Lear were still king and he, the Fool, were still *all-lycens'd*. And Lear has supported him. Secondly, I take it that his behaviour is as much of a disguise as Kent's and, later, Edgar's. He is a professional fool. We don't think him very funny and we are embarrassed by the thought that Shakespeare may have found him a satisfactory clown. It may be to avoid having to condemn Shakespeare for a poor sense of humour that some people have called the Fool a *natural* half-wit and a figure of pathos. It is true our second news of him might seem to point that way—'Since my young Ladies going into France, Sir, the Foole hath much pined away . . .'—and we learn very shortly afterwards that the Fool had changed in his manner of fooling (by singing) since Lear had banished Cordelia. Given the paucity of signs in the text, which makes it hard to reach conviction either way, and, on the other hand, the radical importance of a decision for the actor and producer, this seems to be an instance of the value of a truly experimental theatre which would offer two performances identical save for presenting the Fool in these quite different ways. But however the decision went, I think we should be doing wrong to these scenes if we were induced to attribute to the Fool, as some have done, a passionate love of and devotion to his master, equal to Kent's. By and large it is better to consider his function rather than his motive. His job is to administer medicine to

Lear, the kind that produces madness but prepares the way for the superior brand Cordelia has to offer. The Fool is the ἱερά πικρά Erasmus referred to in the famous letter he wrote to defend his *Praise of Folly*, Bitter Truth; not the whole truth but an uncomfortable kind, based on facts. '—Truth's a dog must to kennell, hee must bee whipt out, when the Lady Brach may stand by th' fire and stinke. —A pestilent gall to me.' And lest we should miss the point Shakespeare repeats it at once:

—This is nothing Foole.
—Then 'tis like the breath of an vnfeed Lawyer, you gave me nothing for't, can you make no vse of nothing Nuncle?
—Why no Boy, Nothing can be made out of nothing.
—Prythee tell him, so much the rent of his land comes to, he will not beleeue a Foole.
—A bitter Foole.

This does not mean that the Fool was never intended to raise a laugh, but that his *major* function was to point a truth, and that we should not be condemning him for heartlessness or tactlessness. The Fool's rôle develops in the next scene. He then, as it were, replaces the stages which inside Lear are bringing on the final outburst. Therefore, though we may find ourselves reflecting that if he had malicious joy in the confrontation he could hardly have spoken differently, yet our thoughts are better employed and applied in trying to imagine what Lear must have been feeling.

Although we do well to be so concentrating on Lear, we cannot help speculating about the 'real' situation. I am anxious that Goneril should have her pound of flesh. We may snort when she professes to speak

in the tender of a wholesome weale . . .

yet she has her point. She is mainly asking for the realities of Lear's renunciation of power. Yet though her language is power-language, the stronger speaking to the weaker, for us it is coloured with dramatic irony, as, for instance, when she says:

I would you would make vse of your good wisedome
(Whereof I know you are fraught) and put away
These dispositions, which of late transport you
From what you rightly are.

Here we may ask: who on the stage knows Lear best? Goneril, too, is giving Lear a hearty dose of medicine, even if it at first stupefies him, then acts as an emetic. At least, when Lear exclaims *Darknesse, and Diuels* we may also ask whether Lear is any less of the Devil's party than his daughter. His is perhaps a different brand of selfishness, the hated kind we call self-righteousness. Who was he to call his daughter *Degenerate Bastard*? Perhaps Lear is the real *all-lycens'd Foole*? He certainly exhibits a looseness of nature, a willingness to curse others that belies the strange image —'Which like an Engine, wrencht my frame of Nature From the fixt place . . .'—he fabricates to explain what had happened when Cordelia committed what he now sees by comparison to have been a *most small fault*. Although I suspect that in ordinary Jacobean life 'Father's temper' was not thought so shocking and degrading as the other members of a family regard it nowadays, yet, I take it, Lear's prayer to nature is a devilish prayer. Edmund's evocation of Nature was genial by comparison. To see that this language is not too strong, we have only to compare it with Lady Macbeth's, where she asks for Nature to be perverted.

> Come you Spirits,
> That tend on mortall thoughts, vnsex me here,
> And fill me from the Crowne to the Toe, top-full
> Of direst Crueltie: make thick my blood,
> Stop vp th' accesse, and passage to Remorse,
> That no conpunctious visitings of Nature
> Shake my fell purpose, nor keepe peace betweene
> Th' effect and hit. Come to my Womans Brests,
> And take my Milke for Gall, you murth'ring Ministers,
> Where-euer in your sightlesse substances,
> You wait on Natures Mischiefe.

In both cases the speeches mean more than they would in the mouths of people to-day. They expressed more than an evil wish, for they were felt as collaborations with unseen powers. Somebody was thought to be offstage listening: the evil in man was thought to be speaking to the evil outside man. We now begin to see that there are *depths* of evil in Lear's mind. His language is far too explicit for the occasion. When an autocratic man first finds his match in his own daughter, we may expect an outburst of baffled rage and the thought Lear finally produces:

> Thou shalt finde,
> That Ile resume the shape which thou dost thinke
> I haue cast off for euer.

But the specificity of Lear's curse suggests a deep poison, at the least a potential hatred of the whole process by which children are brought into the world. Dimly, as yet, he seeks to ally himself with all that could blight the sacred aspect of the parent-child relation. He perverts his own sacred rights, his real authority, by sending out scouts to contact evil. If there is anything in this, we may reinforce the point that the Fool's truth is very limited. There were more important things Lear needed to know than that he had been a fool. He needed to understand the full bearing of what Kent had told him:

Ile tell thee thou dost euill.

# CHAPTER 2

# Manipulating our Sympathies

I T would be ungainly to tumble headlong into a general discussion of the propriety and impropriety of an author's design turning out to be a design on us or to distinguish the limits we put on our general willingness to be led wherever an author proposes. In a commentary on a reading of a play the topic only comes up when we are bothered by something that interferes with what we had been taking to be the general intention or mode of the piece. We don't normally need to formulate conjectures of what steps the artist took to get effects that we find acceptable. I assume as axiomatic that, providing what is shewn as having been has some sort of necessity or inevitability, about it, so that looking back we say both 'so it was' and 'so it had to be', we have no concern as participants in a tragedy with the author's contrivance. When we get art in this form we are as pleased to find it difficult to discover the art concealed as we are shocked when the artist who had seemed to be absent suddenly intervenes to give events a tweak. I feel with those critics who at the end of *King Lear* are bothered to find *contrivances* bringing about the death of Cordelia. It may, however, seem premature to bring up this topic as early as the opening of what is our Act II. It will certainly appear inadmissible if the reader experiences no initial sense of an *interruption* and *diversion* of interest in what, as a trapped spectator in the theatre of the imagination, he is forced to attend to until Lear re-appears. But if puzzlement, however slight, is great enough to make us pose the question of the propriety of certain contrivances, then I think we simultaneously distinguish one here as a stroke of will almost totally lacking in inevitability and another as a deliberate manipulation of our sympathies which later on reveals itself as a stroke of great art.

To take a trifle first: what is this rumour of war between the sisters' husbands? The sisters know nothing of it, and if Edmund has not heard of it either, he is remarkably adroit and quick-thinking in weaving it into his business with Edgar. Is this trifle serious enough to provoke a reflection that I did not think *had* to come up in the previous scenes: that not nature or the facts of the case but the author has passed a law decreeing that neither father nor half-brother shall be able to see through Edmund's devices and that the deceit shall go to the limit? And would the reader who accepts this as the law for Edmund agree that a fine dramatic possibility was thereby diminished? This is to look ahead: the question that comes up at once is whether the effect of Cornwall's

> Natures of such deepe trust, we shall much need . . .

is diminished by our sense that it is contrived when we compare it with Duncan's

> He was a Gentleman, on whom I built
> An absolute Trust.
> *Enter Macbeth* . . .

We may also ask ourselves whether it would have made a difference if the comparison had been with Gloucester's

> of my land,
> (Loyall and naturall Boy) Ile worke the meanes
> To make thee capable. . .

The answer will depend on how strongly we regard as an acceptable contrivance Shakespeare's palpable design to make Gloucester and Lear *converge*. 'Palpable', I take it, is not too strong for

> — how dost my Lord?
> —O Madam, my old heart is crack'd, it's crack'd.
> —What, did my Fathers Godsonne[1] seeke your life?
> He whom my Father nam'd, your *Edgar*?
> —O Lady, Lady, shame would haue it hid.
> —Was he not companion with the riotous Knights
> That tended vpon my Father?[2]
> —I know not Madam, 'tis too bad, too bad.
> —Yes Madam, he was of that consort.
> —No maruaile then, though he were ill affected,
> 'Tis they haue put him on the old mans death,
> To haue th' expence and wast of his Reuenues . . .

This first apparent diversion is followed by a second in the next scene. But when we look at this scene we see that it is not of a piece, and we therefore suspect that it was contrived to serve more than one purpose. First, we must observe with amazement that the Kent who rails at Oswald is a new character. He has a flow and a vivacity quite out of keeping with the rest of his part in the play. This is more than plainness, it is

---

[1] The touch in *Godsonne* is inspired!
[2] Here we may note that Regan must suppose the riot to be public knowledge.

the abundance of riot. If we had not thought it at the time, we now look back on Kent's previous treatment of Oswald and begin to add a further item supporting the view that if Kent stood for the Good Servant he might also have stood for the Bad. This is awkward, since Oswald himself is obviously cast for this part — the loyal servant of a corrupt mistress, a bawd in way of good service. Kent continues in the wrong and blunts the strong antipathy of good to bad when he accuses Oswald of taking Vanity the puppet's part against Lear, since he himself is behaving as if Lear were still fully king and Oswald were the servant of a rebel. This is drawn to a point when Cornwall enters. He was right to say

> You beastly knaue, know you no reuerence?

in reply to Kent's unmannerly outburst: 'my Lord, if you will giue me leaue, I will tread this vnboulted villaine into morter, and daube the wall of a Iakes with him'.[1]

The bringing out of the stocks is one of the characteristic felicities of Shakespeare's art. This gross particular turns out to be an instrument of scientific delicacy for both registering and manipulating our sympathies. It is both a fine precision balance and the focus and generator of a mass of thoughts that contribute to the central issue that has been preoccupying our minds: the rights and wrongs in the case between Lear and his relations. It serves to clarify some of the contradictions of Lear's position as king and no king. Shakespeare had already hit on one excellent contrivance for this purpose: the number and behaviour of the knights. In a novel this could have been made to produce a set of situations to illustrate all the ways in which Lear by his plan of renouncing and yet retaining royalty was sowing disorder in the state. I suppose that Shakespeare could not have used these numbers on his stage to create the significant particulars that speak so dramatically. So the stocks replace the knights. They would remind his audience of all the elements of riot and disorder that they tried to keep in check by this instrument. Once Kent is clapped in them, and we watch the balance swing to the side of guilt, we may well congratulate Shakespeare on doing with Kent what in the name of char-

---

[1] What is puzzling here is that, when Kent is called on to justify his behaviour, he does not seem to be speaking about the Oswald we know:
> such smiling rogues as these,
> Like Rats oft bite the holy cords atwaine,
> Which are t' intrince t' vnloose: smooth euery passion
> That in the natures of their Lords rebell,
> Being oile to fire, snow to the colder moodes,
> Reuenge, affirme, and turne their Halcion beakes
> With euery gall, and varry of their Masters,
> Knowing naught (like dogges) but following.

acter consistency I have deplored. For it may then cross our minds that Kent's uncharacteristic unmannerliness was, as it were, by replacing that of his knights, an extension of Lear. He for the moment *is* Lear's guilt, his unnatural folly.

At the same time, the stocks give us a nice measure of Cornwall's position. If Lear had not studied his duties to his daughters still less had he thought of his duties to his sons-in-law. Cornwall, too, must have his pound of flesh. His act is an exercise of proper authority: he is using a power that became his by Lear's own act. He is seeking to set a precise limit marking off his area of authority from Lear's. Yet almost automatically the balance begins to sway in the other direction. If Cornwall's assertion of power was right the method of doing so gave offence. For heralds and all who served in a similar capacity were *ex officio* or while in office bearers of honour. It was one thing to draw a line by refusing to allow Kent's breach of the peace to pass; it was another to inflict an indignity on Lear by way of his messenger. Kent instantly recovers his dignity, the dignity of a royal ambassador, a king's servant. Indeed Shakespeare now contrives to link him in our minds with Cordelia, and not merely because they are allies, but because they stand for those who are capable of bearing adversity without breaking down. It is not a very deep contrivance, but, when taken up again by Cordelia, it serves as a reminder from inside the play that nothing that happens in it is so bad as to make us forget that courage in the face of misfortune is a reasonable attitude. The extent of the realm of ill-will is fearfully enlarged before the play is out, but an area governed by fortune and her wheel remains uninvaded.

'Edgar is a superfluous character'. Orwell's remark, taken out of context, may look like one of those invitations given to examinees to unload their knowledge in an essay. The verdict is a severe one for Shakespeare in that an enormous amount of contrivance has gone into getting Edgar into the position of poor Tom if it was after all to have been to little purpose. Here I wish to consider only whether his odd entry and his odd speech hold up or forward the play. I call it odd (though as we shall see there are others like it) because in one sense it *is* strictly superfluous, and since it merely *tells* us something we shall be able to judge of much better when we see for ourselves. It is as if Shakespeare had no confidence in his action or in the intelligence of his audience. It is also a singularly faceless speech, one which would justify us in perverting the meaning of

*Edgar* I nothing am.

His disguise is the most real thing about him. And with the contrivance in itself we surely have no quarrel if its principal aim was to give us a concrete sense of one of the items which we must know to the full if we are to be able to judge delicately of Lear's future position as an outcast. I am supposing that Shakespeare, to prepare our minds for what Lear is to undergo, took the most concrete specimen of an outcast he could find. I imagine that the Abraham man was a familiar horror, that he would stand in everyone's mind for the consequences, what it did for man, to be outside society. His appearance therefore was to give body to

> To take the basest, and most poorest shape
> That euer penury in contempt of man,
> Brought neere to beast . . .

The critical question to be decided in the furnace of the intense scenes that are to come is whether this disguise is too solid, too real, and by contrast we dislike the fact that Edgar is play-acting. It may even take off something from the reality of Lear's sufferings in the storm.

\*       \*       \*

We now come to the scene that is obviously in the centre of interest. Now every early thought flowers, everything plays into everything else. This is full drama and here there is no question but that we have everything we want in full presence. We see many things done before our eyes that we now fully understand. I shall therefore pass over the mere intensifications of points already made and dwell instead on the new sense that is emerging that Lear is a man to engage our sympathy and concern. Let me start where sympathy might be hesitant. Although Lear is abominably wrapped up in himself, he is also a man in pain, even if some of the pain is of a kind to do him good. I begin to feel just a little for and with him (where I didn't when he said something similar earlier on) when I hear

> Oh *Regan*, she hath tied
> Sharpe-tooth'd vnkindnesse, like a vulture heere . . .

and

> strooke me with her Tongue
> Most Serpent-like, vpon the very Heart.

I take it we feel confusedly that, though we should name the wounded centre his cursed pride and desire to be master, yet somehow his suffering *is* in the heart. But we hesitate less when we turn from the king to the old man.

This is, as I have said, a value that is fast becoming historical. We are all potential Regans and Gonerils nowadays. They, realists on the surface, see only what the eye sees, that old men are weak, dote, etc. They therefore agree that by the law of nature old men should meekly hand themselves over to the authority of those in the prime of life. They feel, as the modern state to-day, that bare subsistence is the meed of the aged. And if the real *is* what the eye sees, what the intelligence tests measure, we are right to see the fact of senility for what it is. The value Lear appealed to was as much a religious as a social value. Nowadays the man or woman who detects the first grey hair resorts to the tweezers or the dye-bottle. In Shakespeare's day we might almost call grey or white hair a badge of grace, since it provoked deference and religious respect. We must therefore listen to the verse for overtones now grown faint. But none of us misses the note here:

> O Sir, you are old,
> Nature in you stands on the very Verge
> Of his confine: you should be rul'd, and led
> By some discretion, that discernes your state
> Better then you your selfe.

I am not, however, sure whether we participate fully in the effect of this on Lear. Professor G. Wilson Knight has written well of the grotesque element in this play. What do we think of Lear on his knees? It was unsightly, an ugly bit of play-acting, but is that all? Could it also have been enacting the enormity of Regan's attitude?

> Deere daughter, I confesse that I am old;
> Age is vnnecessary: on my knees I begge,
> That you'l vouchsafe me Rayment, Bed, and Food.

(All this, we reflect, is going to furnish contrasts when Cordelia appears: Lear is going to perform in earnest what he now does in bitter jest.) And don't we feel a shudder of pity at this expedient, even though Lear cuts the feeling off as he invokes Heaven to help out his evil desires? But it is the same Heaven he calls on to better purpose a moment later:

> O Heauens!
> If you do loue old men, if your sweet sway
> Allow Obedience; if you your selues are old,
> Make it your cause: Send downe, and take my part.

Here, we feel, Lear has dug down deeper and touched a spring in himself. It's not pure water for he's too full of self-pity and has no sense of mutuality, but if we permitted the thought that in calling down evil he was collaborating with a supernatural power, we can't refuse the thought that here there is at least an aspiration toward the good spirits.

When all is going so well and Shakespeare has us fully under control, there is no need to dwell on one thing more than another as all is of the central stream. Since I am about to present myself in a light that may expose me to the charge of unfeeling, I should like to record how the pathos of Lear's last attempts in delusion and illusion to bear with the ill-treatment comes over me. In particular, here:

> I will not trouble thee my Child: farewell;
> Wee'l no more meete, no more see one another.
> But yet thou art my flesh, my blood, my Daughter,
> Or rather a disease that's in my flesh,
> Which I must needs call mine. Thou art a Byle,
> A plague sore, or imbossed Carbuncle
> In my corrupted blood.

That way knowledge lay. A more terrible knowledge doesn't get further consideration than is given here:

> You see me heere (you Gods) a poore old man,
> As full of griefe as age, wretched in both,
> If it be you that stirres these Daughters hearts
> Against their Father. . .

But we have been wonderfully conducted to the *Storme and Tempest*—to the scenes that make or break the play.

*          *          *

Here I come to the point I forecast in my previous chapter, where the reader has every incentive to give me up as I myself would wish him to if he finds that I am expressing a merely private view. Given the weight and volume of opposing opinion, I would rather start with a modest query: Is there *nothing* wrong in the current ways of taking these central scenes? And in favour of opening an enquiry into an apparently closed subject, my plea would not be on behalf of some special insight granted to me alone but for some very prosaic and commonsense reflections, such as that from now on we are intended to see the play's action as one and not two-fold.

If we allow this, we may conclude that the most significant actions in the third act concern *Gloucester*, and that Lear's appearances serve to intensify our attention when Gloucester's far more real sufferings appear before our eyes. My argument then continues: if we refuse to follow the current of the play and instead blindly follow Lear we may come to see the play too much as a mere story. I regard the story as inferior and, if the story were the main thing, Shakespeare's wilful yanking of events from their probable course would be a serious blemish. What I am advocating therefore is an unusual degree of surrender but a surrender to the obvious as well as to the strange and disturbing. I shall, however, make the obvious more palatable by contrasting it with the following judgements taken from an eminent critic, which to me seem literally misreadings of this act:

> At the centre of [Act III], at once the main protagonist and symbol of the spiritual state of a humanity exposed to fundamental disorder . . . stands the figure of the aged King . . . Lear . . . now clearly assumes a stature that is more than merely personal, becomes man, the microcosm of the universe . . . his situation is . . . a concentration of that of man in general.

It is easier, however, to call statements misreadings than to shew that they are, which requires the production of a convincing true reading. Once this is made a necessity, prudence requires that I use gentler language. The difference I see between the critic's remarks and those I should favour turns on the distinction I drew in a previous chapter in contrasting ways of generalising. The particulars that make up the Lear of this act do not to my mind ever constitute a concentration of man in general. Dull and uniform as we all are, I should hope that a concentration of all mankind would exhibit many more facets and not only than those presented by Lear but by the whole caste of the play.

But the difference is also one of our imaginative response to poetry. What I am holding out for is the view that, however powerfully we are made to feel what Lear takes to be the real state of affairs, we never lose our grip on what we take to be the 'objective' truth. The power of the poetry is never such that we surrender our belief to Lear's. Lear makes a great bid to manipulate our sympathies but the storm is a real storm and not a mere projection of Lear's inner state, even though we judge of its severity in part by Lear's projections. So I claim that we misread the play if we don't begin by allowing the storm to be a purely physical event, a matter of limited importance and impressiveness, a natural event, not in itself any more than its opposite, a mere temporary change in the face of nature. I take it that Shakespeare wanted us to be able to compare and contrast the storm with Lear's behaviour in it. The storm itself can become an excellent lever on our feelings, but not if it is fused and dissolved away entirely into psychology and metaphysics.

The storm is there above all to make one point: that an old man's daughters and his faithful servant could lock him out at night in such weather. *There* is a degree of inhumanity, a sign that the daughters are not merely power-drunk and respect-blind but malevolent. I am sick and tired of hearing people discuss Shakespeare exclusively in terms of order and disorder. I don't wish to deny Shakespeare his metaphysical aspirations, but I do wish to stress his human concern, concern at the level where human beings are still recognizable as such. So here I say we should think *first* of the wickedness of letting Lear loose on such a bad night. (We must dismiss the thought that Lear must have met with far worse physical conditions while out hunting.) Then, when this is firmly before us, it is natural to have another thought, of the extremity from which Lear has moved to the extremity he now reaches. We who occupy the middle and lower-middle ranks of prosperity can appreciate what it might be to topple from higher up to further down, and we can feel adversity assuming fearful proportions. But when I find my critic speaking of 'the tragedy which Lear's outraged fatherhood and shattered royalty embody', I pull myself up short. Chaucer may have thought the situation tragic, but I am afraid I am an impenitent Cromwellian, and worse, for I can see that it might do the mighty good to fall from their seats and I relish the phrase: 'God, doctor! he gart kings ken that they had a *lith* in their neck.' Thoughts like these come with a rush when I hear people calling it a sign of grace in Lear that he now, presumably in his seventies, for the first time realises what it is to be poor and for the first time feels sorry for the poor. I can only say, what appalling spiritual blindness he must have spent his life in, and a blindness hard to credit in the Middle Ages, when the physical and moral facts of poverty were evident to the lord who (by proxy) gave daily alms at his gate and had his duty dinned into him by his spiritual adviser. Poverty was not a tabooed subject then.

My general hypothesis, then, is that Act III starts from and exhibits malevolence and Lear is not the centre. The central current flows through Gloucester and the self-knowledge he acquires in adversity. Lear's spiritual movements, by comparison, are slight. When this view gains tolerance, we are free to attend to an undoubted fact that the movement of the play is all in the direction of generality. Lear is merely one of the personages who are used in this way. But the process does not go on to the point where we have *all* the troubles of the universe in our laps. It is a corollary of this view that Shakespeare left many things in a merely suggestive condition in order that we should be left free to attend to his central point. Thus we do not get any profound psychological insight into Lear's mind, but we do know that he has met conditions which are too much for him; he has no inner resources to meet what rises up in him at the thought of the treatment he received. And because Lear cannot handle his situation we are driven to inspect it for ourselves. But the situation we examine is larger than that which preoccupies Lear. We are made to ponder on *all* that happens in this third act, not merely on Lear's soliloquies.

*      *      *

It remains, however, a fact that Shakespeare first asks us to attend carefully to the relation between Lear and the storm. When we consider how competent Shakespeare was to enact this relation dramatically, we are surprised to find, as with Edgar, that he first explains in commentary what we are meant to see when Lear comes on the stage. Yet for this very reason of contrivance we ought to look carefully at what Shakespeare's mouthpiece, the Gentleman, tells us in the first scene of our third act. He invites us to transfer to Lear Lear's interpretation of the storm; that is to say, he prepares us to see Lear not as struggling to understand what has happened to him nor as striving to bear it patiently but as inviting the storm inside him to do its worst, to blow itself out or to destroy him. If this is so, we may legitimately twist the sense and interpret

> Of how vnnaturall and bemadding sorrow
> The King hath cause to plaine

as a criticism of Lear, and say that his is the wrong reaction to the events in that the storm itself does not justify Lear's language. Yet we borrow our sense of the actual fury of the storm from Lear's language—and it is no service to the drama if the production makes that unnecessary—and we so learn from his state of mind, what is confirmed later on, that although the storm was only a storm it was exceptionally fierce.

What might confirm this hypothesis is the consideration that the storm is at first very *external* to Lear. How much we may measure by a comparison with *Macbeth*. Then we see that Lear is merely mouthing *at* the storm whereas Macbeth is intimately related to the storm that embodies his longings for chaos to come. Consider how hard and noisy Lear is compared with Macbeth. In the first scene of the fourth Act of *Macbeth* we find,

> Though you vntye the Windes, and let them fight
> Against the Churches: Though the yesty Waues
> Confound and swallow Nauigation vp:
> Though bladed Corne be lodg'd, & Trees blown downe,
> Though Castles topple on their Warders heads:
> Though Pallaces, and Pyramids do slope
> Their heads to their Foundations: Though the treasure
> Of Natures Germaine, tumble altogether,
> Euen till destruction sicken . . . ,

which is sufficiently similar to make comparison possible with

> Blow windes, & crack your cheeks; Rage, blow
> You Cataracts, and Hyrricano's spout,
> Till you haue drench'd our Steeples, drown the Cockes.
> You Sulph'rous and Thought-executing Fires,
> Vaunt-curriors of Oake-cleauing Thunder-bolts,
> Sindge my white head. And thou all-shaking Thunder,
> Strike flat the thicke Rotundity o' th' world,
> Cracke Natures moulds, all germaines spill at once
> That makes ingratefull Man.

The reason for this contrast is clear: as yet, Lear is merely addressing the *elements*, not the spiritual forces. So he is in fact talking to himself about himself. He is play-acting humility:

> Heere I stand your Slaue,
> A poore, infirme, weake, and dispis'd old man. . . .

In a sense he is enjoying the spectacle he imagines he is offering.

It is certainly a step forward from this when Lear begins to think of the storm as an agent of *the great Goddes*. He is still posturing, of course, but we begin to suspect that there may be more in this spouting than meets the eye. In a ghostly way Lear's evil now begins to confess. On the surface he declares himself more sinned against than sinning, a remark that would have been more becoming spoken about than by Lear. The storm makes a step forward in another sense when we hear

> Mans Nature cannot carry
> Th' affliction, nor the feare.

Kent's language, 'wrathfull', 'horrid', 'groanes', reflects a thought that would be in most spectators' minds, that such an exceptional storm may have had supernatural causes. We must not pretend to know more than we do, we must not posit uniformity of belief, but we must allow for the possibility here that by some minds the storm would be thought of as about to prove revelatory; it would be supposed that some hidden and hitherto unpunished crime was going to be revealed. The next step forward is Lear's madness. If we ask what actually happens to Lear, we may say that he 'cracks up', he ceases to grasp his whole situation and to distinguish his inner troubles from all the other goings-on in the world. He can only interpret everything in the light of his own suffering. Because he is cold, he supposes the Fool is cold, too. It's not a self-outgoing remark to say

> Poore Foole, and Knaue, I haue one part in my heart
> That's sorry yet for thee . . .

but it's something for a self-centred egoist to say it. Shakespeare takes trouble to see that we do not miss the point:

> the tempest in my mind,
> Doth from my sences take all feeling else,
> Saue what beates there.

Lear 'acts' this state of affairs when he sees poor Tom. In spite of all the evidence that Tom's appearance and behaviour provides, Lear can only see in him a mirror of his own predicament:

> Did'st thou giue all to thy Daughters? And art thou come to this? . . . Ha's his Daughters brought him to this passe? Could'st thou saue nothing? Would'st thou giue 'em all? . . . nothing could haue subdu'd Nature to such a Lownesse, but his vnkind Daughters.

Limited as Lear becomes by his sufferings, we note that nevertheless, inside the narrow range of his painful thoughts, he acquires certain certainties. Some think we should include among them

> 'twas this flesh begot
> Those Pelicane Daughters.

This would mark an advance if it meant recognition of a fact implicitly denied by Lear earlier, when he seemed to regard the daughters merely as his disease, yet the context is not very encouraging. We cannot be sure whether Lear had begun to see himself as in some way responsible for their treatment of him. But a real truth comes over him as he looks at poor Tom. There he sees the ultimate condition of divorce from society: there is one form of the worst. Yet when we meet Lear again, he is still essentially in the old false rut of hatred and one-sided justice:

> To haue a thousand with red burning spits
> Come hizzing in vpon 'em.

More eloquent, perhaps, of his real state is Lear's *acting* while Edgar says

> Looke where he stands and glars

glares with the eyes of a devil, like the figure Edgar evokes later:

> me thought his eyes
> Were two full Moones. . . .

On the other hand, Lear is brought to what ought to be the central question of the play when he asks: 'Is there any cause in Nature that make these hard-hearts?' How much more interesting *King Lear* would be if Shakespeare could have answered this, his central question! We have to wait for *Macbeth* to get any fresh insight. Here we are merely presented with the facts, and in so far as the daughters represent those facts we may feel we are getting something less than the full facts. No contemporary of ours will complain that the bad characters in this play are distortions or exaggerations of the worst we know in this kind, but they are not fully present and lack the extra Shakespearian dimension. They cannot there- fore carry the central current; they merely set the scene for a study of Gloucester. I judge it to be a misplaced reaction to shudder over them, for they are almost mathematical functions. Edmund is merely in the line traced out for him when he says,

> This seemes a faire deseruing, and must draw me
> That which my Father looses: no lesse then all,
> The yonger rises, when the old doth fall.

*       *       *

Gloucester now begins to take on form both as agent and patient. He defines the evil of the rulers and of Edmund by the former's abuse of his hospitality and the latter's abuse of his confidence. He begins to interest us by his political and humanitarian decision. Some critics forget that the reason why Gloucester lost his eyes was not his ancient lechery but these movements of his heart: '. . . these iniuries the King now beares, will be reuenged home . . . we must incline to the King, I will looke him, and priuily relieue him . . . if I die for it (as no lesse is threatned me) the King my old Master must be relieued.' How much more he deserves our sym- pathy than Lear! It is only after he has shewn that he feels for Lear and Kent that he mentions his own sorrow:

> Thou sayest the King growes mad, Ile tell thee Friend
> I am almost mad my selfe. I had a Sonne,
> Now out-law'd from my blood: he sought my life
> But lately: very late: I lou'd him (Friend)
> No Father his Sonne deerer: true to tell thee,
> The greefe hath craz'd my wits.

And Gloucester is only beginning. I suggest that through him we grasp the central thread, which has to do with love and suffering and sticking it out to the end. For the moment, Lear is spared the worst. Gloucester gets it.

He must have been as surprised as we are to meet the sisters with the gloves off. No doubt he was used to the dirty world of power politics, but now he suddenly drops into the unmasked world of gangsters, thugs and neurotic sadists, or whatever is the exact name for the woman who so plucks the beard of an old man. But once again the function of the horror is to exalt Gloucester, who now becomes the author's spokesman. At any rate, here is what I would call the centre of Act III:

> Because I would not see thy cruell Nailes
> Plucke out his poore old eyes: nor thy fierce Sister,
> In his Annointed flesh, sticke boarish phangs.
> The Sea, with such a storme as his bare head,
> In Hell-blacke-night indur'd, would haue buoy'd vp
> And quench'd the Stelled fires:
> Yet poore old heart, he holpe the Heauens to raine,
> If Wolues had at thy Gate howl'd that sterne time,
> Thou should'st haue said, good Porter turne the Key:
> All Cruels else subscribe: but I shall see
> The winged Vengeance ouertake such Children.

(This incidentally suggests how Shakespeare may have produced the play, seeing the night as *hell*, naked exposure to evil, the good wholly unprotected.)

Gloucester knows he is fallen among the damned, living bodies with devils for souls like those in the *Inferno* (Canto XXXIII). But the action is interrupted for one of those little scenes that are of immense depth for all their brevity. I see a world of meaning in the servants who are forced to witness their masters behaving like devils. If anyone ever doubted that service was one of the sacred values for Shakespeare, a bond indispensable for the good life on earth, he might be converted by listening and watching with care at this point:

> I haue seru'd you euer since I was a Childe:
> But better seruice haue I neuer done you,
> Then now to bid you hold.

Because of this my mind will for ever linger on a certain pile of rotting filth and, among the putrefaction, on the remains of a life-long servant in a noble house who paid the full price for an impulse of goodness, an impulse without which social man cannot persist.

These last thoughts, however, are off-stage thoughts, and so out of order here. The stage now demands all our attention for an action which has been severely condemned. So I perhaps ought to go on record as one

so squeamish that he can hardly bear to look on the mildest facial de-
formity, who winces at tear-puffed eyelids, swollen lips, the horrible lines
of a sneer, the distortions of abject envy, before I declare my agreement
with those who judge the extreme horror of Gloucester's blinding not
only right but a necessity. We have had too much play-acting with Lear,
the Fool, Kent and Edgar. Here is the real thing. With our eye proleptic-
ally on the final scene with its

> All's cheerlesse, darke and deadly . . .

here for the first time we meet someone with a right to say,

> All darke and comfortlesse?

And then, wonder of wonders, when Gloucester suffers worse than
mutilation he says:

> O my Follies! then *Edgar* was abus'd,
> Kinde Gods, forgiue me that, and prosper him.

What depths of purity, what wells of goodness must be in a soul that goes
outward in love when the inward-boring pain would make most people
think only of themselves! Here I would appeal to the reader to give imagination the rein and let his mind be filled to the full with the grandeur as
well as the pathos of this moment. For only so can the spectacle offered to
the eyes be tolerated and this seen to be the most telling of the particulars,
the one that would take us to the limits of generalisation. It is helpful,
too, to look back over the scattered references to 'eyes' and 'sight', and to
suggestions that blindness may be the condition of wisdom and that those
who think they see are really blind. We may then be led to say that if
there had to be mutilation of the body to stamp the significance of the
play home, then it was peculiarly right to attack Gloucester's *eyes*.

Once again Shakespeare does not bring to bear his whole sense of the
mystery of the evil we have witnessed. Instead, we have a close with a
*Macbeth*-like chorus. It is a note of simple morality: evil is seen from the
outside as having no intimate share in our lives:

> —Ile neuer care what wickednes I doe,
>   If this man come to good.
> —          If she liue long, and in the end meet the old course of death,
>   women will all turne monsters . . .

This is not wisdom, but simple-minded decency. We know, alas, that in
real life, though rarely in art, the wicked often prosper, and that Mr.
Badman lives the full course and makes a good end. Shakespeare is going

to schematise his plot and sacrifice wisdom to bring about the downfall of the wicked. Gloucester's winged vengeance is like poetic justice, something life knows nothing of.

*    *    *

But those remarks come more appropriately when the play is over. Before leaving this third Act I should like to comment on two puzzles. The first concerns Edgar. I take it that though originally Edgar's disguise was meant to bring home certain truths to Lear, Shakespeare developed the part well beyond this function. We are, I think, forced to consider Edgar's make-believe as reality and must therefore take the 'foul fiend' seriously. For it is this spirit that constitutes the extreme form of adversity, that is what makes Tom feel the cold. He is naked and defenceless against the in-dwelling evil. But if we put it like this, we must at once note that through Edgar Shakespeare approaches evil exclusively in the form of popular superstition. We might almost call it fairy evil. The foul fiend is, as it were, a cousin of 'that very Mab that plats the manes of Horses in the night: & bakes the Elf locks in foule sluttish haires, which once vntangled, much misfortune bodes . . .', at least if we take these lines: 'This is the foule Flibbertigibbet; hee begins at Curfew, and walkes at first Cocke: Hee giues the Web and the Pin, squints the eye, and makes the Hare-lippe; Mildewes the white Wheate, and hurts the poor Creature of earth'. Now engaging in a poetical way as all this folk-lore is, I can't see what it has to do with the overt moralizing Edgar indulges in by way of recipes for avoiding the foul fiend.

My second puzzle is to discover the relevance of the stray references to sexual vices, crimes and monstrosities. In the first place, how much attention should we give to the bawdy or faintly bawdy songs of Edgar and the Fool? Nobody pays attention to them on the stage, should we bother with them? If it were only a matter of clownish asides, the answer, I think, would be, no. But there are one or two remarks we cannot simply pass over. For instance, in Lear's catalogue of crimes, we find

thou Simular of Vertue

That art Incestuous . . .

and there is the strikingly vivid portrait Edgar gives of himself:

A Seruingman, Proud in heart, and minde; that curl'd my haire, wore Gloues in my cap; seru'd the Lust of my Mistris heart, and did the acte of darkenesse with her . . . One, that slept in the contriuing of Lust, and wak'd to doe it.

Then there is the equally striking picture the Fool calls up as he sees Gloucester approaching in the blackness with a torch in his hand: 'Now a little fire in a wilde Field, were like an old Letchers heart, a small spark, all the rest on's body, cold: Looke, heere comes a walking fire'.

Both these puzzles might be used to raise disquieting questions about a failure of focus in this act. Yet the natural order of discussion would be to deal first with the radical incoherence of the *end* of the play. Only when that was generally agreed on would there be point in tracing its origin in this act. Since I am proposing to raise this question in a final chapter I will here make amends to J. Middleton Murry by confessing that I am now troubled by his comments on the play after having yearly dismissed them as aberrations. Though his general account in *Shakespeare* (1936) still does not impress me favourably, I am glad to recall the following formulations which re-reading the play has forced me to take very seriously indeed:

> . . . in *King Lear*, I find disturbance, hesitation, uncertainty, and a constant interruption of the 'predominant passion'. The major and the minor intensities are continually flagging. The imagination of the theme becomes perfunctory or strained, the imagination of the verse spasmodic . . .
>
> It is one of the things which has become, by convention, impossible to say, but *King Lear* makes upon me the impression of the work of a Shakespeare who is out of his depth. He does not really know what he wants to say: perhaps he does not know whether he wants to say anything. . .
>
> I am merely demurring to the almost inveterate habit of Shakespeare criticism with regard to the play, which is to represent it as the sublime and transcendent culmination of a "tragic period". It is not that, to my mind, at all. It does not belong to the same order as *Hamlet*, *Othello* and *Macbeth*; or as *Coriolanus* and *Antony and Cleopatra*. It is, in that sequence, an anomaly. Compared to them, it is lacking in imaginative control, it is lacking in poetic 'intensity'.

# CHAPTER 3

# Radical Incoherence?

Is there the slightest prospect of carrying out successfully in 1969 what J. M. Murry thought impossible in 1936? He was apparently proved right during many years after the publication of his book on Shakespeare, for when his disparaging remarks on *Lear* were noticed they were regularly classed as eccentric and disregarded. It may have been because he had no hope of persuading his contemporaries to qualify their verdict that *Lear* was Shakespeare's supreme masterpiece that he couched his own remarks in language that does not easily lend itself to verification by others. As he has left them, his observations sound too much like one man's findings and too little like the voice of common sense. Certainly a very different note will have to be struck if the normal verdict of today is to be shocked into self-inspection and any of the other preliminaries to self-correction. Some extraordinary arguments will have to be put forward before any sane reader will consent to share in a re-reading of the last two acts of *King Lear* which might have as a result a loss of satisfaction, a lower estimate of the play.

The good-humoured reader may nevertheless give an amused consent in the form, 'I'd like to see you try', and this permission to go ahead would suit me very well. But it is very hard to state reasonable grounds for soliciting such a permission if it is not freely granted in advance. For I can point to no general reason why this play should have been over-estimated for so many years. Worse still, I cannot offer the prospect of new insights. The play I find faulty is virtually the play described by Bradley in his *Shakespearean Tragedy*. The faults or deficiencies I have in mind are those that would have weighed with Bradley if he had taken the third act in a way similar to that proposed in the preceding chapter. What I have to offer now is merely the result of firing questions at Bradley's two lectures on the play and imagining what he would say in reply.

One reason for confining enquiry to the broadest effects is that if a change is going to be brought about, it will involve the shifting of a great deal of mental furniture, and most of the energy for that must come from the reader. How much may be measured by considering the energy needed to re-possess consciously any verdict that has ceased to be personal and is so widely shared as to seem that of common sense. I doubt, in fact, whether anybody can now have a first-hand judgement of a Shake-speare play. Personal efforts have so often merely produced the eccentric. The pain of such reflections is, of course, very much worse for those who as teachers or taught cannot go on living with the stale repetitive stuff that is the product of inert acquiescence in the current view of the play. At any rate this train of thought has made it easier for me to keep to what I hope will be called the painfully obvious if accepted, though if rejected I should like to think it will call for some fresh explanation before the current view can be complacently resumed.

But this restriction to the grossly palpable, which is required from any member who asks the community to grant him a brief hearing for what must start as an outsider's opinion, seriously misrepresents the experi-ence I am reporting on. My distress, pain and bewilderment are far greater than is indicated by the local difficulties I shall list. The impal-pables—and impalpable they must always be as long as we cannot see what Shakespeare ought to have been doing—are more telling to me than the instances that can be more easily handled. They are impalpable be-cause they are experiences that came to nothing and can, if at all, only be indicated negatively. As a sample of my general difficulty I could name my inability to find any imaginative fit for famous remarks whether of apparent pessimism, such as

> As Flies to wanton Boyes, are we to th' Gods,
> They kill vs for their sport . . .

or of apparent consolation, such as

> Ripenesse is all.

To take up the language of Swinburne, I am unable to find any word that would serve as 'the keynote of the whole poem' or anything that would correspond to such a firm image of coherence as 'the keystone of the whole arch of thought'. It is painful, distressing and bewildering to be in such a state, but that is not a matter to go on about until it is widely shared. Fortunately, there are other matters that can be put forward, even to the sceptical, and tentative advances can be sketched which, if accepted, will enable me to drop out in good time for the decisive break (if it comes to that) to be made by each reader for himself.

*        *        *

Although the main trouble is to relate the elements that begin from now on to enjoy a quasi-independent life, there is in everybody's ex-perience, I would claim, and likely to be prominent in the most naif and the most sophisticated, a *malaise* bound up with the way each element spreads out. The rôle of Gloucester seems to me a striking instance. Can it be denied that what happens in the fourth act confirms the importance attributed to him in the third; that he has now become Lear's complement and fills out an important part of a thesis that Lear can no longer illustrate since he has permanently retired from coherent experience? Gloucester himself seems to fill out and complete what he was meant to be. He rises in stature to a major figure and is conscious to the finger-tips of having squared his accounts with life. Like a hero in a Greek tragedy he knows he has reached a limit. He thinks the wrong he has done to his son is irreparable. In the world of a Greek play his attempted suicide would be noble. What are we to make of it here? Is it a case of diabolic possession, and are we therefore glad to see him abused once again and once again the victim of a baby trick? Or if we take his resolution to be noble, is it not a pitiful come-down to find him so easily converted by Edgar? Can we see unambiguously what Shakespeare, what the play wants with Gloucester?

Would it be generally agreed that, when Gloucester speaks at the beginning of the act, we do not for a moment think of him as speaking from his inferior self? He is presented to us as a valuable link in a long chain of service, the deserving master to whom the devoted servant can say:

> I haue bene your Tenant,
> And your Fathers Tenant, these fourescore yeares.

Gloucester now has a ripe simplicity of expression which makes us forget the timidity of his appearances in the first two acts. His language suggests that he has come to the true bottom of himself, that he is speaking from Arnold's 'central stream',[1] that which we so rarely know. It is striking that here and in the corresponding scene for Lear Shakespeare relies so much on monosyllables to get this effect:

> He has some reason, else he could not beg.
> I' th' last nights storme, I such a fellow saw;
> Which made me thinke a Man, a Worme. My Sonne
> Came then into my minde, and yet my minde
> Was then scarse Friends with him.
> I haue heard more since:

Yet monosyllables alone will not produce this effect or Tennyson would be a master of simplicity.

[1] Cf. the lines quoted in my *Preface*, taken from *St. Paul and Protestantism* (1870) p. 142.

When an author's main point is not clear, it is natural to turn to any minor clues to see if they can provide a suggestion. We have one such possibility in the speech where Gloucester offers Tom a purse. Some critics have denied that there is any point and called the scene vain repetition of what Lear had said generally when addressing all the poor. Could it be that Shakespeare wished us to contrast the language of true feeling with that of rhetoric and wished us to see Gloucester as the maturer, more reflecting figure? Experience has taught me that the confrontation of the two texts does not bring instant agreement, yet as I have a further use for it, here is the possible point or pointless repetition:

> Poore naked wretches, where so ere you are,
> That bide the pelting of this pittilesse storme,
> How shall your House-lesse heads, and vnfed sides,
> Your lop'd, and window'd raggednesse defend you
> From seasons such as these? O I haue tane
> Too little care of this: Take Physicke, Pompe,
> Expose thy selfe to feele what wretches feele,
> That thou maist shake the superflux to them,
> And shew the Heauens more iust.

> Here take this purse, thou whom the heau'ns plagues
> Haue humbled to all strokes: that I am wretched
> Makes thee the happier: Heauens deale so still,
> Let the superfluous, and Lust-dieted man,
> That slaues your ordinance, that will not see
> Because he do's not feele, feele your powre quickly:
> So distribution should vndoo excesse,
> And each man haue enough.

A final reflection on these two passages might be that *King Lear* is the beginning of a series that ends with *The Winters Tale*; that so many of the speeches are put in not to make us aware of how one man responds to a situation but to suggest how mankind is placed generally. Although I thought the play was asking us to resist any temptation to dissolve Lear into Humanity during the storm scenes, it is harder to resist in the fourth act the invitation to generalise everything and to suspend our normal expectations of probability. But are we happy at the transmogrification of Gloucester that now occurs? Do we think Shakespeare could stand a stiff cross-examination here?[1] I find I don't mind my inability to say more to

---

[1] See Henry James' letter of July 17, 1912 to R. W. Chapman, where, in answer to the charge of not seeing fully all the aspects of Mrs. Brookenham in *The Awkward Age*, he wrote: 'I really think I could stand a stiff cross-examination on that lady'.

questions such as 'What is this *Drang nach Dover*?' 'Why did it have to be
that cliff? Were there not a thousand easier ways to die?' than that we
must think of Gloucester as having undergone a spiritual elevation, that
there is a smack of tragedy in

> from that place,
> I shall no leading neede...

and that the spirit that seeks release is more than that of an abused courtier. I am willing to give the sympathy I feel I am being asked for when
Gloucester speaks what he supposes are his last words on earth:

> O you mighty Gods!
> This world I do renounce, and in your sights
> Shake patiently my great affliction off:
> If I could beare it longer, and not fall
> To quarrell with your great opposelesse willes,
> My snuffe, and loathed part of Nature should
> Burne it selfe out. If *Edgar* liue, O blesse him:
> Now Fellow, fare thee well.

The whole 'logic' of Gloucester in the play seems to be that he should
stand *dans le vrai* in a world where so many others are merely playing a
part. So when we find him forced into a kind of game and, worse still,
when he is made to acquiesce in Edgar's moralising, something in us
protests and starts to worry. When I hear

> I do remember now: henceforth Ile beare
> Affliction, till it do cry out it selfe
> Enough, enough, and dye...

I want to object that mere moral saying-so isn't enough to achieve such
a tremendous change. It's a fine ideal to bear free and patient thoughts
but it ought not to be something one could expect a mere injunction to
bring about.

  This objection is diminished by the time Shakespeare's full plan for
Gloucester is revealed. He is to suffer in fact what Lear escaped by madness:

> The King is mad:
> How stiffe is my vilde sense
> That I stand vp, and haue ingenious feeling
> Of my huge Sorrowes? Better I were distract,
> So should my thoughts be seuer'd from my greefes,
> And woes, by wrong imaginations loose
> The knowledge of themselues.

Yet I cannot help wishing that Shakespeare had given the character more flashes of inner life such as the revealing remark when the melodramatic Oswald draws his sword and Gloucester says:

> Now let thy friendly hand
> Put strength enough too't.

Gloucester's indifference to the killing of Oswald makes it impossible not to take his silent participation in this scene as a dramatically convincing proof that he has been pushed to the limit and past it.

*     *     *

This method of treating a part as if it were the whole has certainly brought one area of discomfort into view but the light on it is rather dim. We see through the Gloucester element in this act that Shakespeare has introduced severe strains into his structure by having no settled systems of morality or religion to draw on. The imagination is not satisfied whenever a deep draught is needed, as it is whenever we want to be sure that some ultimate value is being posited. For this reason I would deprecate any further pondering of the main trouble, the apparent conflict between the claims of a morality which falls short of the highest and a nobility which is not supported by the action, until other elements have been considered. That there is an element of cramping morality in the play is only too apparent, and growing distaste for it, amounting at moments to nausea, may divert one from the other sense, that the play has a 'logic' of its own. At the moment the inverted commas are a necessary protection for a frail being that has gained little substance from the Gloucester scenes. Fortunately, as soon as we open our minds to the rest of the act, we find abundant evidence.

A hypothesis to be tested is that from now on the play wants, and suffers for the want of, an element to control the other elements. This special want is created by the madness of Lear, which in this context means his failure to make sense of what is happening. We clearly cannot have the hero superseded by a more overpowering person, but we must have lights on the experiences that are now beyond Lear to interpret. What I am hankering for would be a few dramatic ultimates, things which cannot in the context of the fiction be questioned or made to look subordinate to anything else. Such a hypothesis is dismissed by those critics who find the disparate claims set out by the various elements in this act themselves forming what will ultimately be seen by the spectator of the last act to be a satisfactory pattern. What I would ask the impartial reader to judge is whether such critics have themselves been impartial or whether they have not silently promoted one of the voices in this act to the position of master voice. This I take to be the central question of the play and the main task handed over to the younger generation to sift and, if possible, to solve.

A little hint that Shakespeare has not in fact 'weighted' any one element with the stamp of authority may be seen if we take a fresh look at the 'bad' characters. 'Give a bitch a bad name and have done with her' has been the usual report on both Goneril and Regan. Some commentators have found the master key for interpreting the scene between Goneril and Edmund in this act by applying to it every word of Lear's soliloquy on copulation and in particular these lines:

> . . . the Wren goes too't, and the small gilded Fly Do's letcher in my sight. Let Copulation thriue . . . Downe from the waste they are Centaures, though Women all aboue: but to the Girdle do the Gods inherit, beneath is all the Fiends. There's hell, there's darkenes, there is the sulphurous pit; burning, scalding, stench, consumption. . . .

Centaurs, says one critic, that's a happy image for Goneril and Regan: 'these free minds unburdened by any conventional or traditional allegiances become slaves to the uncontrolled animal desire, mechanisms for the attainment of irrational objectives.' Yet when I lay Lear's outburst and this critical comment alongside the little scene between Edmund and Goneril, I feel something of the shock Professor G. Wilson Knight received when he asked himself where his sympathies lay between Hamlet and his uncle as the latter was struggling to pray and the former licking his lips at the thought of the King's possible damnation. We don't forget for a moment that the couple are immoral, but is the word *animal* right for this exchange:

> —           This trustie Seruant
> Shall passe between vs; ere long you are like to heare
> (If you dare venture in your owne behalfe)
> A Mistresses command. Weare this; spare speech,
> Decline your head. This kisse, if it durst speake
> Would stretch thy Spirits vp into the ayre:
> Conceiue, and fare thee well.
> —Yours in the rankes of death . . .?

I cannot believe that this was written to provoke a dirty snigger. On the contrary, I would claim for it a power to exhilarate such as could be got from the Ruritanian novels of my childhood or the adulteries of the Round Table. After all, Edmund has real advantages over Albany, which do not need a depraved eye to discover. Something noble is suggested by

> Oh, the difference of man, and man,
> To thee a Womans seruices are due,
> My Foole vsurpes my body.

Yet Goneril is a voice of very limited authority. If by using her eyes we see Albany as milk-livered and a moral eunuch, we cannot refuse to hear him as a representative of that foolish, superstitious popular morality which within its limits has something genuine to say. Lady Macbeth *was* a fiend-like queen: Goneril *is* a fiend. Yet again, don't we escape from reality by such language and miss the mystery of things? Isn't it childish to find the finger of God just where poetic justice expects it? Isn't it it to put the human clock back to see God at work in Cornwall's death? I shall be protesting in due course against critics who see special point in the *brevity* of Edmund's career. The following does not seem to be the point of the play, the voice of authority:

> This shewes you are aboue
> You Iustices, that these our neather crimes
> So speedily can venge.

Shakespeare having once resolved on a limited conception of the evil of the 'bad' characters, felt free to endow them with 'good' aspects. In the face of the extravagances of moralising critics I am prepared to find the villains providing us with comic relief. I have in mind that admirable little scene between Regan and Oswald. It is presumably idle to play with the speculation that Shakespeare occasionally yielded to the temptation to make fun of real contemporaries. But if we consider Oswald's part as a whole, we can see how it lends itself to mild farce. And in this scene we have the repetitions of 'madam' . . . I break off short, however, since his final scene is marred for me in the same way as the preceding fall of Gloucester by Shakespeare's weighting things in favour of Edgar. Was it necessary that Oswald's skull should prove so easy to smash with a mere ballow? If we are getting into one part of Shakespeare's mind by seeing Oswald's would-be villainy as laughable, we are prevented from taking Edgar at his own valuation when after committing murder (when all that was needed was to knock hard on Oswald's sword hand and clout his backside and the coward would have dropped his packet and run for his life) the moral exquisite is only troubled in conscience about the propriety of peeping into a letter not addressed to himself. We may ask ourselves how many degrees he is removed from Cornwall consigning the slave's body to the dunghill when he says

heere, in the sands
Thee Ile rake vp, the poste vnsanctified
Of murtherous Letchers

or from Hamlet when he replied to Horatio's remark

So *Guildensterne* and *Rosincrance*, go too't

with

Why man, they did make loue to this imployment
They are not neere my Conscience.


The unsophisticated reader (the ideal figure, who has been untouched by or who has emerged unscathed from academic criticism) may complain of an artificial impartiality in this attempt to weigh the claims of other would-be authoritative voices against the two infinitely more important centres of Lear and Cordelia. Matters central to and crucial for the play now occur in rapid succession. So far as I know, they do not call for much discussion. We must simply look and feel as people have always looked and felt and we recognize the immeasurable greatness of Shakespeare at his best. They are also scenes that take a lot out of us, that we must brace ourselves to live through. For this reason I should like to protest against any attempt to diminish the *horror*. It was fearful in the third act to see Lear's wits beginning to unsettle, it is appalling to recognize that he is now completely ruined. The governing picture is that Cordelia gives us:

Alacke, 'tis he: why he was met euen now
As mad as the vext Sea, singing alowd,
Crown'd with ranke Fenitar, and furrow weeds,
With Hardokes, Hemlocke, Nettles, Cuckoo flowres,
Darnell, and all the idle weedes that grow
In our sustaining Corne.

This is a powerful picture of a state from which there can never be complete recovery. Cordelia was asking for a miracle when she prayed,

O you kind Gods!
Cure this great breach in his abused Nature,
Th' vntun'd and iarring senses, O winde vp,
Of this childe-changed Father.

Lear is as appalling a spectacle in his way as Hamlet was to Ophelia:
STL H

> O what a Noble minde is heere o're-throwne?
> The Courtiers, Soldiers, Schollers: Eye, tongue, sword . . .
> . . . I . . .
> Now see that Noble, and most Soueraigne Reason,
> Like sweet Bels iangled out of tune, and harsh . . .
> > Oh woe is me,
> T'haue seene what I haue seene: see what I see.

Shakespeare presents us with two forms of Lear's distress. One is of
ordinary delusion: actions and thoughts pass through his mind in a kind
of private drama. In a modern play those would be the central thing, and
we should be expected to piece the scraps together like amateur psy-
chiatrists. Shakespeare was obviously interested in psychiatry and we
must not dismiss these glimpses. They suggest that Lear had been a more
interesting figure than he ever showed himself to us while sane. We discover a Lear wide-awake to practical life, like a vigorous snapping hun-
ting-dog[1]: a swaggering fellow, quick on the draw, who relishes both his
own physical strength and political power. He is proud of his terrible
glare

> When I do stare, see how the Subiect quakes . . .

and there is terrible glee in his plan to sneak up on his sons-in-law

> Then kill, kill, kill, kill, kill, kill.

Through these fragments we get what we could not obtain from the
opening of the play, a flash-back to a vigorous, passionate youth. (There
is blind Cupid, too.)

The second aspect, and the greater, of Lear's madness is the fouling of
the imagination. I take the phrase from Hamlet:

> > my Imaginations are as foule
> As Vulcans Stythe.

These are the remarks that are called *Reason in Madnesse*: they are maddeningly coherent and meant to have their own direct effect on the audience. Two different views have been taken of these speeches. One is that
the fouled imagination is Shakespeare's not Lear's, the other is that the
speeches are of great importance for uncovering the central meaning of
the play. I think the critical path lies in resisting both and taking something from them. I should not wish to force alternatives, but I certainly

---

[1] And so, looking back, we are less astonished by his stamina and physical prowess
in extreme old age.

do not find myself using these tirades to explain what had been pressing on Lear's mind at any period of his life. He seems to be rather in the position of a prophet for whom madness had been a revelation of painful general truths. The general formula appears to be this: there are certain truths about life which, if they were the whole truth, would break our hearts or drive us mad. As long as we think they are the whole truth, life on earth is hell. To recover sanity is to see, or at least believe, that they are partial.

> O the mind, mind has mountains: cliffs of fall
> Frightful, sheer, no-man-fathomed. Hold them cheap
> May who ne'er hung there. Nor does long our small
> Durance deal with that steep or deep.

If such thoughts got a hold over us, we could not attend to any play. Although we escape from the worst because we do not know whether they are actually tormenting Lear as they would a sane man, although we are not *obliged* to see only these truths, yet they strike at us and appal us since they seem to come from the greatest depth touched on so far in the play. They make what was merely fantastic in the storm scenes a grim reality.

All this helps us to say with conviction that whatever else Cordelia is— and enormous claims have been made for her—she is that which makes for unity and sense in the play, she is that which opposes the general drift toward hopelessness and chaos. For the last time, when we think how successful Shakespeare was in dramatising her, we note with surprise that Shakespeare has written a stilted and formal scene of preparation. I don't know why Kent is made to speak so stiffly to the courtier: 'Did your letters pierce the queene to any demonstration of griefe? . . . Made she no verball question?' We are made to endure some insufferable conceits of which the worst is

> As pearles from diamonds dropt. . . .

Yet the human note prevails. Hope springs up when we learn that Lear is in a state where love might be able to operate. Lear, we are told,

> . . . some time in his better tune remembers,
> What we are come about, and by no meanes
>       will yeeld to see his daughter. . .
> A soueraigne shame so elbows him his own vnkindnes
> That stript her from his benediction turnd her
> To forraine casualties gaue her deare rights
> To his dog-harted daughters, these things sting his mind
> So venomously that burning shame detaines him from *Cordelia*.

The preparation scene does, however, give us a true foretaste of what we see when Cordelia appears. She is, in a way, a formal figure, hard to reconcile with the daughter of our memories. She is evidently a power, and what is noteworthy is that her power is in league with nature rather than with heaven. Cordelia's view of Lear is much narrower than ours and we are now forced by her to see Lear as a lost child of nature. Her first concern is for Lear's health. These remarks become more pointed when we contrast the medical view of Lear's lunacy with that of Lady Macbeth. Her doctor was much less hopeful of being the right man for the job:

> More needs she the Diuine, then the Physitian:
> God, God forgiue vs all.

And when Macbeth asks him,

> Can'st thou not Minister to a minde diseas'd,
> Plucke from the Memory a rooted Sorrow,
> Raze out the written troubles of the Braine,
> And with some sweet Obliuious Antidote
> Cleanse the stufft bosome, of that perillous stuffe
> Which weighes vpon the heart?

he gives the gloomy reply:

> Therein the Patient
> Must minister to himselfe.

But what Shakespeare has most prepared us for is the intimate association between the good natural forces and Cordelia's *tears*:

> All blest Secrets,
> All you vnpublish'd Vertues of the earth
> Spring with my teares . . .

which cancels the Gentleman's frigid formality:

> there she shooke
> The holy water from her heauenly eyes.

The scene closes with the central point: Cordelia is not essentially august benevolence but love: that is the healing and restoring power.

The wonderful meeting between father and daughter is the place where above all I feel like Hazlitt. Here we see the whole action for the first time through the eyes of love. Where all is so moving, it is hard to decide if there is one thing that ought to stand out. Is it Cordelia's failure to effect the cure she wishes that moves us most? Or is the deepest note

that Lear cannot really meet his daughter? I am full of wonder at seeing
Cordelia able to find her way back and say the words she could not bring
out when commanded. As she finds her way back, she helps us to find
ours. If I were asked what human speech were like when perfect, I should
choose her lines, for there we have the keen delicate touch of true feeling
missing nothing.

> Had you not bene their father these white flakes,
> Did challenge pitie of them. Was this a face
> To be opposed against the warring winds,
> To stand against the deepe dread bolted thunder,
> In the most terrible and nimble stroke
> Of quick crosse lightning to watch poore *Perdu*,
> With this thin helme? Mine Enemies dogge,
> Though he had bit me, should haue stood that night
> Against my fire. And wast thou faine poore father,
> To houill thee with swine and rogues forlorne,
> In short and mustie straw, alack, alack,
> Tis wonder that thy life and wits at once
> Had not concluded all. . .

And what a rush of joy comes when Lear finds the only right way left to
him![1] Lear does more for Cordelia and Kent than they can do for him.
They are enabled to express love and reverence, Lear can only express his
loss. But he lays hold on something that is as near reality as he can get and
as near as he will get until the end of the play, when he loses all:

> Pray you now forget, and forgiue,
> I am old and foolish.

The note of wonder is as confining as it is enlarging. It seems as if the
condition of possessing one ultimate in this play—love—is that it shall
for ever remain a mystery. Consequently the scene that in one sense cen-
tralises the play remains in another a thing apart. The critic's duty,
therefore, is never to lose sight of these two senses; constantly to respond
to their opposing tugs. Although in an earlier chapter I took it upon myself to deprecate the use of *King Lear* for edification, no mind that could

---

[1] It is a pity that we do not see people on their knees on all the occasions, from the
merely formal to the deepest and most solemn, as any Elizabethan or Jacobean would.
We can get the feel of the occasion from the words, but it would help if we had their
memories, for we must believe that more than kind thoughts passed to and fro when
one human being knelt to be blessed or forgiven.

not expand in the spirit of Professor L. C. Knights's remarks on what love
meant to him in this play could deserve to be called critical. Similarly, I
admire Bradley's generosity of spirit, which made him confess that he
wanted the play to end, if not here, at least in keeping with the feelings
aroused by this scene:

> Doubtless we are right when we turn with disgust from Tate's sentimental
> alterations, from his marriage of Edgar and Cordelia, and from that cheap
> moral which every one of Shakespeare's tragedies contradicts, 'that Truth
> and Virtue shall at last succeed'. But are we so sure that we are right when we
> unreservedly condemn the feeling which prompted these alterations, or at all
> events the feeling which beyond question comes naturally to many readers of
> *King Lear* who would like Tate as little as we? What they wish, though they
> have not always the courage to confess it even to themselves, is that the
> deaths of Edmund, Goneril, Regan and Gloster should be followed by the
> escape of Lear and Cordelia from death, and that we should be allowed to
> imagine the poor old King passing quietly in the home of his beloved child to
> the end which cannot be far off. Now, I do not dream of saying that we ought
> to wish this, so long as we regard *King Lear* simply as a work of poetic
> imagination. But if *King Lear* is to be considered strictly as a drama, or
> simply as we consider *Othello*, it is not so clear that the wish is unjustified. In
> fact I will take my courage in both hands and say boldly that I share it, and
> also that I believe Shakespeare would have ended his play thus had he
> taken the subject in hand a few years later, in the days of *Cymbeline* and the
> *Winter's Tale*.[1]

Yet the play does not so end, and the organising and unifying power of
this scene is thereby curtailed.

*          *          *

If we now look back on the experience of the fourth act, as an ideal
spectator might if it were followed by an *entr'acte*, I would be content if
there were agreement that the predominant feeling of trouble is not
deeper than might be expected with one further act of resolution still to
come. But a full experience of the fifth act must, I would argue, bring the
conviction that the play has permanently split into two parts, one of which
is so bad that it cannot be seriously attended to. (In saying this I am
ignoring what is generally conceded, that nobody could recapitulate the
plot after a single sitting through the act.) This last act is full of stuff
which varies from the merely dull through the ludicrous to the mildly
distasteful. It also contains some very poor writing, of a kind that makes

[1] *Shakespearean Tragedy*, pp. 251–252.

it hard to believe that Shakespeare felt himself deeply engaged. For an analogy of my general impression I would therefore offer 'a fine cathedral surrounded by slums'.

To leave matters in those terms, however, would mean, for a minority view, that it would expire in the desert air. To ask for a patient hearing would be to treat the majority view with graceless contempt. For what common features could the experiences of those final scenes have if the verdict at the end is to find room for both 'a pattern in which all the elements come together in a supremely satisfying way' and 'a fine cathedral surrounded by slums'? Since the main object of these chapters is to bring out what can be shared in our experience of the play, I am faced with an apparent absurdity, to put it in the most favourable light for me. I think, however, that my eirenic purposes can be achieved. Firstly, although I am about to try to support two propositions which run counter to views put forward very persuasively by critics such as Bradley and Derek Traversi, my arguments do not presuppose any gulf of *general* disagreement. I admire and to the limits of my capacity share in all the values they appeal to. Both critics are always saying things that command my respect. That I believe they fail to speak for all where they fail to speak for me doesn't lessen the interest of their championing a 'moral pattern' or a 'redeemed' Lear. If these views are imperfectly supported by the play, they at least do credit to the minds that conceived them.

Secondly, I should not have used these words 'minority' and 'majority' so loosely. Is it not the fact rather that *nobody* has sat through the last act without *some* qualms over the disparity of its constituent elements? Here I would appeal confidently to the readers of Professor Muir's introduction to his Arden edition of the play: is there not in every theatre-goer a potential Bradley who would smile at Professor Muir's confidence (see pages xlviii-li) that he could afford to treat the real Bradley as relatively incompetent to report on even an ideal stage performance? The truth, if we could know it, might well turn out to be that there is some incoherence in this last act, but for a number of people, representing an opinion which at least overlaps with the ideal common judgement of our day, that incoherence does not deserve to be called radical.

Thirdly, we could do with some precise language about what does or does not constitute a 'moral pattern'. Although I should like all reputable authors to sign a ten-year agreement to abstain from using the word 'pattern', I do not find its use objectionable in the series of articles on *King Lear* by D. A. Traversi printed in *Scrutiny* in Volume XIX (1952). What makes it a pleasure to take these articles as a target of criticism is that Mr Traversi, unlike many critics who find themselves discussing the

play as if the last act contained the answers to the many moral perplexi-
ties raised in the minds of spectators of the preceding four acts, would
not be indifferent to the charge that the last act was not what Shelley
called the whole, 'the most perfect specimen of the dramatic art existing
in the world'. For if I have understood Mr. Traversi's general position,
his moral pattern is first of all a matter of *poetry*, and therefore even a mild
excursion into literary criticism, if it brought the conviction that the act
contained bad writing, would compel him to readjust his verdict on the
pattern. It is therefore of general interest to ask whether Mr. Traversi so
badly wanted that pattern to come out that he was willing to mark up very
bad writing and treat it on the same level as the best. (The impartial
reader is referred to *Scrutiny*, Vol. XIX page 213, where he will find Mr.
Traversi's favourable commentary on the passage ending

> As pearls from diamonds dropp'd.)


Here is one of the places I had in mind when accusing people of over-
collaboration with the author and supplying the significance he had
failed to give. The wicked characters in this act seem to me to be mere
stage villains and their downfall pure melodrama. They are not people we
can be concerned with or concerned for. Looking back I will grant that in
claiming to find them amusing in the fourth Act I was really saying that I
had detached myself from them or that they had ceased for me to stand
for anything significant. Are there not signs in this fifth Act that Shakespeare himself was deliberately diminishing their stature? Everybody, I
hope, would agree that the critic has got the proportions badly wrong if
he attributes an intensity of feeling matching that caused by Iago's

> From this time forth, I neuer will speake word

to Goneril's

> Aske me not what I know.

But would there be as wide agreement that Regan's lewd approaches to
her fancy man are comically incongruous?

> —Tell me but truly, but then speake the truth,
>    Do you not loue my Sister?
> —In honour'd Loue.
> —But haue you neuer found my Brothers way
>    To the fore-fended place?
> —That thought abuses you.

It will surely be granted that Edmund's reflections on the sisters do nothing to raise their status or his:

> To both these Sisters haue I sworne my loue:
> Each iealous of the other, as the stung
> Are of the Adder. Which of them shall I take?
> Both? One? Or neither?

Mere numbers cannot decide critical questions, but I should certainly like some samples of actual theatre experience to estimate whether everybody registers the lurch into incongruity and melodrama when Albany says,

> *Edmund*, I arrest thee
> On capitall Treason.

What is language like this, which might have passed in *The life and death of King Richard the Second*, doing at the climax of *The Tragedie of King Lear?*

> I protest,
> Maugre thy strength, place, youth, and eminence,
> Despite thy victor-Sword, and fire new Fortune,
> Thy valor, and thy heart, thou art a Traitor:
> False to thy Gods, thy Brother, and thy Father,
> Conspirant 'gainst this high illustrious Prince,
> And from th' extremest vpward of thy head,
> To the discent and dust below thy foote,
> A most Toad-spotted Traitor.

What offends me more than this absurd bombast is the wrong decision Shakespeare gave in the knightly ordeal. But to justify that remark I have to appeal to something that I may be accused of supplying—the logic of the play, what has been the upshot of all the scenes we have sat through. Since this involves me in a plain condemnation of a twist Shakespeare gave to his own play, I seem to be in the awkward position of claiming to know better than the author which was his stronger side and which his weaker. The reader might therefore prefer to hear a commentary which finds the 'philosophy' of the play exemplified in Edgar's triumph. Here is Mr. Traversi's formulation:

The last Act . . . brings the two actions, the personal and the political, finally together. . . . For all [Edmund's] self-confidence . . . the forces which are shortly to combine to undo . . . [him] are already gathering for the final resolution. Chief among them, and in accordance with the 'philosophy' prevailing in the play, is the passion which he has roused in each of the two sisters. . . . [Edmund] is playing with forces which he does not understand, but which bear within themselves the seeds of their own disintegration and will therefore destroy him. The capacity of irrational and predatory desire to exercise a decisive influence upon political events is something which Edmund . . . fails to allow for; so . . . is the deference to the claims of conscience . . . Behind both these forces, which are on the point of slipping finally out of the control which Edmund still believes he can impose upon them, lies, as the instrument of final vengeance, the disguised Edgar, already associated with the 'trumpet sound' which is to announce the final 'arbitrament'. That Edmund himself still believes that he can play off one against the other the two sisters . . . is, in the long run, part of the blindness which underlies his practical capacity. . . . He has still to learn that the forces he has helped to raise are greater than he can hope to control, and that they will, in the hour of apparent success, bring about his downfall.

In the face of this, I am inclined to protest that what brings about Edmund's downfall is not so much any inner incapacity or failure to measure the forces in his exterior world as Shakespeare's deliberate decision to sacrifice him, to give Edgar yet another opportunity for cheap moralising:

> The Gods are iust, and of our pleasant vices
> Make instruments to plague vs:
> The darke and vitious place where thee he got,
> Cost him his eyes.

No doubt I should instantly be challenged to name one other eccentric beside myself if I said that *we* have been longing for somebody to wring Edgar's neck. But even when we dwell on all that is noble in Edgar's moral *suffisance*, must we not admit that the play would have been more satisfactory if Edgar had been taught, like all the 'good' characters, a lesson appropriate to himself, that it is nonsense to suppose that

> My strength is as the strength of ten,
> Because my heart is pure.

Yet I would rather abandon this thought if by doing so I could lead the reader to ask himself whether accepting Edgar's voice as authoritative does not result in falsifying the play. Here, at any rate, is how Mr. Traversi continues:

In the moment of death . . . and faced by the revelation of his brother's identity . . . [Edmund] too in his own way admits, as never before, subjection to the prevailing pattern. To Edgar's affirmation that the gods are 'just' and that Gloucester's punishment . . . has been the consequence of his original reversal of 'natural' ties, he replies with a gesture of acquiescence:

> The wheel is come full circle, I am here

In this admission, the political and the personal processes, which seem so far to have developed on parallel lines, are at last brought together. 'The dark and vicious place' in which Edmund was 'unnaturally' begot brought the father in due course to blindness and his bastard son, in the very moment that should have been that of his triumph, to his fall. The action of the 'wheel' of fortune, genuinely if mysteriously impelled by the 'gods', covers the whole of human life and to it the successful adventurer is not less subject than the betrayed and erring father. Relief from the sense of enslavement to circumstance which this recognition seems to imply must be preceded by due acceptance of this subjection to a universal process.

This seems to me to be making a virtue of a weakness in the play. Certainly, if this were the true account, I should not place *King Lear* very high among the world's tragedies. Secondly, it seems to be confusing all the issues it takes up. Where in the play is it said that Fortune is under control and the gods turn her wheel? Which of the 'good' characters decides that submission to Fortune is the condition of relief from the sense of enslavement to circumstance?

> My selfe could else out-frowne false Fortunes frowne.

*       *       *

Cordelia leaves us as a brave and sensibly-balanced woman. Lear is obviously less than this. When he comes in with her, he seems partly to be fixed in the state in which we last saw him and partly in one of the phases of his earlier madness. The beauty of the one state may blind us to the fact of the other, a fact which prevents us, I am convinced, from sharing in Bradley's view of how we should take the end of the play. However difficult it is to speak of Lear *knowing* anything now, we must say that he has got hold of something — the point of Cordelia's reappearance. It is true that his vision is selfish, for it is only as it concerns himself that he can, like characters in Pirandello's play, live over and over again one wonderful moment:

> When thou dost aske me blessing, Ile kneele downe
> And aske of thee forgiuenesse.

He never recovers the initial insight of the opening of the play, when he

knew that the condition of having Cordelia's company for the rest of his
life must be that he became her child.

It would be a stern moralist indeed who would condemn the passion
that breaks out in

> He that parts vs, shall bring a Brand from Heauen,
> And fire vs hence, like Foxes . . .

Yet I think we must ask what is the glee that inspires these lines:

> So wee'l liue,
> And pray, and sing, and tell old tales, and laugh
> At gilded Butterflies: and heere poore Rogues
> Talke of Court newes, and wee'l talke with them too,
> Who looses, and who wins; who's in, who's out;
> And take vpon's the mystery of things,
> As if we were Gods spies: And wee'l weare out
> In a wall'd prison, packs and sects of great ones,
> That ebbe and flow by th' Moone.

In bringing out the answer it may help to have the following lines before
us from a different play:

> Sir, to a wise man, all the world's his soile.
> It is not *Italie*, nor *France*, nor *Europe*,
> That must bound me, if my *Fates* call me forth.
> Yet, I protest, it is no salt desire
> Of seeing *Countries*, shifting a *Religion* . . .
> . . . hath brought me out; much lesse,
> That idle, antique, stale, grey-headed proiect
> Of knowing mens mindes, and manners, with *Vlisses* . . .

(I omit a passage dealing in detail with court news. The play continues:)

> —It seemes, Sir, you know all?
> —          Not all, Sir. But,
> I haue some generall notions; I doe loue
> To note, and to obserue: though I liue out,
> Free from the actiue torrent, yet I'ld marke
> The currents, and the passages of things,
> For mine owne priuate vse; and know the ebbes,
> And flowes of *State*.

I am not suggesting that Lear speaks exactly like Politique Would-Bee
in *Volpone* but that this plan is not that of a man in a 'blessed' or 'resur-

rected' state. It does not seem compatible with his good self but rather to be preparing us for Lear's last burst of savagery, when he kills the man who hanged Cordelia.

\* \* \*

If I have had to suffer throughout this commentary from the invidiousness of the task of reducing the stature commonly allotted to the play, when we come to the very last moments I feel the exhilaration of enjoying (if that's the word) and approving every trait of Lear's behaviour. So I weigh and relish, as in keeping with the whole play, Lear's having the leisure to contemplate complacently his bloody vengeance:

> I haue seene the day, with my good biting Faulchion
> I would haue made him skip.

For me the play ends with a particular; the final experience is *exclusively* of Lear and his dead daughter. We forget the slums when we sight the cathedral. The gods become trash the moment

> The Gods defend her

is followed by '*Enter Lear with Cordelia in his armes.*' (I did not think they could survive our instant rejection of Albany's earlier remark on the production of the corpses of the two elder sisters:

> This iudgement of the Heauens, that makes vs tremble.)

At any rate in the rest of his part, Albany, along with all the other characters, makes no mention of gods.

We have no eyes or ears for the prattling of the half-men who interrupt our vision of Lear moving finally out of play-acting into the real. There is the paradox: to call real what is in no ordinary sense the inevitable, since it had to be manipulated. It certainly does not seem to be an answer to the question, what is man? The very reasons that would lead us to reject the extreme view that everything comes together in a satisfactory way bar us from the complementary view that Lear's end suggests that everything is for the worst in this vale of tears. What is compelled on me by repeated returns at well-spaced-out intervals is that the couple seem real just in proportion as they have power to rivet our eyes and feelings. We rage if we are asked to turn aside. At least I felt myself protesting when I found Professor Knights saying: 'But the question, ultimately, is not what Lear sees but what Shakespeare sees. . . . At the end . . . we are still concerned with nothing less than the inclusive vision of the whole. . . .' Yet, gauchely as I have no doubt occasionally expressed myself, it is not part of my case that I *know* whereas Professor Knights merely opines! In concluding with some personal remarks I nevertheless offer them to the open forum. Doesn't the text sharply point to such a dismissive ending as I have been describing? Is it not significantly blank? Can we seriously maintain that it is as hopefully forward-looking as the end of *Macbeth*? Mr. Traversi strangely omits to comment on the last words of the play, which I take it find their point in

> The oldest hath borne most.

The silence of all on the stage when Lear dies should itself have sufficed to dismiss as an intrusive quirk of fancy the conjecture that Lear dies of joy or in bliss or has a death in any way like Gloucester's, as reported by Edgar. But I would rather stress the inherent rightness of this death as making sense of the play. It seems to me the right solution to have pushed Lear to the only worst he could know in his ruined state. The worst thing that could happen was the right thing: separation for ever from the only being he still had contact with. Lear thus dies in the real. We have had to wait a long time for it, but here is finality:

> she's gone for euer.
> I know when one is dead, and when one liues,
> She's dead as earth.

'We feel also that everything external has become nothingness to him.' I should like to tack on to this phrase of Bradley's, "how savagely Lear dismisses mankind and all mortality!" Bradley seems to think of Lear's mind as blank when he is not contemplating Cordelia, but there is a continuous substance represented by:

> He'le strike and quickly too, he's dead and rotten.

Lear dies an obstinately unreconstructed rebel.

# Anthony and Cleopatra

# CHAPTER 1

# Angelic Strength – Organic Weakness?

THE acrimony which, every time I have tried them out in public, has regularly greeted most of the views that emerge in the next two chapters has been of a quality to tempt me not to let them go further forward into the rigidity of print. Not that I have as a consequence of sharp criticism wavered in the least in my conviction that first thoughts about this play might well be stimulated in response to the general conclusions summed up in my two chapter-heads. What has daunted me is rather that the acrimony has been aroused as much by the critic as by the critic's views. I have both heard and read accounts of myself that astonish me and make me renew Burns' famous prayer:

> O wad some Pow'r the giftie gie us
> To see oursels as others see us!

These accounts prove that I have failed to get out of the listener's and the reader's way, and, therefore, since I know I have become obtrusive, that I have a plain duty to make myself less opaque. So I will, in an effort to move in this direction, confess that, although I have mounted my counter-positions so as to dislodge and upset the critics I most admire, whose views I have generally been guided by, the man who was meant to be getting the most smarting punishment was always myself, and my chief hostile target was the body of impressions and verdicts I had been carrying with me during thirty years of contact with the play before I was made to take myself strictly in hand by the responsibility of joining in public discussion, as described in my introduction. What is more, I have only to relax slightly or to be caught a little off my guard to go under once again before the powerful spell which, I shall be suggesting, holds in thrall those who accuse me of desiccation and harshness. In many moods it still seems that the right, the generous, thing to do is to go along with Shakespeare's will, since the reader's imagination is filled with something more solid than wind when he yields to the suggestive language of the play. I do not think that the strength of Shakespeare's language in this play is less than an angel's, and I certainly have had a task which I hope it is neither ludicrous nor blasphemous—*toutes proportions gardées*—to compare to Jacob's to keep on top.

Furthermore, this strength of poetry cannot be isolated from another element in the whole experience. We are also under the spell of the two chief personages. Indeed, I do not know what a reading of this play can mean if it has not included submitting to every one of their moods and aspirations. A man should quietly drop out from the discussion who does not in imagination re-enact *with relish* all the follies and extravagances of the lovers. I would have every bawdy joke expounded, every indecent wrinkle unfolded, and every effort made to connect them with the sub-limities of the play. The world must be many times well lost for the spec-tator—however great the contradictions that are thereby set up. We might be well advised to read the play in the spirit of the Keats who wrote in a sonnet 'On sitting down to read *King Lear* once again':

> once again, the fierce dispute
> Betwixt damnation and impassion'd clay
> Must I burn through. . . .

But here I would say that, if the reader can take my word that I do feel and have felt for and with Anthony, he should leave me behind and look into the play for Shakespeare's adverse criticism of him; for I do not think that I am harder on him than the author. I am merely more consistent. My plea to the reader is to forget the critic if in this respect he gets in the way and to allow the text to have its *full* effect, or, after galloping along with some other critic who fancies he is travelling on the viewless wings of Poesy, to consider whether there are not clear signs of Shakespeare's own retarding action from the very first scene of the play.

On the other hand, I must not shrink from the odium of having found fault with *Anthony and Cleopatra*. In asking for fair play here I invite the reader to consider the following extract: 'The reader, if he surrenders himself to the play's spell, finds himself borne steadily onwards at a height of unqualified delight. . . . The impression left in his memory is of a har-monious radiance. . . .' If the reader has had an experience like mine of asking his friends whether anything of this sort happened when they were trying to be judicious spectators or reflecting readers, and getting a nega-tive answer, he may be curious to know what can have happened to make a man give such a uniformly enthusiastic report. It might then be reason-able to raise the question whether we need to make a distinction in read-ing this play comparable with that we make in life when contrasting deeds with words. And from there we might find ourselves reasonably and naturally proceeding to ask whether we must distinguish poetry that is dramatically effective from poetry that merely conditions or colours the sense of fact arising from the dramatic fiction. This in turn might bring on the question whether, if we aspire to the condition of common readers, we must not resist the 'spell' of the 'poetry' whenever it turns out that Shakespeare is substituting spell-binding for the manacling power of true drama.

The question that most concerns me in these chapters, whether the play is in any sense an organic whole, has been given a special twist by this struggle with the 'poetry', for the language in its suggestive play seems to offer us a prospect of discovering an organization like that of a poem. The following extract will give some idea of the claims that are made in the course of reading the play as if it were merely a poem:

> The poetry of Antony no longer turns, like that of even the later tragedies, upon a cleavage between 'good' and 'evil' within the unity of experience. It depends rather upon a perfect continuity between the 'flesh', with its associations of earth and death, and the transcendent justification of passion in terms of emotional value and vitality. This continuity is in no way vague or sentimental, but is splendidly realized in a harmonious scale of related imagery; to reconstruct this scale step by step is the critic's task in dealing with Antony.

I am taking it for granted that the reader will at once exclaim that there are other things we must do if we wish to have Anthony than to reconstruct a scale of imagery. I hope that he will include among the other things the old-fashioned considerations about Shakespeare's success in dramatising narrative materials, for it will be one of my main arguments that, whereas at times the play lapses into a none too glorified chronicle, Shakespeare at least began to work dramatically on the historical materials he had before him and at least in outline found a subject and so raised expectations like those we find gratified in *Macbeth*. My argument will be that in the play our expectations or some of them are not gratified, and that the 'line' Shakespeare took landed him in difficulties which he could only emerge from by magnificent subterfuges. I shall be obliged to contest the view that the final scenes of the play are like the Everest apex of a Himalayan range, and the claim made for the very last scene that 'The whole development of the play has moved consistently towards this point'.

\* \* \*

A strong argument in favour of the view that Shakespeare had more than a chronicle in mind is the power of the opening words of the play. Here we have a passage of a kind we meet with in the centre of other plays, when everything is growing to a point. This first scene has a clear function and a correspondingly clear structure; an observation is made in the form of a statement; the statement is corroborated immediately by an exemplary action, and to make the point clear, the statement is repeated. The function I take to be communication from author to audience of a point that will, as it is driven home in different ways, grow into the subject of the play. It is an undertaking that there will be a focus, a stress, even a selection from the many incidents that make up the chronicle.

The point of the scene, it seems to me, is to present Anthony in an unfavourable light rather than in two conflicting lights, one good, one bad. But here in the very opening of the play we meet with opposition and the debate about the whole play must be rehearsed over this first scene. Our play is unusual in presenting us with so much comment and so little dramatic action. More is said of and by the two chief characters than is ever performed by them. I should be exaggerating foolishly if I said that the hero and the heroine never act heroically but I would hope to argue successfully that the *extremes* of heroism are given to us in words rather than deeds. We can thus speak of Anthony and Cleopatra as having two existences. One is indubitable from the moment we lend ourselves to the dramatic fiction. We see with our own eyes, if the play is well performed, or judge in full possession of the facts. But from the beginning of the play there is a shadowy alternative of imputed being which threatens towards the end of the play to juggle us out of our sense of the real. Part of the critical task is to assess at each moment the relation of substance to shadow, and to decide when what is thrown out as a possibility is embodied in a dramatic actuality.

For our debate the most important things said about the two chief personages are those which go beyond anything that could be said of any human beings, however heroic. Of the instances in this first scene we have to ask whether they blend, or form an extension continuous with, the human beings we see before us or whether they remain as spots of oil on water. Later on, the crucial and painful question will arise: what are we to think if we suppose the author meant us to take them in one of these ways and we feel forced to take them in the other? The first of such phrases would hardly arrest our attention in the fiercer interest of what is going on, but might well be used by us when we are going over the experience of the play:

> those his goodly eyes
> That o're the Files and Musters of the Warre,
> Haue glow'd like plated Mars . . .

Grammatically, it is true, his eyes are merely *compared* to the god in armour, but the god-like fire passes back and would turn Anthony at the very least into a demi-god of war (something of a higher order of being than that of a great general at a moment of intense dignity and power, performing his proper function) as soon as it could combine with the right dramatic material. But if we are considering this scene again, as we are made to do later on when the question of

> that great Property
> Which still should go with *Anthony*

comes up for final judgement, we may prefer to fall back on the suggestions of

> His Captaines heart,
> Which in the scuffles of great fights hath burst
> The Buckles on his brest

which bring us into overwhelming intimacy with the man both as a spirit and as a body. Yet if we do so, it will not be on poetical grounds but on our judgement of what has been made good in the course of the action. We are therefore driven to distinguish good poetry from good dramatic poetry. It seems to me characteristic of this play that the best poetic bits are not dramatically anchored. And if this example is too slight and questionable to take as a first instance there is a more obvious case later in the first Act. Everyone admires the passage beginning

> When thou once
> Was beaten from *Modena*. . .

—and those who have read North have grounds for even greater admiration. Yet what does this passage do for the play? We are obliged to accept it as one of the preliminary 'facts' and we may (though I would not) reflect on the person who can so command our language and make this observation, yet does it accompany us through the play like the first intimations of Macbeth's soldierly qualities? Would it figure in our epitaph over the freshly-fallen hero? Can we resist the suggestion that it intrigued Shakespeare because he found it in North, and do we then suppose that he never bothered whether it was going to figure in his final creation of the 'sworder'?

*Sed nunc non erat his locus.* The question to be settled here and now is the import of Philo's judgement:

> —Take but good note, and you shall see in him
> (The triple Pillar of the world) transform'd
> Into a Strumpets Foole.

It is not that Anthony has debased himself by falling in love with a female Othello, but that he has become the professional clown, the hired entertainer of a courtesan—something less than her fancy man. Precisely what Shakespeare meant by 'fool' is immediately shown on the stage. 'Behold and see', says Philo, and we see it. What we see is an exchange between a woman and her clown like that between Desdemona and Iago while they are waiting for Othello's ship to come in. There Iago is set the clown's task to discuss in a witty form the topic: how should a woman be praised? So here Anthony has just been asked to show his paces on the topic: how to measure love?

This is not how the critics see it. A representative figure once commented on the lines

> CLEO. If it be Loue indeed, tell me how much.
> ANT. There's beggery in the loue that can be reckon'd
> CLEO. Ile set a bourne how farre to be belou'd.
> ANT. Then must thou needes finde out new Heauen, new Earth.

'Their first words express the essence of romantic love, a tacit contradiction of all that Philo seems to have just suggested.' Leaving aside for the moment the implication that Cleopatra is being presented as just as infatuated as Anthony claims to be, it is surely a fair argument to ask the reader to reflect on the time, manner and place of these remarks. Since I am appealing to a natural reaction I will go somewhat far afield to illustrate what I take to be the norm. There is a passage in Stendhal's novel *Le Rose et le Vert* where the heroine, Mina, is surrounded by several suitors, *tous parlant sensibilité profonde et sentiments intimes*, which provokes the following conversation among three women of sense:

> —Ces messieurs, dit Mina à sa mère, n'ont même pas appris que la sensibilité a sa pudeur.
> —Tout homme qui raconte son amour, dit Madame de Strombek, par cela même prouve qu'il ne sent pas l'amour et n'est mû que par la vanité.

I am not here forgetting the 'conventions' (as they are called) of the stage, nor that Anthony was reported by Plutarch to be a gifted orator.[1]

Whether or not Anthony actually blushes, it seems clear that Cleopatra's taunts reveal a head free from romantic nonsense and respect for

---

[1] Indeed it seems to the point to bring in here Plutarch's comment, as it appears in North:

He vsed a manner of phrase in his speeche, called Asiatik, which caried the best grace and estimation at that time, and was much like to his manners and life: for it was full of ostentation, foolish brauerie, and vaine ambition.

Anthony. Anthony, however, in a sense rises to the occasion and covers up his unawareness of the realities of his situation whether political, moral or amorous by giving us a specimen of the grand nonsense he can spout in the lines beginning

> Let Rome in Tyber melt. . .

It is exactly what Cleopatra tells the audience it is: excellent falsehood, first-class rhetoric; that is to say, if we stop to look at the lines we find them wanting in intelligent grip and consequently judge that Anthony is still making an ass of himself; he is now merely garlanding his ass's head with flowers. And just as Desdemona distances herself from her fool and tells us

> I am not merry; but I do beguile
> The thing I am, by seeming otherwise . . . ,

so Cleopatra dissociates herself from Anthony by telling us (though she no doubt means her fool to overhear),

> Ile seeme the Foole I am not. Anthony will be himselfe.

The further point in the demonstration:

> There's not a minute of our liues should stretch
> Without some pleasure now. What sport to night?

seems unambiguous. But though the charge against Anthony seems to be grounded, the case is opened, not closed. For there is a possibility that Anthony may come to his senses and the turn of the phrase:

> I am full sorry, that hee approues the common
> Lyar, who thus speakes of him at Rome . . .

delivers us from the necessity of identifying ourselves with Rome when we dwell on Anthony's faults. We are perhaps given a hint that the Romans may not be fit to pass a final judgement.

\*       \*       \*

I register a drop in firmness in the next two scenes. I feel that Shakespeare could easily have deepened them or made them more pointed. Consequently, beyond quarrelling with those who are sure that we get a more definite lead, I have no points to make. We are at any rate moving forward in the direction indicated in the first scene. But the two principal characters seem only half awake. 'A Romane thought hath strooke him' is not adequate to what comes over Anthony. He is certainly now in a business mood and willing to attend to his duties. But, although the 'Asiatic' style is dropped and he has ceased to be an actor, he does not seem to be all there. There is certainly nothing god-like about him. In fact, at times, he is more like a commentary on himself than a real man:

> Speake to me home,
> Mince not the generall tongue, name
> *Cleopatra* as she is call'd in Rome:
> Raile thou in *Fuluia's* phrase, and taunt my faults
> With such full License, as both Truth and Malice
> Haue power to vtter. Oh then we bring forth weeds,
> When our quicke windes lye still, and our illes told vs
> Is as our earing . . .

And even more so here:

> I must from this enchanting Queene breake off,
> Ten thousand harmes, more then the illes I know
> My idlenesse doth hatch.

It may, of course, be in character: Anthony in the morning may be feeling like the heavy drinker who says, 'I really must cut down on the whiskey, it'll be the death of me.' We know how little such speeches mean.

My interest rises with the entry of Enobarbus. His prose makes me sit up more than Anthony's would-be judicious verse. It is prose of character. You feel that a man who can talk like this—on a restricted occasion, with obvious limits imposed on him—could enlarge wonderfully, given better circumstances. When an age can command wit such as this, it is in a finer condition than that of the years following the restoration of Charles II or the early years of the eighteenth century. What charms me most in this manner—which I like to fancy resembled Shakespeare's own—is that the wit is not like a corset or the smart uniform that goes over it. This wit does not mark a limit or set up one part of the mind over another. When this wit is in the saddle, the literary vices of the Elizabethans, the exuberant fancies and conceits, the over-intrusive moral apophthegm, give way to something far more imaginative. The excursus on dying is at any rate a great relief from the usual Shakespearian 'word-play'. I can't say what exactly it is I am enjoying, but I know it has to do with the passage from obvious sense to obvious play that we get, for instance, here: '*Cleopatra* catching but the least noyse of this, dies instantly: I haue seene her dye twenty times vppon farre poorer moment...'

There we have an aristocratic, an in every way more elegant Iago. Enobarbus, however, finishes his sentence like this: 'I do think there is mettle
in death, which commits some louing acte vpon her, she hath such a
celerity in dying.' I am not here thinking of the impression we all get
that this scene might have been composed just after Shakespeare had
finished the final scenes of the play, but of how the mind is led on further
than usual and below the hard protective surface of the man who apparently takes only a man's view of how women behave. It's a discreet subtlety
—far more palatable than the displayed subtlety of, say, Sir Thomas
Browne—and it's far too subtle for poor Anthony. It opens a vista: we
feel at once that Enobarbus could be drawn into other modes of considering the human body and soul, that he could bring insight and not merely
bawdy and fancy to bear. And this pleasant largeness I feel in Enobarbus
extends in another direction, for it encompasses the homely proverb. It is
always a sign of intelligence to know how to bring them in, as we see from
the poems of Horace and Chaucer: 'This greefe is crown'd with Consolation, your old Smocke brings foorth a new Petticoate, and indeed the
teares liue in an Onion, that should water this sorrow.'

The advantage gained by Shakespeare is that if he did indeed find his
historical matter hard to shape and so had to do much of the shaping
through commentary, he now had a commentator capable of saying for
him the highest and lowest things and a figure whose words we should
always attend to even if we had never heard of 'conventions' or 'choric
figures'. The immediate gain is to bring home to us how far Anthony
tolerates and so presumably in part shares what may be called the
Baconian view of women. Since this is one of the points that will be
growing as the play progresses, I draw attention to two of its aspects:
first, 'It were pitty to cast them away for nothing, though betweene them
and a great cause, they should be esteemed nothing . . .' and, second, the
implied appreciation in calling Cleopatra the sort of thing a traveller
should prize: 'Oh sir, you had then left vnseene a wonderfull peece of
worke, which not to haue beene blest withall, would haue discredited
your Trauaile.'

\*     \*     \*

Nothing is clear to me in the following dissembling scene between
Anthony and Cleopatra. The two characters themselves do not quite
know where they stand. Anthony may speak as if Cleopatra could command him, but somehow, from somewhere, he is free enough to get away
to deal with the emergency. But neither he nor she can ever speak out

honestly. Cleopatra looks for a moment as if she were going to drop play-acting, but her speech dissolves away:

> Courteous Lord, one word:
> Sir, you and I must part, but that's not it:
> Sir, you and I haue lou'd, but there's not it:
> That you know well, something it is I would:
> Oh, my Obliuion is a very *Anthony*,
> And I am all forgotten.

Cleopatra does not rise to the occasion like Dido, though Anthony sinks to the lameness of Aeneas. The toils are about them both: after this scene we cannot go on with any simple account of their relation. I don't find it helpful to think of Lady Macbeth, though there is a smack of her in these lines:

> Nay pray you seeke no colour for your going,
> But bid farewell, and goe:
> When you sued staying,
> Then was the time for words. . .

I can sum up my impression like this: I try to enter into the action but I am kept at a distance, forced to be merely a watcher, a reporter with an almost empty notebook. This stinted feeling may have been a stroke of art, particularly if Shakespeare had wanted to ensure that while we are taking in the events that are developing in Italy we shall be puzzling and repeating the question: what *is* the relation between Anthony and Cleopatra?

\*　　　\*　　　\*

The very favourable opportunities I have had in recent years of being present at discussions of this play have proved to me that statistically I am eccentric in the impression I regularly receive from pondering the fourth scene of the play. I have therefore worded my conviction of its function more emphatically than is compatible with good manners. But I do not have to ask for more than a temporary suspension of disbelief while I state a minority verdict. If the reader is convinced that its principal function is to give us insight into the character of Octavian, I can only beg him to consider the verse. I should be surprised if anyone faced with a few lines from this scene could distinguish one speaker from another. Every-one, I take it, would grant that the messengers speak with extraordinary power, more like principals than anonymous subordinates. Now, since we all imagine that to differentiate speakers by their style was almost second nature for Shakespeare, we should ask, particularly when he is bringing on two new personages for the first time, why they are not given more than a modicum of particular character. The answer, I suggest, might include the following thoughts: that Shakespeare was not intending to develop them into 'characters' at all or that he had some far more important business in hand which would suffer if the audience gave all their attention to making out the motives behind each speaker's remarks.

My conviction is that Shakespeare was inviting us to bring our intelligence to bear on what he has proposed as the subject of his play and to pause to bring some general considerations in to get our proportions right as we try to make up our minds and form a judgement on Anthony's conduct. I find it hard to characterise the special form of intelligence Shakespeare exhibits in this scene and so fall back on general words such as 'ordonnance' and 'grip'. It is blank verse without the smallest hindrance to dramatic expression. If we wrote it out as prose and then studied how to speak it best, where to put a slight stress, where to pause for longer or shorter intervals, a delicate blank verse pattern would emerge. Occasionally Shakespeare preferred the natural movement of prose to the iambic restraint, once at least with emphatic rightness. Is there a syllable wrong here?

> Hardly gaue audience
> Or vouchsafe to thinke he had Partners. You
> Shall finde there a man, who is th'abstracts of all faults,
> That all men follow.

The scene, then, seems to me in important respects like a similarly 'intellectual' scene in *Macbeth* where the function also seems to be to provide the standards we need when we try to assess the faults of a man 'in an imperial charge'. There we find the two leading thoughts we need when we are judging Anthony's intemperance, the comparative innocuousness of lust in a ruler:

> This Auarice
> Stickes deeper: growes with more pernicious roote
> Then Summer-seeming Lust . . .

and the grounds for condemning and fearing it:

> Boundlesse intemperance
> In Nature is a Tyranny.

This scene, then, has as its primary function to bring out the importance of a phrase in the first scene that might at first hearing have been passed over:

> reneages all temper.

We now hear the clear announcement of one of the main subjects of the play:

> As we rate Boyes, who being mature in knowledge,
> Pawne their experience to their present pleasure,
> And so rebell to judgement.

Nevertheless, admirable as this scene is, we have been treated to a bloodless, abstract way of looking at life. Even political *wisdom* sees passion from the outside; the temperature of passionate, inarticulate feeling in the common people is measured as it were with a thermometer and becomes:

> This common bodie,
> Like to a Vagabond Flagge vpon the Streame,
> Goes too, and backe, lacking the varrying tyde
> To rot it selfe with motion.

*   *   *

The next scene plunges us to the other extreme, to life seen near the quick of feeling. This switch seems to me the most potent hint so far in the play. Here is life as well as feeling and here is drama fully rounded. Although, as Bradley found when offering to lecture on Cleopatra, the decencies of the public platform clash with the demands Shakespeare makes on the imagination, yet I think the emphasis here is plain as we pass from the eunuch to the horse and to the recalls of Anthony, Caesar and Pompey, and so to the messengers unpeopling Egypt. All the commentators seem to find their account here. Shakespeare is wonderfully at home and at ease: all the possible aspects of Cleopatra are immediately and simultaneously present to him. The consequence for us is that our usual terms become at once too thin and too narrow to describe what we feel. We can all draw up a scale for love with something heavy at the lowest end, an undifferentiated ache, and with gradations mounting to feelings of rarefied intensity. But Cleopatra can't be fitted into such a scheme. She is an Ariel in the very evocation of what we are pleased to call the most earthly feelings. Is there one expression here we wish away? Here we have a surprisingly dramatic fulfilment of Anthony's remark in the 'prologue':

> Fye wrangling Queene:
> Whom euery thing becomes, to chide, to laugh,
> To weepe: who euery passion fully striues
> To make it selfe (in Thee) faire, and admir'd.

Who now wishes to 'name *Cleopatra* as she is call'd in Rome'? Yet though in a general way we can say that Shakespeare is proposing to arouse wonder and admiration, he is not proposing to disturb the moral categories or to set up Cleopatra alongside a Bérénice. But, granted these limitations, we have the promise of a large vista opening, the prospect of being made to combine things we usually keep separate and to separate what we normally combine.

*     *     *

Technical jargon is a great help to the university lecturer but almost as great a hindrance to the general reader. I was going to write: 'Shakespeare has now completed his *donnée*.' The word avoids any too explicit commitments and allows for all the complexity of dramatic composition. We have suffered too much from abuse of the word 'theme' for me to rescue it and re-apply it. 'Subject' seems too blunt and narrow. We can at least say that Shakespeare has kept an implicit promise to work on the chronicle material so that our interest is concentrated on one happening among the many things that happened. What he has done is also promising and fills us with expectations. I have more than once found myself using the word 'vista' to suggest that one of them is an enlargement of our experience. Well, Cleopatra makes me open my eyes, but the presentation of 'top-level' goings-on in Rome doesn't. I am therefore obliged to ask whether the *donnée* now gets the kind of intense treatment and development that deepens our wonder by rapid extension of insight.

When I contemplate the emptiness of what follows Act I and fills the interval until Act III scene vii[1], I am bound to go further and ask whether Shakespeare found that he had landed himself in an impossible position and was genuinely 'stuck' and unable to progress. I had rather, however, put these questions from the other end, as it were, and ask the candid reader whether he can suppose that Act I was given the form it has in order that precisely *these* scenes should follow? I am not anxious to damn this interval too heavily. It won't do, for instance, to say that like Cleopatra we sleep out the gap between the end of Act I and the beginning of Act III scene vii. Rather would I ask the reader who feels that the play is a fully-worked-out dramatic poem, possesses organisation and a satisfactory structure, whether he feels that Shakespeare never puts a foot

[1] I have adopted the scene divisions of the Arden edition (1954, M. R. Ridley).

wrong and so can give an account of the necessity for everything being as we find it.

One of the expectations that is not fulfilled is that the play will turn into a tragedy. Looking back we can see the beginnings of an ominous decision in Lepidus' judgement:

His faults in him, seeme . . .
Hereditarie,
Rather then purchaste: what he cannot change,
Then what he chooses.

If this becomes a true account then Anthony is doomed from the start. This is a pity because we cannot be so involved with a man already fated to take a certain line as with one who is going to struggle before our eyes and we finally judge to have had fate as his adversary. The scenes of this 'gap' make clear that Anthony is never going to be so close to us as Macbeth. His temporary removal from Egypt is not used to give his whole nature a chance to come to a challenge. In fact I would say that he merely marks time and even *recedes* from us. We can only conjecture, for example, what he thought he was doing when he contracted marriage. I should also say that just as Anthony is not brought to an inward test, he is not faced with the full outward test, since the government of the world is seen consistently, as it were, down the wrong end of the telescope.

These are the chief but only some of the reasons why as I sit through these scenes in my imaginary theatre I find myself fidgeting and wishing that most of what I hear had been cut. I am certainly not 'borne steadily onwards' by a sense of the glorious inevitable rightness of everything that is put before me. And when feeling out for the considerations that might justify so much dissatisfaction I come upon two. The first is regret that Shakespeare did not give his whole mind to the question thrown up by his play, the division in our minds when we try to assess the absolute and relative claims to importance of love and lust. Shakespeare constantly plays on this division, yet does not contribute from his inwardness to enable us to set anything substantial against what I shall call the 'normal' view—for it is a mistake to think of it as specifically Roman. Yet we get it constantly from Roman mouths, as in this passage:

but all the charmes of Loue,
Salt *Cleopatra* soften thy wand lip,
Let Witchcraft ioyne with Beauty, Lust with both
Tye vp the Libertine in a field of Feasts,
Keepe his Braine fuming. Epicurean Cookes,

Sharpen with cloylesse sawce his Appetite,
That sleepe and feeding may prorogue his Honour,
Euen till a Lethied dulnesse. . .

This is a belittling view, and if it is indeed allowed to become the norm, that towards which reality is striving, then the nobler aspirations of the chief personages must be condemned as deviations and lapses into unreality. Experience has strongly suggested to me that sooner or later every persistent group of enquirers in their determination to open their minds to the breadth of Shakespeare's vision have to break away from the play to compare notes and pool their prejudices and passions. We certainly need to be sure that here we may go on using the word 'we' when claiming that we are not wholly and all the time of one mind on the whole complex of questions and issues which come before us when we feel invited both to enter into, relish and pass judgement on the lives of Anthony and Cleopatra as they are presented on the stage. The share of each participant in such strategical temporary withdrawals from the play is determined by what comes into the pool. The drawback of discussing a play alone in a book is like that of the first contributor to such a pool: he inevitably says more and less than what is finally found to be the adequate airing of common thoughts and feelings. In this dilemma of needing to be both personal and yet inviting and winning general assent, I recall a modern instance of such a division that struck me hard at the time when it first appeared, and has become very much more significant as we have come to know more of the circumstances and the people involved.

The following anecdote is taken from J. M. Murry's autobiography, *Between Two Worlds.*[1] The time is 1914.

This was the first time I had been with Lawrence for long together, and I had my first real taste of an experience that was pretty constant throughout my relation with him—a feeling that I did not really understand what he was 'driving at'. At this particular moment his novel *Sons and Lovers* had been discovered by some of the Freudian psycho-analysts, who were enthusiastic about it because it exemplified some of Freud's main theses: and Dr. Eder then called more than once on Lawrence to discuss the doctrine, when I happened to be there. I was, as usual, quite ignorant about Freud; I knew his name and the significance he attached to dream-symbolism, also the word *Traumbedeutung*; and that was about all. But I was bewildered by the tone of the discussion. I could not understand why the matter should be taken so seriously, as though it were one of life and death. When Dr. Eder was gone,

[1] Jonathan Cape Ltd., 1935, pp. 287–288.

Lawrence would take me to task for my insouciance and my scepticism, and imply that I in particular ought to be very concerned about the Freudian theory. I felt that I was being indicted, rather unreasonably, for not taking SEX seriously.

I was, indeed, quite incurious about my complexes and my repressions; and I could see no good reason why I should get bothered about them, supposing that they existed. The dogs were asleep, as far as I knew, so why not let them lie? Moreover, I hadn't the faintest notion of how to make them bark: they had no visible tails for me to pull. No doubt a psychoanalyst could have set them in motion; but why should I consult an analyst? On the sexual side of my being I felt normal, positively commonplace indeed. The specific problem of sex had never been a reality in my life and never could be. Yet Lawrence seemed to feel, and to be anxious to make me feel, that this immunity of mine was wrong, and that somehow I was evading reality and behaving irresponsibly. That attitude was perplexing: for I did feel that, in comparison with Lawrence, I was somehow evading reality – but my evasion was not in the province of sex at all. On the contrary, it was precisely there that I felt myself on firmer ground than he. And though I was aware, from his books and from his conversation, that he had vastly more experience of sex than I, I did not feel that he had come to any better conclusion than myself – if one as good.

Neither Katherine nor I could really understand Lawrence's point of view in the matter. He appeared to think that we, simply because we had nothing to correspond with his intense and agonising sexual experiences, were flippant about sex. And that we rather resented. If we were abnormal, our abnormality lay in the fact that we were unusually happy as lovers, and we felt that, in this one thing, we were a good deal happier than Lawrence and Frieda. To have this vaguely imputed to us as a crime seemed rather extravagant. Perhaps neither of us fully appreciated quite how fortunate we were; it struck us as quite exorbitant that Katherine should be regarded as a butterfly and I as a child, merely because our sex-relation was exempt from agony. We tended to retaliate by making fun of Lawrence's Freudian entourage – a game which Katherine played like a master; but it only confirmed Lawrence in his suspicion that we were flippant about the Holy of Holies.

What I am quietly assuming is that a comparable division of opinion has always been present in our civilisation and that a debate of this kind goes on in everybody's mind. On the one hand, when we take men in the mass, there is a dreadful, boring normality in their behaviour. A confessor, for example, rarely comes upon matter for an extraordinary story. The possibility of what is called by some the 'comedy' of 'sex' lies in this clockwork propensity, the fixity of the pattern at any one moment. But if we consult individual experience we often become aware of significant deviations, and when we consult the great artists we learn indeed of new heaven and new earth. But the artist's creative vision does not supersede the confessor's.

Here, then, in rough terms is the basic contrast. Man is only a matter for wonder, 'fearfully and wonderfully made,' when the soul and body are thought of as a 'knot intrinsicate', when all his functions are considered in their inter-actions. Take them separately and man becomes a machine. So we can isolate part of man and in Murry's terms we find we have 'sex' on our hands. In such lines from the play as those just quoted we don't get the word, but the same abstraction. Lust is thought of as something simple, very like hunger. A hungry man is not interested in what he eats but that he eats. When he has eaten he is satisfied and his hunger disappears leaving not a wrack behind. This hunger is thought of as limited, easily satisfied, and automatically shutting itself off when satisfied. Left to function in its natural way it is like Murry's sleeping dog in that it does not rise to consciousness. Hence what a man does in the brothel or the marriage bed is not of the faintest interest. It might almost be described as 'time-off' from living. The only remarkable thing, on this view, about Anthony and Cleopatra is their capacity to defeat this natural functioning. 'Sex' is on the normal view something that switches itself on and off like an automatic washing machine. It is strictly periodic, a thing quickly on and quickly off. It is an appetite soon cloyed, soon blunted. What makes Cleopatra a witch for Anthony is that she can

> Sharpen with cloylesse sawce his Appetite.

Now this is something that Nature cannot sustain. The consequence of amorous surfeiting is exactly that of over-indulgence in eating and drinking—a heavy stupor. I need hardly stress the extent to which Shakespeare follows this account. And we need to immerse ourselves in this view to appreciate the full contrast which is given in Act II scene ii. At least, this is how we might be tempted to put it when we think of that famous description of Cleopatra on her barge, but when we look at the scene as a whole, do we feel we have moved forward?

When Shakespeare does so much for everybody in the way of healing the division and enabling us to make previously impossible transitions from extreme to extreme we clearly cannot wish to make much more than I have of feelings of dissatisfaction. So I would here like to glide and blend into my central *grief* and come closer to the debate about substance and shadow, dramatic reality and imaginative play and about the characteristic strength of the most admired passages of *Anthony and Cleopatra*. Fortunately for this point in the argument we can draw on a classic piece to support the view that the 'Cydnus' passage represents substance rather than shadow. If the reasons grow rather than diminish for passing a harsh verdict on much of the writing on Shakespeare done in the last fifty years, there will be some things that can only gain by being tried in the fire. One of these, I would claim, is the commentary by Professor Leavis embedded in his contribution to *Scrutiny*, volume five, number two, of September, 1936, entitled *'Antony and Cleopatra' and 'All for Love': A Critical Exercise*. It would be desirable to have every word of this article present now, for there a number of general terms, required for pushing this argument on, receive public definition and their full force. Before we can argue about the characteristic dramatic life in Shakespeare's verse we need to know and feel what 'life' there is in this 'Cydnus' passage. Without the particular analysis we cannot appreciate what can be meant by the general observation that 'Shakespeare's verse seems to enact its meaning, to do and to give rather than to talk about' or what is implied in speaking of Shakespeare's characteristic sensuous strength.

But my chief reason for wishing that the reader would leave my argument for these pages in *Scrutiny* is that I am now going to draw a different conclusion about what the 'Cydnus' passage is doing for the play. Professor Leavis was not directly concerned with this question and certainly did not state and perhaps did not imply that Cleopatra and the play as a whole gain in actuality from this passage. At any rate I wish to put on record that, having benefited from the heightened reading Professor Leavis has bequeathed to us, I feel that for the duration of the passage I am carried both out of reality and out of the play and out of the company of the three men on the stage.

The whole effect of the passage on me is to place Cleopatra in an extra-natural setting. Professor Leavis did not dwell in his commentary either on the lines

> O're-picturing that Venus, where we see
> The fancie out-worke Nature . . .

or on

> At the Helme.
> A seeming Mer-maide steeres. . .

If we go along (as we can't help) with Professor Leavis, we are bound to feel when we hear 'The Windes were Loue-sicke', that the winds really were more than what the meteorologists might tell us. We do not think of ordinary river or sea water but of a new non-material liquid endued with feeling. In short, we feel ourselves in a world where fancy has outworked Nature.

The effect of this is to reduce human participation in the scene in favour of extra-natural sympathy of the inanimate. It is this feeling, I imagine, that led Shakespeare to assimilate the spectators to inanimate objects in the phrase:

> hits the sense
> Of the adiacent Wharfes.

The consequence is that there is no imaginative passage in and out from this scene. Can we, for instance, succeed in putting on that barge among

> Her Gentlewomen, like the Nereides,
> So many Mer-maides

who

> tended her i' th' eyes,
> And made their bends adornings

the company we meet in the second scene of the play? Is it possible to imagine the goddess in the barge hopping through the public street—though that is the most genuine clue we have had to Cleopatra so far in this play?

Enobarbus had mingled with Charmian and Iras and had seen Cleopatra on other occasions, yet the contrast between reality and fancy does not now occur to him. It was this power of contrasting and linking the two that fascinated me in our first glimpse of him. Here I miss that power in the supreme moment of fancy that closes the passage:

> *Anthony*
> Enthron'd i' th' Market-place, did sit alone,
> Whisling to th' ayre: which but for vacancie,
> Had gone to gaze on *Cleopater* too,
> And made a gap in Nature.

Enobarbus and the other two men do not seem to be so affected by the purple passage as we are. They remain fixed in the 'normal' view of the relation between Anthony and Cleopatra. I seem to have read somewhere that we should allow the grand suggestions of fertility to work and see Cleopatra as an Earth Mother when we hear the lines:

> She made great *Caesar* lay his Sword to bed;
> He ploughed her, and she cropt.

But my mind somehow refuses to work in that direction. Surely *this* does not mark any shift from the 'normal'?

> Age cannot wither her, not custome stale
> Her infinite variety: other women cloy
> The appetites they feede, but she makes hungry
> Where most she satisfies.

It might be said that we get a new response here:

> For vildest things
> Become themsleves in her, that the holy Priests
> Blesse her, when she is Riggish.

Yet this strikes me as a 'try-on': we see an intention, but in art only realization counts.

Finally, there seems something abrupt, shapeless and anticlimactic about this scene. It is as if a curtain fell on the word 'Riggish', for Maecenas abruptly changes the subject and Agrippa is in a hurry to get off the stage. When we examine this irrelevant appendix we find it is a rarelessly slapped down piece of Plutarch:

> There-vppon euerie man did set forward this mariage, hoping thereby that this Ladie Octauia, hauing an excellent grace, wisedom, and honestie, joined vnto so rare a beawtie, that when she were with Antonius (he louing her as so worthy a Ladie deserueth) she should be a good meane to keepe good loue and amitie betwext her brother and him.

If on further reflection it becomes clear that there are other passages ike this and that the Horatian tag

> inceptis grauibus plerumque et magna professis
> purpureus, late qui splendeat, unus et alter
> adsuitur pannus[1]

begins to apply to our play, then we can hardly resist the felicitous 'angelic strength' offered by Coleridge, and we are bound to ask ourselves whether this virtue had in any sense to be paid for. I shall be arguing in the next chapter that these passages are some of the 'magnificent subterfuges' I referred to earlier on. At the moment I should merely like to raise the question: are these the passages to quote when we wish to illustrate Shakespeare's virtues as a dramatic poet? I cannot bring myself to say

---

[1] *Ep. ad Pisones*, lines 14–16, translated by T. S. Dorsch in Penguin Classics as Works that begin impressively and with the promise of carrying on in the heroic strain often have one or two purple passages tacked on to catch the eye'.

that these passages of 'angelic strength' are less than fine poetry, but I gladly point to places where Shakespeare's strength is better described as that of a very *human* intelligence.

\*       \*       \*

Since the bias of my commentary may have led the reader to conjecture that I find it easier to reject than to accept the good things offered, I append some notes of appreciation of the two scenes between Cleopatra and the messenger. I am impatient at having to sit through the interval between them, for Shakespeare's comic touch is so inferior when hand-ling the Romans that I long for the superior reality and life that fill every syllable of the two Cleopatra scenes. If these large words 'reality' and 'life' seem to be doing nothing, I would willingly exchange them for the remark that the mind lingers over these scenes, gladly returns to them, and always with fresh admiration for the intelligence that created them. And when I ask myself what I mean by intelligence here I find I want to exalt it over other exhibitions of intelligence in the play. For it is an in-clusive intelligence and an applied intelligence. We don't want to extract it from what it is applied to. Indeed its felicity is inseparable from the exact expression it gets at each several moment in these scenes. So I should like to contrast the intelligence shown here with an instance of intelligence which merely makes a point, and proves that Shakespeare had made a successful general observation about life. We salute the point and pass on. In these two scenes with the messenger, as I said, we linger and come back again and again.

There is something for the 'tablets' of the eager young man on the make in the first scene of Act III:

> Who does i' th' Warres more then his Captaine can,
> Becomes his Captaines Captaine: and Ambition
> (The Souldiers vertue) rather makes choise of losse
> Then gaine, which darkens him.
> I could do more to do *Anthonius* good,
> But 'twould offend him. And in his offence,
> Should my performance perish.
> —                Thou hast, *Ventidius*, that,
> Without the which a Souldier and his Sword
> Graunts scarce distinction: thou wilt write to *Anthony*.
> — Ile humbly signifie what in his name,
> That magicall word of Warre we haue effected. . .

Here we salute the kind of intelligence we meet in Bacon's *Essays*. First we reduce the statement to a maxim, and consider whether it holds good in life as we know it. Then we applaud the phrasing—the compactness, the sharpness obtained in such points as

his Captaines Captaine

and

a Souldier and his Sword.

After that 'there is no more to say': the truth is a felt one, a bright penny that rings true, but if I may continue these images, it has no other facets or overtones.

The intelligence in the two Cleopatra scenes is a matter of mental play, of the poise between many attitudes. The over-all mode is comic, but it is not crudely or simply comic. The structure of the progressive revelations of the messenger suggests farce—it is simplified and schematic—but the intelligence weaves in and out and is never subdued by the ground plan of the scheme. A little instance of the so much more added by intelligence may be seen here:

—Giue me some Musicke: Musicke, moody foode
   of vs that trade in Loue.
—The Musicke, hoa. . .
—Let it alone, let's to Billards. . .

I think the commentators are right in suggesting that our first thoughts on hearing this should be of the commonplace, such as we get in the opening of *Twelfe Night*:

If Musicke be the food of Loue, play on,<br>
Giue me excesse of it: that surfetting,<br>
The appetite may sicken, and so dye.<br>
That straine agen, it had a dying fall:<br>
O, it came ore my eare, like the sweet sound<br>
That breathes vpon a banke of Violets;<br>
Stealing, and giuing Odour. Enough, no more,<br>
'Tis not so sweet now, as it was before.

But our second thoughts might well be that Cleopatra, too, had heard the Duke of Illyria. She is both the Duke and a critic of the Duke. Her escape from mere 'type' comes in the compression and pregnancy of 'Musicke, moody foode of vs that trade in Loue.' The phrase lifts us above the immediate point, the broadly comic. Of course, the intelligence here would be impotent if it could not command the fine ear that gives us just this chain of syllables. I don't pretend to know the exact phonetic value in Shakespeare's day, but I would throw out the suggestion that these sounds have *overtones* like those we hear when Macbeth says:

> Light thickens,
> And the Crow makes Wing to th' Rookie Wood. . .

Similarly we feel the intelligence in slight touches when Shakespeare illustrates the point that North sums up when he describes the 'sport' Anthony and Cleopatra filled up the long day hours with as 'delighting in these fond and childish pastimes'. First, he shows us how closely we must identify Cleopatra with the mood of her maids as we saw it in the second scene of the play, in the idle play on the two meanings of play: 'As well a woman with an Eunuch plaide, as with a woman'. Then we have the episode of the fishing. It took no intelligence to see that North's anecdote would serve. But what are we to call the stroke that gave us

> which he with feruencie drew vp . . .?

Similarly, we may contrast as *abstract* intelligence the summary—

> Is not more manlike
> Then *Cleopatra*: nor the Queene of *Ptolomy*
> More Womanly then he.

—and as *concrete* the exemplification:

> Ere the ninth houre, I drunke him to his bed:
> Then put my Tires and Mantles on him, whilst
> I wore his Sword Phillippan.

That last word does it. We advance *dramatically* here, not merely circle round the point made by Octavius.

The trembling balance in the first passage with the messenger needs delicate handling. It could easily be taken merely coarsely or wholly pejoratively. I don't think that we should overlook the coarse and pejorative implications. Our basic situation is that Cleopatra has very little discipline or regard for decorum and no feeling for what Jane Austen called Principle. She is indeed cruel and savage. But there are mitigating touches. The messenger is, I think, from the beginning, something of a Clown. At any rate he takes a Clown's liberty in this exchange:

—He's bound vnto *Octauia*.
—For what good turne?
—For the best turne i' th' bed.

Even exalted members of the court could not risk this tone when report-
ting to their Queen. As an instance of the hair-breadth that divides our
feelings I would take Cleopatra's words:

> and heere
> My blewest vaines to kisse: a hand that Kings
> Haue lipt, and trembled kissing.

We may start from the thought that kings are two-a-penny in this play,
but does not *trembled* arrest our smile here?[1]

Another tempering thought comes when we consider the resemblances
between Cleopatra here and Macbeth in those scenes where he, a prey to
saucy doubts and fears, interviews people on whose news his fate depends.
For if we allow that to some extent Cleopatra is 'acting' a tragic part it
releases our minds to enjoy the sense in which she improves on the tragic
mode. There is an extraordinary intensity in some of her expressions. If
Macbeth is masculine here:

> The diuell damne thee blacke, thou cream-fac'd Loone:
> Where got'st thou that Goose-looke . . .

there is an admirable feminine turn in Cleopatra's aside:

> so tart a fauour
> To trumpet such good tidings,

But she explodes with power here:

> I do not like but yet, it does alay
> The good precedence, fie vpon but yet,
> But yet is as a Iaylor to bring foorth
> Some monstrous Malefactor. Prythee Friend,
> Powre out the packe of matter to mine eare,
> The good and bad together.

There we have Shakespeare's mind opening out, and when it opens we
are engulfed. We cease to be merely spectators, we are drawn in. But the
point at which I cease to be merely a judge sizing up a woman's character
and become surrounded by Nature, the point where Cleopatra merges in
Humanity, comes for me when after the gypsy lapse

> Rogue, thou hast liu'd too long . . .

[1] Would it stand up to the severest, the most acid test I can think of, comparison
with the use of the same word by Francesca in Canto V of the *Inferno: La bocca mi
baciò tutto tremante?*

she struggles to recover herself. At the point where she is most a woman, she becomes all mankind.

The scene, however, remains bathed in the light of humour, even though I don't for a moment feel like laughing, for now I feel *with* her and she is sufficiently aware of her true self now to dispense with our judging eye. Everything is now real and we retire with her to digest something which has now become as much a fact to us as to her. It is only when she returns and we note how her attendants humour her, that we feel for the first time that Cleopatra needs our sympathy. If this scene does not dissolve away the hardness whether of admiration or of condemnation in our attitude, nothing will.

These two scenes seem to have an extra dimension for the want of which the rest of the 'interval' seems to me to lack commanding interest.

CHAPTER 2

# Telling *versus* Shewing

WHEN making a critical point in the face of opposition there is always a danger that the energy generated to drive the point home may carry the critic beyond his true mark. But without opposition there would be no energy, and here, if there were not the pressure of a valued *consensus* of opinion making high claims for the dramatic merits of the play, there would be no dialogue. Nor would there be any point in seeking to establish that the play is not a supreme dramatic masterpiece if Shakespeare had not provided us with our criteria for the supremely dramatic, and made us long for it, so that we are impatient even when, as in this play, we are getting a great many other pleasures than that given by a great dramatist in full control of his material. I am assuming that the pleasures of drama are what we above all want in a play, and that it is a fault in a critic if other pleasures blind him to dramatic defects. My main contention is that, whether or not as a consequence of Shakespeare losing his grip, the fall of Anthony comes as an improper shock, comes, that is to say, too much from outside, from the known facts of history, and too little from what has been built up in our minds as the original *donnée* was developed. More particularly I would suggest that in the portion of the play beginning with our Act III scene iv and continuing to scene ix, what we are merely told takes on an illegitimate prominence over what we are shewn, and I shall try in this chapter to make comments and put forward arguments that forced me to abandon tenaciously held views. It is from my own inner opposition that I have learned to respect the dissent of other judges. May my eventual capitulation be favourable to a verdict commanding the judgement of my peers!

In Act III scene iv we find that even in the plot the important action has taken place 'off'. Shakespeare has, as it were, simply pushed the hands of the clock forward. For although nobody would expect the world alliance to prove durable, our expectations—necessarily vague ones, of course —would be of something like what actually happened in history. We should suppose that the alliance would take some time to break up; the time, say, for the birth of one or two children to Anthony and Octavia. There is thus something unpleasantly theatrical in being suddenly presented with so much development in the wings. I should not, however, want to make very much of this, because I cannot see much inherently dramatic life in the 'political' scenes. (My impression is that Shakespeare felt he, as it were, owed them to Plutarch). But occasionally the play suffers from the decision to give us narration instead of action, notably in this incident:

> — Where's *Anthony*?
> —He's walking in the garden thus, and spurnes
> The rush that lies before him. Cries Foole *Lepidus*,
> And threats the throate of that his Officer,
> That murdred *Pompey*.

And in scene iv we are also left badly in the dark. If Anthony is being sincere, why has this meeting with Octavia no sequel for him? Can we in fact say with any confidence how he is treating her? Can we easily dismiss our inability to answer a query about how he must have been treating her before this scene? Is the reality what in scene vi Caesar gives us in his summary to Octavia?

> You are abus'd
> Beyond the marke of thought: and the high Gods
> To do you Iustice, make his Ministers
> Of vs, and those that loue you.

This is the language of the 'good' characters in *Macbeth* when they are bringing the villain down:

> *Macbeth*
> Is ripe for shaking, and the Powres aboue
> Put on their instruments. . .

Anthony is certainly ripe for shaking, but are we getting the merited fall of a villain? And, is our interest to be diverted to the political fall from the initial interest, which was the inner collapse of the hero?

At this point, however, where we might have the impression of a slight hiatus, Shakespeare refers us firmly back to the *donnée* and extends straight from it. We are once again made to examine the Roman thesis, as presented by Caesar:

> *Cleopatra*
> Hath nodded him to her. He hath giuen his Empire
> Vp to a Whore. . .

and in the 'choric' underlining by Enobarbus:

> Your presence needs must puzle *Anthony*,
> Take from his heart, take from his Braine, from's time,

> What should not then be spar'd. He is already
> Traduc'd for Leuity, and 'tis said in Rome,
> That *Photinus* an Eunuch, and your Maides
> Mannage this warre.

Here it is remarkable how prominent this single unifying line is allowed to become. The scenes hereabouts are clearly designed to demonstrate one point:

> our Leaders leade,
> And we are Womens men . . .

Hence we can say that here Shakespeare is appealing chiefly to our moral interest. The principle of unity is manifest: if dramatically the great shock is the total loss of honour, the dramatic point to which the preceding scenes lead up is the wonderful speech about judgement—about what led to the loss of honour. We are thus powerfully challenged to apply our ordinary moral sense and to join with Anthony when he says:

> But when we in our viciousnesse grow hard
> (Oh misery on't) the wise Gods seele our eyes,
> In our owne filth drop our cleare iudgements, make vs
> Adore our errors, laugh at's while we strut
> To our confusion.

There we have a felt commonplace, and one suggesting that if Anthony was doomed, he had nevertheless previously enjoyed freedom but had lost it through his viciousness.

If we follow Shakespeare we cannot exaggerate the great disgrace of Actium. We see an Anthony who threw away his chances by an act that irreparably destroyed his honour as a man of the world. To concentrate our judgement, Shakespeare wrote in a 'verdict' scene which leaves no room for evading his intention. First, we have the repeated horror expressed by Enobarbus:

> Naught, naught, al naught, I can behold no longer . . .
> To see't, mine eyes are blasted . . .
> Mine eyes did sicken at the sight, and could not
> Indure a further view . . .

Then the second chorus figure:

> The greater Cantle of the world, is lost
> With very ignorance, we haue kist away
> Kingdomes, and Prouinces.

Then the explicit judgement:

> I neuer saw an Action of such shame;
> Experience, Man-hood, Honor, ne're before,
> Did violate so it selfe.

After that, we hardly need the repetition of the *donnée* from the first scene of the play:

> Had our Generall
> Bin what he knew himselfe, it had gone well.

We might therefore well feel that, had Shakespeare been writing a free tragedy, he would have ended his play about here. And, if he *had* treated Anthony as a supremely heroic figure, there would be little more to say. As it is, Shakespeare has drawn for us the degradation of the extinguished hero beyond the point where life could ever be fully lived again. Although, paradoxically, some of the finest things in the play are just about to occur, we ought to be clear that, coming so late, they cannot have the resonance they could have had when life was all to play for.

As it is, fallen Anthony is a paler version of the fallen Macbeth: we therefore hardly need to recall the more vivid expressions which are merely echoed here:

> Hearke, the Land bids me tread no more vpon't,
> It is asham'd to beare me. Friends, come hither,
> I am so lated in the world, that I
> Haue lost my way for euer.

Anthony, we may say, fell from a lower height: he still only half knows what he has done, whereas Macbeth knew the heaven he lost for ever. The issues for Anthony are less momentous: he has not broke open the Lord's anointed temple, he has merely lost his honour. Consequently, there is an immense difference between

> Oh,
> I follow'd that I blush to looke vpon

and

> I am afraid, to thinke what I haue done:
> Looke on't againe, I dare not.

Yet in one sense Anthony falls lower than Macbeth. Macbeth never reproached his wife with instigating him to crime. When we hear Anthony saying:

> Egypt, thou knew'st too well,
> My heart was to thy Rudder tyed by' th'strings,
> And thou should'st stowe me after. O're my spirit
> The full supremacie thou knew'st, and that
> Thy becke, might from the bidding of the Gods
> Command mee...
>    You did know
> How much you were my Conqueror, and that
> My Sword, made weake by my affection, would
> Obey it on all cause.

our feelings must be tinged with contempt.[1] Equally weak if not more is the attempt to pretend that no loss has occurred:

> Fall not a teare I say, one of them rates
> All that is wonne and lost: Giue me a kisse,
> Euen this repayes me.

Once again Shakespeare stages a verdict scene: Enobarbus will not let us or Anthony off:

> —Is *Anthony*, or we in fault for this?
> —*Anthony* onely, that would make his will
> Lord of his Reason. What though you fled,
> From that great face of Warre, whose seuerall ranges
> Frighted each other? Why should he follow?
> The itch of his Affection should not then
> Haue nickt his Captain-ship, at such a point,
> When halfe to halfe the world oppos'd, he being
> The meered question? 'Twas a shame no lesse
> Then was his losse, to course your flying Flagges,
> And leaue his Nauy gazing.

Enobarbus, too, underlines the stupidity of Anthony's challenge to single combat:

> Yes like enough: hye battel'd *Cæsar* will
> Vnstate his happinesse, and be Stag'd to th' shew
> Against a Sworder. I see mens Iudgements are
> A parcell of their Fortunes, and things outward
> Do draw the inward quality after them
> To suffer all alike, that he should dreame,

[1] Are these repetitions a mark of weakness or a failure by Shakespeare to settle on a decisive phrase?

> Knowing all measures, the full *Cæsar* will
> Answer his emptinesse. *Cæsar* thou hast subdu'de
> His iudgement too.

It is once again Enobarbus who tells us how to take the wonderful scene when Anthony passes through to his final stage before he kills himself:

> Now hee'l out-stare the Lightning, to be furious
> Is to be frighted out of feare, and in that moode
> The Doue will pecke the Estridge; and I see still
> A diminution in our Captaines braine,
> Restores his heart; when valour prayes in reason,
> It eates the Sword it fights with. . . .

'Now hee'l out-stare the Lightning'—to this has come the figure of whom it was said:

> those his goodly eyes
> That o're the Files and Musters of the Warre,
> Haue glow'd like plated Mars.

Much as we relish these scenes and admire their dramatic execution, we cannot help noticing the extent to which Shakespeare was content to reproduce the Anthony given him by North: 'There Anthony showed plainly, that he had not only lost the courage and heart of an emperor, but also of a valiant man, and that he was not his own man. . .' If we compare the scenes in North with those in Shakespeare, we can say that, passing from one to the other, we are not aware of any marked difference in intelligence. The insight into the fall of Anthony seems about equal, which means, given the order of time, that Shakespeare was not putting much into the play: hereabouts he is merely Plutarch's man. If an exception is made for the scene where Anthony surprises Thidias kissing Cleopatra's hand, it must be conceded that the structure corresponds to the account given by North together with the comment. Its exceptional liveliness, its many felicities of expression, do not make Anthony more real, but underline his unreality. Anthony exasperated expresses himself with more vigour than Macbeth but he moves us less seriously. We are now outside Anthony: he is a man to be abandoned: he may say, 'I am *Anthony* yet', but everything he says tells us he is not. This is partly due to the paucity of human relations in the Roman story. There is no dense value-world round Anthony. Consider what is called up by Macbeth when in exemplification of the comment:

> Now do's he feele
> His secret Murthers sticking on his hands,

> Now minutely Reuolts vpbraid his Faith-breach:
> Those he commands, moue onely in command,
> Nothing in loue: Now do's he feele his Title
> Hang loose about him, like a Giants Robe
> Vpon a dwarfish Theefe. . .

he reveals how he moves swathed in an atmosphere of real human value-relations all fatally violated and destroyed:

> I haue liu'd long enough, my way of life
> Is falne into the Seare, the yellow Leafe,
> And that which should accompany Old-Age,
> As Honor, Loue, Obedience, Troopes of Friends,
> I must not looke to haue: but in their steed,
> Curses, not lowd but deepe, Mouth-honor, breath
> Which the poore heart would faine deny, and dare not.

Macbeth, we feel, is a fine soul, who cares for real social relations, but when Anthony says:

> Authority melts from me of late. When I cried hoa,
> Like Boyes vnto a musse, Kings would start forth,
> And cry, your will. . .

we know that he never felt the moral bond involved in being the head of society. He is more like a retired Colonial governor, lamenting in Bournemouth or on the Riviera his inability to boss his European servants as he used to boss the 'boys' of Africa. So Anthony may prate of judgement, but substituting judgement for temperance, we may turn his unworthy taunt (unworthy, coming from him) against himself:

> For I am sure,
> Though you can guesse what Temperance should be,
> You know not what it is.

And if we withhold our sympathy from Othello when he roars at the thought of being cuckolded, what are we to think of Anthony when he says:

> O that I were
> Vpon the hill of Basan to out-roare
> The horned Heard, for I haue sauce agause,
> And to proclaime it ciuilly, were like
> A halter'd necke, which do's the Hangman thanke,
> For being yare about him. . . ?

Of course, we understand that Anthony, so far from being what his judgement might tell him he was, is by every means trying to 'drown consideration'. One of his means is to substitute big words for big thoughts, and one such evasion is dressing up the ugly facts in fine astrological language:

> my good Starres, that were my former guides
> Haue empty left their Orbes, and shot their Fires
> Into th' Abisme of hell. . .
> Alacke our Terrene Moone is now Eclipst,
> And it portends alone the fall of *Anthony*.

Here, surely, we counter with

> The fault (deere *Brutus*) is not in our Starres. . .

or better still:

> This is the excellent foppery of the world, that when we are sicke in fortune, often the surfets of our own behauiour, we make guilty of our disasters, the Sun, the Moone, and Starres.

Do these particular observations lead us towards a general remark: that Anthony is an unconscionable time a-falling, that Shakespeare had nothing further to reveal after the initial fall and that therefore he was not working on a deep level? Once again the challenge is to say what kind of organisation holds together all that part of the play which directly or indirectly bears on Anthony. We must ask about the quality of the interest and how deep it goes, and about the quality of the revelation and how much of reality is being brought to our attention. We may ask, but it is very difficult to feel quite sure of anything in this part of the play. Can we, for instance, say that we get what the newspapers call 'the moment of truth' here?

> —*Eros*, thou yet behold'st me?
> —I Noble Lord.
> —Sometime we see a clowd that's Dragonish,
>   A vapour sometime, like a Beare, or Lyon,
>   A toward Cittadell, a pendant Rocke,
>   A forked Mountaine, or blew Promontorie
>   With Trees vpon't, that nodde vnto the world,
>   And mocke our eyes with Ayre.
>   Thou hast seene these Signes,
>   They are blacke Vespers Pageants.
> —I my Lord.

STL K

—That which is now a Horse, euen with a thoght
the Racke dislimes, and makes it indistinct
As water is in water.
—It does my Lord.
—My good Knaue *Eros*, now thy Captaine is
Euen such a body.

But the question I find hardest to decide is whether, if Shakespeare intended to shew how unreal Anthony had become after Actium, he was always himself firmly in the saddle. Here the lapses, if there are any, are not crude: much of the very highest interest is occurring: dissatisfaction is therefore to be measured against expectations that Shakespeare satisfied only at his best moments. Each of the following points would seem a trifle if isolated, yet taken together they may be found suggestive and worth developing into a judgement.

The development given to Enobarbus here seems to me a symptom of Shakespeare's failure to focus his mind. His death is quite out of keeping and seems to belong to the cluster of thoughts that we find under the title *Timon of Athens*. Anybody who had formed the same impression in the theatre that I am trying to describe might find his experience confirmed by turning to North. At this point in his narrative North interrupts his account of Anthony to tell the story of Timon and he also describes the death of one of Anthony's followers who regretted leaving his master. It might well strike such a reader how many of the items in this part of the play seem to be the result of versifying North rather than the consequence of trying to write a play. But the theatre-goer's question is whether anything in the play justifies Enobarbus' scruples and self-reproach. Can we point to behaviour in Anthony that sets up the moral situation which Enobarbus both describes and implies? Does it come over us, as we attempt to make up the necessary sum, that Shakespeare is now beginning to attempt by mere telling to undo what he has shewn; that he is illegitimately restoring to Anthony the heroic virtues he properly robbed him of?

It is here that I come into conflict with Bradley, in that I find myself taking differently the import of many scenes in this part of the play. For example, I cannot discover the imaginative unity that binds the music scene (taken from North) into the play. But before introducing Bradley's comment, a slight prefatory digression is unavoidable. I have so far passed over in silence all the references to Fortune and Fate in this play because I judged each and all to be without serious authorial backing. Indeed, I was tempted to complain of Shakespeare's irresponsibility in letting so many of them in when he clearly wasn't doing anything with them. Now Bradley was always looking for Fate, since without the idea of Fate he could find no tragedy, and he found what I thought a trivial passing reflection by Caesar significant:

> Be you not troubled with the time, which driues
> O're your content, these strong necessities,
> But let determin'd things to destinie
> Hold vnbewayl'd their way.

On these lines Bradley wrote[1]:

> In any case the feeling of fate comes through to us. It is aided by slight touches of supernatural effect; first in the Soothsayer's warning to Antony that his genius or angel is overpowered whenever he is near Octavius; then in the strangely effective scene where Antony's soldiers, in the night before his last battle, hear music in the air or under the earth:
>
> > 'Tis the god Hercules, whom Antony loved,
> > Now leaves him.
>
> And to the influence of this feeling in giving impressiveness to the story . . .

Yes, that, I fear, is what Shakespeare hoped. The impressiveness is an external dodge. When has anything corresponding to a god been present in the play? The references to the gods have all been perfunctory.

The central issue, however, concerns what Bradley calls Anthony's 'inward recovery'. Since my account of the fall owes so much to Bradley's, it is awkward not to be able to subscribe to the sequel:

> Then Shakespeare begins to raise him again. First, his own overwhelming sense of shame redeems him. Next, we watch the rage of the dying lion. Then the mere sally before the final defeat—a sally dismissed by Plutarch in three lines—is magnified into a battle, in which Antony displays to us, and himself feels for the last time, the glory of his soldiership. And, throughout, the magnanimity and gentleness which shine through his desperation endear him to us. How beautiful is his affection for his followers and even for his servants, and the devotion they return! How noble his reception of the news that Enobarbus has deserted him! How touchingly significant the refusal of Eros either to kill him or survive him! How pathetic and even sublime the completeness of his love for Cleopatra! His anger is born and dies in an hour. One tear, one kiss, outweighs his ruin. He believes she has sold him to his enemy, yet he kills himself because he hears that she is dead. When, dying, he learns that she has deceived him once more, no thought of reproach crosses

[1] A. C. Bradley, *Oxford Lectures on Poetry* (1909), p. 290.

his mind: he simply asks to be carried to her. He knows well that she is not capable of dying because he dies, but that does not sting him; when, in his last agony, he calls for wine that he may gain a moment's strength to speak, it is to advise her for the days to come. Shakespeare borrowed from Plutarch the final speech of Antony. It is fine, but it is not miraculous. The miraculous speeches belong only to his own hero:

> I am dying, Egypt, dying; only
> I here importune death awhile, until
> Of many thousand kisses the poor last
> I lay upon thy lips;

or the first words he utters when he hears of Cleopatra's death:

> Unarm, Eros: the long day's task is done,
> And we must sleep.

If he meant the task of statesman and warrior, that is not what his words mean to us. They remind us of words more familiar and less great—

> No rest but the grave for the pilgrim of love.

And he is more than love's pilgrim; he is love's martyr.[1]

The tone, manner and rhythms of this passage have led me in the past to dismiss it as 'tosh', yet it is only with people capable of siding so extremely with Anthony that I would care to advance the opposing thesis, that in his closing scenes Anthony both talks himself out and is talked by others out of reality.

A mild beginning towards this conclusion might be made by noticing a deliberate device employed by Shakespeare to throw a classical aura round Anthony. Every classical reference takes Anthony off the earth we know and delivers him over to hyperbole and bombast. Taken one by one, we may not find these allusions out of place. For instance, when the soldier tells Enobarbus—

> Your Emperor
> Continues still a Ioue . . .

—we may only murmur, 'generous, yes, but not quite so superlative as to require the introduction of the divine.' Yet, as they accumulate, we both become aware of the author's intention and build up our resistance to the 'try-on'. When Anthony tells his men, 'you haue shewne all *Hectors*', we note that Anthony is characteristically inflating a petty skir-

---

[1] *Op. cit.*, pp. 297–298.

mish into a major campaign. The whole mode of this scene smacks of
Marlowe:

> —Ile giue thee Friend
> An Armour all of Gold: it was a Kings.
> —He has deseru'd it, were it Carbunkled
> Like holy Phœbus Carre. . .

and ends on a crude boyish note:

> Trumpetters
> With brazen dinne blast you the Citties eare,
> Make mingle with our ratling Tabourines,
> That heauen and earth may strike their sounds together,
> Applauding our approach.

The effect on me of Anthony's self-comparison with Herakles, so far
from casting over him a heroic or mythical tragic grandeur, is to make
him a mere stage figure:

> The shirt of *Nessus* is vpon me, teach me
> *Alcides*, thou mine Ancestor, thy rage.
> Let me lodge *Licas* on the hornes o' th' Moone,
> And with those hands that graspt the heauiest Club,
> Subdue my worthiest selfe.

Cleopatra reinforces the impression:

> Oh hee's more mad
> Then *Telamon* for his Shield, the Boare of Thessaly
> Was neuer so imbost.

This is stock Elizabethan rhetoric: it mars Anthony's efforts to meet
death squarely. He is ranting in the same vein here:

> The seuen-fold shield of *Aiax* cannot keepe
> The battery from my heart. Oh cleaue my sides.
> Heart, once be stronger then thy Continent,
> Cracke thy fraile Case.

Weighing more heavily against Anthony is this speech:

> Stay for me,
> Where Soules do couch on Flowers, wee'l hand in hand,
> And with our sprightly Port make the Ghostes gaze:
> *Dido*, and her *Æneas* shall want Troopes,
> And all the haunt be ours.

This was a never-never land, even for a Roman. It makes a terrible draught on the previous scenes of the play and forces us to weigh once again the relative significance of what we have seen for ourselves and what has been merely said about the lovers. This speech itself has power, but cannot remove the impression of weak evasion: instead of living in the present and ending as a full person, Anthony projects himself into an unreal future.

What turns the scale for me is the emphasis on the admiration Anthony thinks they will get from the Elysian spectators. Shakespeare seems anxious to support this conceit by praising Anthony up well beyond any deserts shewn in the play. First, we have the repeated assertion that suicide is noble as well as prudent, and then the various forms of commentary. The most ludicrous, to my mind, is that of the two soldiers who find that Anthony was unable to make a clean job of his own death:

> The Starre is falne
> And time is at his Period.

*Qui est-ce qu'on trompe ici?* Is Shakespeare inviting our irony or an implicit acceptance? For Cleopatra merely says the same in more moving words:

> Oh Sunne,
> Burne the great Sphere thou mou'st in, darkling stand
> The varrying shore o' th' world.

It is the same Shakespeare who makes Cleopatra joke at the ludicrousness of the scene where sixteen stone of dying Anthony are lugged into the monument, and immediately after makes her say:

> Had I great *Iuno*'s power,
> The strong wing'd *Mercury* should fetch thee vp,
> And set thee by *Ioues* side.

Here, quite inconsistently, I find in the context this allusion helps. For Anthony goes off by contrast with pleasing sobriety: he merely says what North said.

But what can we do with the wonderful epitaph Cleopatra speaks before she faints?

> Oh see my women:
> The Crowne o' th' earth doth melt. My Lord?
> Oh wither'd is the Garland of the Warre,
> The Souldiers pole is falne: young Boyes and Gyrles
> Are leuell now with men: The oddes is gone,

    And there is nothing left remarkeable
    Beneath the visiting Moone.

I am unable either to feel it as generated out of her own mind or to relate it to the Anthony of the play. The lines are written in by Shakespeare, and it is a pity that he did not organise a play around them. When I compare these lines with their repetition in Cleopatra's next speech this impression is reinforced. The former seem to come all the more from a mind such as we may imagine was Shakespeare's—they are his commentary on a situation he has imagined but not embodied: the latter strike me as theatrical in the best sense. They are what make Cleopatra a 'fat part', good to declaim . . . at the lips' ends, but not going deep.[1]

    A possible sign of a general loss of grip is that Anthony is not the only leading personage to become the slave or dupe of words. The consequence of Cleopatra's lending herself to the self-deception of the pacification after the quarrel over the messenger may have been the frigidity of:

        Ah (Deere) if I be so,
  From my cold heart let Heauen ingender haile,
  And poyson it in the sourse, and the first stone
  Drop in my necke: as it determines so
  Dissolue my life, the next Cæsarian smite,
  Till by degrees the memory of my wombe,
  Together with my braue Egyptians all,
  By the discandering of this pelleted storme,
  Lye grauelesse, till the Flies and Gnats of Nyle
  Haue buried them for prey.

And even before Anthony's death Cleopatra has played up to his illusion about the grandeur of his petty operations:

        Lord of Lords,
  Oh infinite Vertue, comm'st thou smiling from
  The worlds great snare vncaught?

Yet though Cleopatra speaks like this to his face, she may still have a shrewd idea of the real proportions, for behind his back, we must not forget, she had said:

    He goes forth gallantly: That he and *Cæsar* might
    Determine this great Warre in single fight;
    Then *Anthony*; but now. Well on.

[1] Who, for instance, could believe she is fully 'there', *all* behind
      Then is it sinne,
  To rush into the secret house of death?

What puzzles me more, and makes me wonder what Shakespeare thought he was doing, is the deliberate insertion of a favourable Roman epitaph for Anthony. We have had the Roman verdict before our eyes throughout the play. Although there have been many small suggestions that it was not to be taken as the last word on Anthony, since it was based on an external view of his behaviour, yet it has often enough been substantiated by internal evidence. Nothing, for instance, coming from within, has mitigated the verdict on Anthony's flight at Actium. Yet now we find the Romans uniting to lament Anthony as a fallen *hero*. We cannot mistake the author's intention here. Shakespeare lets himself go in his self-indulgent delight in hyperbole and incongruously gives to Caesar the following words:

> The breaking of so great a thing, should make
> A greater cracke. The round World
> Should haue shooke Lyons into ciuill streets,
> And Cittizens to their dennes. The death of *Anthony*
> Is not a single doome, in the name lay
> A moity of the world.

This is reinforced by 'choric' commentary:

> —His taints and Honours, wag'd equal with him.
> —A Rarer spirit neuer
> Did steere humanity.

But what brings out the contrast between the Anthony who walked the earth and the fiction that might have been but never was, is Cleopatra's scene with Dolabella. This is the true counterpiece to the description of Cleopatra at Cydnus:

> I dreampt there was an Emperor *Anthony*.
> Oh such another sleepe, that I might see
> But such another man.[1]

This at any rate is what Cleopatra says she saw in her dream:

> His face was as the Heauens, and therein stucke
> A Sunne and Moone, which kept their course, & lighted

---

[1] Which might remind us of Caliban:
> and sometime voices,
> That if I then had wak'd after long sleepe,
> Will make me sleepe againe, and then in dreaming,
> The clouds methought would open, and shew riches
> Ready to drop vpon me, that when I wak'd
> I cri'de to dreame againe.

The little o' th' earth . . .
His legges bestrid the Ocean, his rear'd arme
Crested the world: His voyce was propertied
As all the tuned Spheres, and that to Friends:
But when he meant to quaile, and shake the Orbe,
He was as ratling Thunder. For his Bounty,
There was no winter in't. An Automne it was,
That grcw thc more by reaping: His delights
Were Dolphin-like, they shew'd his backe aboue
The Element they liu'd in: In his Liuery
Walk'd Crownes and Crownets: Realms & Islands were
As plates dropt from his pocket.

But then comes the significant exchange where, as in the piece on Cleopatra, Fancy is played off against Nature:

— Thinke you there was, or might be such a man
As this I dreampt of?
— Gentle Madam, no.
— You Lye vp to the hearing of the Gods:
But if there be, nor euer were one such
It's past the size of dreaming: Nature wants stuffe
To vie strange formes with fancie, yet t'imagine
An *Anthony* were Natures peece, 'gainst Fancie,
Condemning shadowes quite.

What a remarkable play, we might reflect, *Anthony and Cleopatra* would
have been if Cleopatra had shewn in her behaviour that she had often had
such dreams in Anthony's life-time! Yet this is the only mode in which
Anthony can now be presented. It is equally significant that when Cleopatra prepares to meet Anthony in the other world she recalls the part
they played at Cydnus.

Do these observations taken together and shorn of what is merely
personal in them call for a judgement on the play? Will it now be generally agreed that the promise of the first scene was never realised? The
Anthony we were to see was never shewn. We are *told* I don't know how
many times that he was a supreme specimen of humanity, so lofty indeed
that to indicate the scale it was necessary to suppose that his nature par-
took of the divine. The Anthony who is presented dramatically never
makes us believe in these reports. Shakespeare's Anthony, in fact, is not
markedly more heroic and god-like than what we divine to have been
Plutarch's conception. The critics who have defended Shakespeare
against the charge of selling his soul to Plutarch (North) could easily

point to many departures in the plot, they could also tell of departures in the drawing of Anthony's character, but they say nothing of the relative stature of the two figures in the narrative and in the play. I cannot believe that Shakespeare tried very hard to make us feel, feel intimately, what he so often talks about. He has not made us know what it is for a man to be like Mars, nor has he brought us near knowing what it would be for a man to be like Bacchus. We do not get near enough to the roots and springs of action that could make a life of love-making and drinking and general jollity seem the expression of a force of nature. And for those who do not require the values of Love and War to seem god-like before they can be deeply roused by them, I would say that on the human level we do not get the effective answer to the common-sense moral judgement on Anthony's behaviour. I am quite sure that Shakespeare could have challenged the Elizabethan norms and given us the inside picture of a valuable love with all its attendant stresses as it conflicted with the normal judgement of decent men. I can't feel that Shakespeare could not have endowed his hero with the necessary articulateness or made us feel what was going on inside a man who could not tell us directly. So I am bound to conclude that Shakespeare was seduced by his 'angelic strength' into organic weakness. Nobody can deny that Shakespeare was playing with the heroic suggestions he failed to make dramatic. Though he certainly strikes me as too often having taken the will for the deed, Professor G. Wilson Knight was not making his Anthony out of nothing. The will is plainly in the text—which makes the failure very painful to contemplate. Humanly, of course, we can understand that a poet might not want to repeat the agony of pushing matters painfully home. We are so greedy for the supreme pleasure of tragedy that we overlook what it costs the poet to provide it. When I call this play a failure, I do not mean that Shakespeare tried for tragedy and failed: it seems to me he just did not try.

We have still to ask whether the organisation of the play required most of what is now the last act. If the centre of the play concerned Anthony, then this last act is an appendage. We must then suppose that Shakespeare simply took over the story as he found it in North, where, after recounting the death of Anthony, he continues the story down to the death of Cleopatra. But those critics who regard the play as beautifully organised, so well organised in fact as to deserve the title dramatic poem, do not feel that the play comes to an end with Anthony's death. They see the play mounting steadily to a climax when Cleopatra dies—Professor G. Wilson Knight wrote of this climax as of the crest of an Everest. To pick out the path of a common experience here is not easy. I shall start from Bradley because he is not committed to an extravagant view of the play yet finds himself using extravagant language about Cleopatra. Indeed I do not know how to reconcile his praise of Cleopatra with his conclusion that the play is not a great tragedy. In the fifth act, he says, Cleopatra becomes unquestionably a tragic character, and what raises Cleopatra at last into pure tragedy is in part her love for Anthony. Yet when he comes to describe Cleopatra's last scenes, though his language is ecstatic, his conclusion is chilling:

> Why is it that, although we close the book in a triumph which is more than reconciliation, this is mingled, as we look back on the story, with a sadness so peculiar, almost the sadness of disenchantment? Is it that, when the glow has faded, Cleopatra's ecstasy comes to appear, I would not say factitious, but an effort strained and prodigious as well as glorious, not, like Othello's last speech, the final expression of character, of thoughts and emotions which have dominated a whole life? Perhaps this is so, but there is something more, something that sounds paradoxical: we are saddened by the very fact that the catastrophe saddens us so little; it pains us that we should feel so much triumph and pleasure. In *Romeo and Juliet, Hamlet, Othello*, though in a sense we accept the deaths of hero and heroine, we feel a keen sorrow. We look back, think how noble or beautiful they were, wish that fate had opposed to them a weaker enemy, dream possibly of the life they might then have led. Here we can hardly do this. With all our admiration and sympathy for the lovers we do not wish them to gain the world. It is better for the world's sake, and not less for their own, that they should fail and die . . . when the splendour [of their passion] vanishes, we do not mourn, as we mourn for the love of Romeo or Othello, that a thing so bright and good should die. And the fact that we mourn so little saddens us.[1]

The difficulties facing all critics of this act are inherent in the play. Comment can only challenge when it refers to the palpable. So much of the play is now a matter of suggestion, of response to an almost magical play with words, to activities of what I must be content to style the imagination without providing a working definition of the word, that one man's say-so becomes unusually impertinent. I shall therefore confine my comment to a few marginal notes on Bradley, which query some of the terms but do not point to a radical difference of judgement.

First, then, as to the love that has been before us for most of the play, and now comes up for a last scrutiny. Cleopatra, says Bradley, ruins a great man but shews no sense of the tragedy of his ruin. This seems true: it is fatal to the continuity of the play, if Anthony's ruin has mattered to us,

[1] *Op. cit.*, p. 304.

for it simply disposes of the question of honour. The difficulty of this is that it takes the grandeur out of her contempt for the world Anthony and she have lost. Since her pronouncements on that world have not the merit of 'weighed and found wanting', we must look to what she puts in place of all that she fails to understand and respond to. A greater difficulty is that it severely qualifies the meaning we can give to her 'love'. We do not require Cleopatra to be herself a great warrior—though we think the less of her as a *queen* when having claimed the right to lead her contingent at Actium she funks the issue and turns tail: but we do expect a woman in love to be able to imagine what it must mean for a man, a great general and leader of men, to imitate her. So, as our first point, we might say that after Actium Cleopatra sinks back and is no longer a sustaining partner in the love relation, somewhat as Lady Macbeth ceases to be a help to her husband after the banquet scene. She seems dazed and puzzled by the catastrophe and has to question Enobarbus—and then makes no comment when she hears his verdict. Bradley thinks she seriously meditated giving up the fallen Anthony: Enobarbus clearly thought so too:

> Sir, sir, thou art so leakie
> That we must leaue thee to thy sinking, for
> Thy deerest quit thee.

The meaning of 'love' is narrowly circumscribed by what follows the reconciliation:

>                                        Come,
> Let's haue one other gawdy night: Call to me
> All my sad Captaines, fill our Bowles once more:
> Let's mocke the midnight Bell.

Cleopatra does not suggest that their love requires a different celebration; she yields to the invitation. Although I have not been able to find the texts to support Professor L. C. Knights when, starting from this point, he comments:

> Antony . . . is galvanized into feeling; there is no true access of life and energy . . . Looking back, we can recall how often this love has seemed to thrive on emotional stimulants. They were necessary for much the same reason as the feasts and wine. For the continued references to feasting . . . serve to bring out the element of repetition and monotony in a passion which, centring on itself, is self-consuming . . .[1]

nevertheless it reminds us how restricted are the lights Shakespeare throws on the love relation: an awful lot has to be taken for granted.

[1] Reprinted in: *Some Shakespearean Themes* (1959), p. 147.

Nevertheless, we must not press everything equally hard in making out the case against Cleopatra. Some critics, for instance, have included Cleopatra's failure to understand what was happening to Anthony in the second scene of the fourth act. I would suggest that the presence of Cleopatra and Enobarbus in that scene is merely as *ficelles* to help the author 'dramatise' the following passage from North:

> So being at supper (as it is reported), he commaunded his officers and house-hold seruauntes that waited on him at his bord, that they should fill his cuppes full, and make as muche of him as they could: for said he, you know not whether you shall doe so much for me to morrow, or whether you shall serue an other maister: and it may be you shall see me no more, but a dead bodie. This notwithstanding, perceiuing that his frends and men fell a weeping to heare him say so: to salue that he had spoken, he added this more vnto it, that he would not leade them to battell, where he thought not rather safely to returne with victorie, then valliantly to dye with honor.

But though this detail may not be telling, we cannot avoid a general impression. Suppose a man entered the theatre during Act IV, would he have supposed that love between Anthony and Cleopatra was the central theme? More than this, would he have understood that Cleopatra was the dominant partner who had caught Anthony in her toil? Although one can't measure these things, I should say we are more engaged with Cleopatra in the early part of the play when Anthony is in Rome than we are in the fourth act when she is always popping in and out.

Again, if we were not already convinced that the couple were tied by love, if we merely followed the text, what would we say was uppermost in Anthony's mind when he hears the false news of Cleopatra's death? Anthony's mind is not easy to know: at one moment in a rage, at the next unmanned. At least he knows he ought to be dead but that he must kill Cleopatra first. When the eunuch says:

> My Mistris lou'd thee, and her Fortunes mingled
> With thine intirely.

Anthony replies:

> Hence sawcy Eunuch peace, she hath betraid me,
> And shall dye the death.

And when he takes in the news, it never crosses his mind that it might have been the result of his rage. He immediately thinks, 'she has done the noble thing I ought to have done', she recovers stature in his eyes and becomes a queen. We see this again when Eros kills himself:

Thrice-Nobler then my selfe,
Thou teachest me: Oh valiant *Eros*, what
I should, and thou could'st not, my Queene and *Eros*
Haue by their braue instruction got vpon me
A Noblenesse in Record.

Now although we must allow for the conventions of the theatre—
Anthony is going to have another dying speech—dramatically Anthony
thought those were his last words on earth. He returns to them when he is
brought to Cleopatra:

Not *Caesars* Valour hath o'rethrowne *Anthony*,
But *Anthonie's* hath Triumpht on it selfe.

And his actual last words are:

A Roman, by a Roman
Valiantly vanquish'd.

And the more I ponder this death scene the harder it becomes to think of
the lovers as united. The lines that stand out are:

Hast thou no care of me. . .
Come, away,
This case of that huge Spirit now is cold.

Secondly, some notes and a judgement on the final scene of the play. In
a sense the play picks up from Act IV scene 2. The remainder of the play
makes a continuous whole, but closes on a less ambitious note, it draws to
a fine single point. There is, however, a certain amount of vain repetition.
The interview with Proculeius goes over the same ground as the earlier
interview with Thidias, and Cleopatra's rage against Seleucus is pale
after her previous outburst and Anthony's. One repetition, however,
Act V scene ii lines 51–62, is an improvement on Act III scene xiii lines
158–167 (quoted above). Cleopatra is still play-acting, but she is truer
here to her theatrical self. We feel she is rapidly trying out all her reper-
toire, and the contrast between her poses and her real calculating self is
thrilling. Especially after the dream fantasy about Anthony, this line is
very moving:

Know you what *Caesar* meanes to do with me?

This contrast is even more poignant after the play-acting with Caesar:

He words me Gyrles, he words me,
That I should not be Noble to my selfe.

Yet Iras' reply, though in itself impressive, seems without relation to its context:

> od Lady, the bright day is done,
> are for the darke.

But when C          mes to grips with her probable fate, she surpasses anything           aid about suicide. Here we touch reality, for if Cleopatra in           an diminish the greatness of Rome as an imperial power,           ny Caesar the most piquant element in his triumph. What           does is in fact to stage a *rival show*, a final show as like as possi          which began her career with Anthony, a show which requires dre   g up—only this time there will be words.

These words are the natural focus for a debate on the play. The extreme at one end may well be Professor G. Wilson Knight's remark, 'We find an imaginative parallel in the Crucifixion'.[1] When we think of the manner of the two deaths, we may wonder whether 'parallel' is the right word for

> Now no more
> The iuyce of Egypts Grape shall moyst this lip . . .

and 'I wyll not drinke of the fruite of the vine, vntyll the kyngdome of God come.' For Cleopatra's is to be a painless triumph:

> As sweet as Balme, as soft as Ayre, as gentle.

I should not dare to assert that Shakespeare had no interest at this point in possible forms of after-life and immortality, but I would advance confidently that full participation in the text requires us to note the paradox of the apparent claim to be leaving the body and the recurrent stress on 'lip' and all the other allusions to the body. If we say that Cleopatra now refines her essence, it is still an exquisite sensuality that goes out with her dying words. Her power is to be able to keep it up to the last and to shew her sensual nature dominant, to end with velvety jokes drawn from memories of love passages involving the complexities of bodily touch. Unlike Bradley, I find myself now recapturing the mystery of Cleopatra, the sense that she somehow brings the qualities we associate with the spirit to bear centrally on matters we normally classify as of the flesh. Not that I find myself tempted to create a 'mystique' or 'philosophy' of the extremes of love. I come naturally to the literary query: how to characterise what I have just called her jokes? They have something of the conceit in them and extend from the merely fanciful to the 'metaphysical' or

[1] *The Imperial Theme* (1931), p. 321.

Donne-like play of the mind. I have elsewhere in this book[1] spoken of the finest intelligence as that which is one with what it works on. Sometimes her mind seems distinct from what she is attending to, but in the lines that move us we surely have to ask what faculty is at work, and what she turns death into in such flights?

The more I am willing to grant that there is no limit to the reverberations in the imagination of lines such as

> Now boast thee Death, in thy possession lyes
> A Lasse vnparalell'd

the more I would contend that what we have is a flight of imagination rather than an embodied dramatic creation. And difficult as it would be to contrast the supreme imagination and the real when we are thinking of a play, yet if we agree with Bradley that this death does not trouble us, if we feel that its import is seriously diminished by the sense that Cleopatra could have died saying, 'All's had, nought's spent,' then we can say that the interest aroused by Cleopatra at the end is too ideal and that she has ceased to be part and parcel of the real. In claiming that the play draws to a fine point, I am expressing a feeling that the end does not bring the whole of our minds into play and as it were set a new pattern on our being.

[1] Chiefly in the pages on *Othello*. See pp. 136–161 and the index under *Intelligence* and *Shakespeare's intelligence*.

# Index